# THE
# HINDU
# CONNECTION

CONCORDIA
SCHOLARSHIP
*Today*

# THE
# HINDU
# CONNECTION

## Roots of the New Age

**A. R. Victor Raj**

CPH™
SAINT LOUIS

The OM (or AUM) pictured on the cover is the most popular and perhaps the most original of all mantras. OM is the Brahman in the form of sound. OM is the beginning and the end of everything. This mysterious sound of eternity is the "Amen" of Hinduism. Every hymn, every prayer, the reading of every sacred text, and every religious rite begins and ends with OM.

The Upanishads describe AUM as the four stages of consciousness: A represents waking state, U stands for dream, and M symbolizes deep sleep. The three together constitute the transcendent state (Cf. the discussion of mantras, p.66).

Copyright © 1995 Concordia Publishing House
3558 S. Jefferson Avenue, St. Louis, MO 63118-3968
Manufactured in the United States of America

Library of Congress Cataloging-in-Publication Data

Raj, Victor A. R., 1948–
    The Hindu connection : roots of the new age / A. R. Victor Raj.
        p.        cm.        (Concordia scholarship today)
    ISBN 0-570-04802-8
    1. New Age movement. 2. Hinduism—Influence. 3. Christianity and other religions—Hinduism. 4. Hinduism—Relations—Christianity.
I. Title. II. Series.
BP605.N48R348 1994
294.5—dc20                                                94-43623

1 2 3 4 5 6 7 8 9 10        04 03 02 01 00 99 98 97 96 95

To Christ Memorial Lutheran Church
St. Louis, Missouri

Committed to communicating the true saving Gospel
throughout the world

# Contents

# Foreword

Like all volumes in the Concordia Scholarship Today series, *The Hindu Connection* offers useful insights as it examines and clarifies current concerns. It offers these insights in the light of a broadened and deepened understanding of the Christian faith, thereby aiding us in making considered and responsible applications of that faith and helping us "comprehend the love of God in Christ."

*The Hindu Connection* appears at a time when it is almost a truism that Americans are deeply "into" spirituality. Manipulated by the mass media, particularly television, and hardly aware of their ideological captivity, Americans are unwittingly taken in by enthusiasts of the New Age. New Age ideas have become especially attractive to-day in our world of feeling that thrives on the relativity of truth.

Not too long ago the notion still prevailed that ultimately all "truth" could be ascertained, given sufficient time and the free, imaginative yet objective manipulation of human reason. A concomitant series of near cataclysmic events has changed all that: the surrender of absolute-truth claims of the Enlightenment as the "broken promise of the historical-critical method" became evident, open cynicism toward government and politicians, the failure of communism, marked by the fall of the Berlin Wall in 1989, the growing notion that moral standards (an aspect of religion) are relative, and the popularity of deconstructionism and a false pluralism. These and other changes have left society confused if not in disarray. Perhaps Americans have therefore embraced the burgeoning New Age Movement with its attraction for feeling and mystery as a kind of counterpart to the excesses of the Enlightenment or as a refuge from the confusion of the day.

Whatever the reason, do-it-yourself religion is flourishing. Authority is "out." In many quarters, relativity of truth—and morals as well—is "in." But it is only natural then to cast about for useful spiritual sources—unwittingly recognizing authority after all. The resulting cafeteria-style selection of spiritual values has produced an endless variety of New Age beliefs, with some features regularly appearing. *The New Age Is Lying to You* (Concordia, 1994), one of many books analyzing the movement, details much of that variety. *The Hindu Connection* shows that in the final analysis Hinduism is the base from which the New Age Movement has emerged.

One objective of the author is to provide sufficient background into the development of Hinduism so the reader will understand how Hinduism grew like an amorphous banyan tree and became not only a religion but a way of life for India and has now become attractive to the West. Chapter 6 sketches similar patterns among Christian theologians in the West. And because in both instances these developments grew out of human efforts to understand the mysteries of religion, there are interesting parallels between the two.

Above all, *The Hindu Connection* is an effort to analyze Hinduism and its relation to the New Age, believing that understanding the historical and theological aspects of Eastern religions will be useful for Christians, overwhelmed by the love of God in Jesus Christ, who are looking to understand the New Age and its roots.

*The Publisher*

# Introduction

The New Age transcends definition. It defies analysis and classification. Obviously, its faith and practice fluctuate between religion and irreligion. Nonetheless, its religious nature can neither be ignored nor underestimated. In terms of its persuasion, cultic nature, spirituality, and superstition it surely falls under the category of religion. It strives to outlast (traditional) religion as it exploits modern disciplines of psychology, psychiatry, astronomy, and ecology. The New Age returns to where it hesitates to belong—among its cohorts, the religions of the world.

Human nature by design has in it a spiritual void that needs to be filled in one way or another. Historically, in the West this void has been filled by faiths and values that have emerged from a Judeo-Christian milieu. One needs to remember only that even today the average Easterner views Christianity as the religion of the West, despite the fact that it emerged in the Near East. To be sure, in recent times a notable section of the Western population has exhibited a growing discontent toward the faith of their fathers. In its place they have chosen to embrace the Eastern ideas of transcendence and mysticism. Perhaps disgusted with the Western notions of structuralism and institutionalism, these individuals venture to "fly as a bird" into the Eastern vistas of solipsism and universalism.

Over the years the West has built up for itself a reputation for being the explorer of the earth, the sea, and the sky. Apparently some of these explorations have led also to a certain exploitation of our natural resources. Paradoxically, by way of paying a ransom, a faction of the same society today chooses to stoop down before nature and the things therein, with a view to venerating them as objects of worship.

In the recent past the West has spread the umbrella of progress over the world by accenting an orientation to mechanization and industrialization. The warm welcome accorded nowadays to the New Age thinking, nevertheless, supports the notion that progress has not altogether overridden the significance of religion in the life of modern man, although it may have created a certain repugnance towards existing religions.

While determined to keep his mind preoccupied with thoughts and ideas that transcend religion, in his search for absolutes man finds himself seized by and confined to some form of religion. By denying the role of religion in life man may have thought that he kept his mind "unoccupied, swept clean and put in order" (Matt. 12:44). The emergence and perseverance of the New Age verifies that the contrary is the truth.

The New Age is a religion in a broader sense, more than the sense in which modern humanism is a religion. It is not necessary that a religion by definition should preserve and promote a doctrine of God. As a case in point, in the sixth century before the common era, both Jainism and Buddhism first made their appearance in India as atheistic religions. The New Age is not a cult, for it is not limited to the leadership of one individual or to a few conclaves. It is not a fad, for its glory is not fading even after a score of years of its coming into being. The New Age is a religion, like its closest ally, Hinduism.

It may very well be that the evolutionary process of the New Age has not been one of design, but of accident. The followers of this lifestyle may not have realized that they have indeed given themselves into another "religion" as they bid farewell to the so-called traditional religions or as they have embraced New Age ideas with a view to supplementing what seemed to be lacking in the traditional religions. The concepts and formulations that draw the New Agers closer have long been in existence in Hinduism and in other sources. Just as Christianity has it base in the Old Testament, and just as the New Testament writers, moved by the Holy Spirit, availed themselves of various Greco-Roman expressions, innumerable concepts from Hinduism and from various other modern disciplines have made their way into New Age thinking.

The New Age is the New Testament of Hinduism. It is intrinsically Hindu in its faith and practice. Like its eastern precursor, Hinduism, the New Age Movement does not have a founder, nor does it operate on the basis of well defined creeds or confessions. Especially by the turn of the 20th century, Hinduism began to penetrate the soul of the West, and in the passing of time, some of its teaching began to surface in the form of the New Age Movement.

Hinduism admittedly has a philosophical as well as a popular dimension to it. Popular Hinduism does not limit its operation to the confines of well-established guidelines and rigid regulations. Instead, it appears to be absorbent, inclusive, and all-encompassing. The same may be said of the New Age inasmuch as it is considered a religion.

Against this background we will pursue an analysis of the New Age, bearing in mind that "religion is the human experience of the sacred and what people do with it."[1] We will begin with a chapter on various theories of religion. This will help illustrate our position that the New Age has in it several characteristics that match these theories on many counts.

The chapters that follow will deal with the salient features of the New Age Movement in terms of its philosophy and theology. Here we will see how some hard-core aspects of both philosophical and popular Hinduism steadily gained acceptance in New Age thinking. We will also see how, for the New Agers, many of these Hindu thoughts may be providing hidden answers for some of their ultimate questions in life.

In the second half of the book we will explore the various ways in which the Hindu view of life was introduced to the Western audience. Initially, this may have occurred because the Hindu scriptures were available in the European languages. Hinduism was identified, familiarized, and acknowledged by Christian missionaries who dedicated their lives for the cause of Christ in India. Secondly, a resurgent Hinduism was introduced to the West by such great Indian minds as Swami Vivekananda and a host of other Hindu scholars who succeeded him in the worldwide Hindu philosophical enterprise. And thirdly, in an attempt to make Christ all things to all men, several modern Christian theologians ventured to discover and acknowledge Christ in the Hindu religion.

Consequently, the West was fascinated by the philosophical, universal, and somewhat fanciful nature of the Hindu religion. Thus Hinduism shed its primitive, Eastern clothing and was well-clad in its scholarly and contemporary attire, appealing to the Western mind. Christianity was watered down as one of many ways of salvation, and Hinduism was acclaimed as the bride whose wedding with Christ was yet to be consummated.

We will conclude our study with a proposal to respond to the challenges of the New Age from a Christian point of view.

A number of good books already are availaable on the New Age Movement, written mainly by Christian authors. These volumes depict the New Age as a powerful sensation that exerts a certain magnetic force to lure people away from the Christian religion. They are also very helpful for identifying the various ways in which the New Age thinking is influencing the American mainstream.

Douglas Groothuis, for example, in his *Unmasking the New Age*, describes how a counter culture steadily gained acceptance in contemporary society through entertainers, therapists, books and media, and has now become a challenge to Christian faith and worship. *Understanding the New Age* by Russell Chandler provides an analysis of the subtle ways in which society falls victim to New Age ideas, without noticing the damage they do to Christian spirituality. Walter Martin describes this movement as a cult in *The New Age Cult*. An outstanding compendium of the sources of the New Age is perhaps Gordon Melton's *The New Age Almanac,* which presents a historical overview of the diverse ways and forms in which New Age ideology became prevalent in Western society. Elliot Miller in his *A Crash Course on the New Age Movement* identifies the features

14

of the New Age and explains how convincingly it tries to appear to be the bedfellow of Christianity. Recently, in his *The New Age Is Lying to You*, Eldon Winker has demonstrated how subtle and deceptive the New Age thinking is.

The above books and many others like them are extremely helpful for recognizing the anatomy of the New Age as it is recognized in the West. The present book deals basically with the monistic philosophy of the New Age. In our opinion, this is the consequence of the erosion in Christian spirituality. Modern Christian theology, perhaps unwittingly, nurtured the New Age, particularly through its encounter with other world religions. Thus the notion of a certain "Christian monism" evolved from this meeting of the minds that became the basic source of the New Age worldview.

I would like to express my thanks to my colleague Gene Edward Veith, Jr., who encouraged me to put into book form some of the ideas I have tried out on him in our hallway discussions. I am grateful to the members of the theology division of Concordia University who successfully blend sound theological scholarship with true Christian spirituality. I am deeply indebted to our reference librarian, Rev. Richard Wohlers, who aided me amply in this endeavor by making available a number of basic books and periodicals.

A study like this would not have been possible had it not been for my students who represent a variety of religions and cultures. They have been very kind to listen to some of the ideas in the book, because they were among the first to hear them, and because they usually knew from where I was coming. I thank President R. John Buuck for his inspiring leadership with the vision to foster Christ-centered education as a means of reaching the world with the Gospel of Jesus Christ. Thanks also to Wilbert Rosin, editor at Concordia Publishing House, for his constant support and encouragement to put this book together and to polish the rough edges of its language and style. His own direct exposure to India's faith and culture has also been a major backing for the production of this volume.

I thank my family, especially my wife, Anie, and children Anand (joy), Seemanth (love), and Nishant (peace). All of them have known and believed that the faith of Abraham, Isaac, and Jacob is theirs too, though their culture is different from the fathers.

# 1
# Theories of Religion

Religion undoubtedly plays a significant role in the life of humankind. Religious convictions and ceremonies hold people together. More than in any other aspect of human discipline, in religion people find answers to ultimate questions in life. For many, if not for all, in a trouble-filled world, religion is the wellspring of life.

The relevance of religion for human beings does not diminish even as the world comes of age. Progress and technological advancement may pose threats to religion and tend to undermine its hold on human lives. Nevertheless, religions and religious beliefs refuse to yield to such challenges, and, in the end, survive with permanent endurance. Evidently "there is something eternal in religion: it is the cult and the faith."[1]

Cults and faiths remain with people. Basic religious beliefs, rituals, rites, and ceremonies tag along even as people move from place to place. Given a choice, a person does not easily give up one's faith. Unless the powers have ulterior motives, no nation or government will purposely infringe on an individual's freedom of religion.

The Jews of the sixth century before Christ lost their homeland to the Babylonians. Nebuchadnezzar, the invader, deported the people of Judah and held captive their political and religious leaders. The Jerusalem temple, which for the Jews symbolized God's presence with them, was ransacked, leaving no stone unturned. But the faith of Israel lived on, in spite of such atrocities. In place of the temple, Israel reclaimed its identity by assembling in synagogues for worship. In the absence of a sacrificial system, God's people regained their solidarity through the study of his revelation in the Torah.

We ought not be agitated if today we should encounter a mosque on a street of New York or a Hindu temple on a hillside in Pittsburgh. Mosques and temples are symbols,

17

respectively, of Muslim and Hindu collective identity. No bewilderment should strike us if, somewhere in the United States, one morning we should wake up to the call of the Minaret, or if we should find ourselves in earshot of a Hindu mantra echoing from a sacred gathering. The call from the mosque's tower is an invitation to every Muslim, announcing the time of worship and prayer. Mantras are words or verses with spiritual power that enable a Hindu enthusiast to come to terms with his own self. The hold religions have on people does not diminish even after they leave their homeland and settle elsewhere. Religions continue to travel with people.

A quarter of a century ago, Professor E. E. Evans-Pritchard made the claim that religion had "ceased to occupy men's minds in the way it did at the end of the last century."[2] Extinction of religion, according to this Oxford professor of social anthropology, was only a matter of time.

To be sure, our century has witnessed a remarkable change in the way in which we handle the issue of religion. The Christians of the 19th century were intent on evangelizing the entire world in their lifetime. The emergence of the schools of comparative religion, on the other hand, required students to exercise a "scientific" approach to the study of religions. Such studies led the lion's share of scholars to conclude that religion is the pursuit of truth, and, after all, that there is truth in every religion. Consequently, the missionary emphasis of the Christian religion shifted from the proclamation of its own truth claims to the church's involvement in issues of social and political concerns. Not surprisingly then, today we encounter theologies of liberation, humanization, development, and pluralism.

Religion has not become extinct, however, despite Professor Evans-Pritchard's prediction. Religions will continue as long as humanity continues to occupy the face of the earth. Religion is where people are. Religious affirmations hold fast with people. People do not easily give up their religious persuasions, regardless of the social and cultural changes that take place in their own lives. Religious ideas seem to make every effort to resist change. Instead of succumbing to the threat of extinction, religions today learn and borrow from one another ways to establish their lasting imprint on human lives.

A case in point is in order. Historically, the concept of mission and evangelism has been associated with Christianity. Missionary enterprise enabled the Christian faith to span the globe. By contrast, traditional Hinduism in its essence is not a missionary religion. The ethos of Hinduism is such that a Hindu is born a Hindu. This self-contained Hindu disposition, however, shifted dramatically since the launching of the grand-scale Christian missionary enterprises in the modern era.

Missionary efforts today are not an exclusive feature of the Christian religion. Reportedly, in the year 1991, the United States alone was visited by 90 Hindu "travelling or itinerant evangelists."[3] This relatively new trend in Hinduism first began with the formation of the Brahmo Samaj and the Arya Samaj.[4] These movements emerged in the 19th century primarily as militant Hindu responses to the approaching Christian missionary challenge. In defense against the Christian religion then, Hinduism revived its purity in accordance with its scriptures, the Vedas. A striking demonstration of this endeavor was the tremendous influence Swami Vivekananda made on the World Parliament of Religions in Chicago in the year 1893.[5] Modern Hindu resurgence has been making tidal waves in India's social as well as political climate. The Hindu tradition so far has not spoken to the challenge of clearly separating the "Church" from the State. Consequently, a significant majority of the Hindu population in India today operates on the assumption that all Indians are meant to be Hindus. Undoubtedly, the appearance and survival in India of other religions, such as Islam and Christianity, is irksome to Hindus. Small wonder then that, in the name of religion, riots and revolts continue to occur in various parts of this great nation that is renowned for its variety and diversity.[6]

We have seen that, for the most part, religions do not wane, but grow. Religions thrive against struggles and survive hardships. Religious ideas unite people and persuade them to stick together in homogeneous groups and communities. All these must be because religion is accorded a central place in the fabric of human society. Religion has pioneered in almost every human effort toward progress and advancement in life. As Durkheim perceived, "The fundamental categories of thought, and consequently of science, are of religious origin."[7] Religion is the hub of the wheel of human life.

In his exhaustive study of the phenomenology of religion, Garadus van der Leeuw arrives at the conclusion that "religion is the extension of life to its uttermost limit."[8] Van der Leeuw observes that there are two ways of looking at the whole theory of religion. The first is to view religion as an incomprehensible revelation coming from God. According to this view, man accepts himself and all that surrounds him as things are, all together serving a revelatory function. Revelations from God are authenticated by humanity's own ready acceptance of, and response to, them in the course of human history.

The second way to approach religion is to understand it as an "intelligible experience." Man has always been in pursuit of discovering the breadth and depth of life's meaning. In his search for meaning, he confronts something superior to himself, something that is more powerful than he is. While the search continues, man either worships this power in wonder and amazement, or tries to subdue it to serve his own purposes.

The purpose of this book is to study New Age thinking and analyze its implications from the point of view of religion. Conceivably, the followers of the New Age do not want themselves to be branded as religious people. In fact, the majority of them may have espoused this new phenomenon because they were disillusioned by the traditional environment of established religions. But religion follows them as a shadow, only with a different scaffold. After all, to be religious is to be human. And, if religion is stretching life to its utmost limit, then there would be no limit to the ways in which the New Age could be understood as a religion.

In any case, the New Age is a religion in more than one sense. A certain mystery is attached to this new movement, which is typical of many religions. It is amorphous and does not claim for itself a particular founder or a specific creed. While the New Agers strive for their selfhood and independent identity, they also yearn for inner communion and a universal, cosmic consciousness. Immanence as well as transcendence is reflected in this new religion. Although there is a deep seated ecological consciousness (down-to-earth, existential, and environmental) among the New Agers, they do not shy away from the idea of reincarnation (other worldly, spiritual, and transcendental). The New Age may not sustain a clear teaching on God; and, according to certain modern definitions, a religion can also be atheistic.[9]

Webster's Dictionary defines religion as "belief in, acceptance of God or gods, with the emotion and morality connected therewith; rites or worship, any system of such belief or worship."[10] Religious scholarship today, however, does not want to limit religion to any dictionary definition. And no two scholars agree on the exact way in which religion is defined. As W. Richard Comstock rightly observes, religion

> has been described as the sense of the sacred; as ultimate concern; as loyalty to the Good, the love of Man, allegiance to the Gods. It has been said that it is what we do in our solitude; but also what we do to maintain our society; that it is about limit-situations; but also about everyday life. It has been called resignation, but also hope; release from this world, but also a way of living in this world more effectively. Some claim it is an encounter with the Wholly Other; others that it is the crucial meeting with one's own Self.[11]

The above observation is descriptive, comprehensive, and representative of all that has been going on until now in the study of religion. For our purposes, we will highlight from the above four major viewpoints and explain how they relate to an understanding of the New Age as a religion. We will call these the philosophy, psychology, sociology, and theology of religion.

# The Philosophy of Religion

Religious studies experts have shown a preference for a variety of engaging expressions for articulating the philosophy of religion, such as the "sense of the sacred" and the "ultimate concern." Scholars approach the study of religion in this manner primarily because, according to them, God, the alleged common denominator of religions, connotes different meanings for different people. For example, a Jew or a Christian easily understands the sacred as one God, personal, and separate from human beings and the rest of the universe. And Jews as well as Muslims swiftly part ways with Christians who make confession of the one God as Father, Son, and Holy Spirit.

Ironically, the Christian understanding of God applies only to less than a third of today's world population, and Islamic theology is confined to much less than one-tenth of the modern world. This means that a significant majority of the human race views the sacred in ways other than that of a personal God.

In his Large Catechism, Dr. Martin Luther raises the question, "What is God?" He answers, "A God is that to which we look for all good and in which we find refuge in every time of need." The Lutheran Church—Missouri Synod *Catechism* develops this point in Luther's Small Catechism by answering the question with a direct quotation from the Gospel of John: "God is a Spirit." *The Catechism* says God is all-powerful (omnipotent), all-knowing (omniscient), and present everywhere (omnipresent). Although the query *What is God?* (as opposed to *Who is God*) is unbiased and objective, a thoroughly biblical basis is presupposed in the answer(s). The God-question is approached more philosophically in the latter part of the answer. Even there, God is described as a person, and his dealings with the world are understood in terms of his power, knowledge, and presence. Philosophy must remain just a handmaid of theology.

Nevertheless, philosophy today, and particularly the philosophy of religion, prefers to leave the God-question unanswered. Instead of acknowledging ultimate power and authority as God's prerogative, men and societies choose to worship power itself.[12] Power is a wonderful phenomenon. Few people, races, and nations have not coveted power. Power fantasies transcend time, race, and nationality. Power can control one's own self and others. Power enables a person to rise to the occasion. Possession of power builds up in us the confidence that we are on top of the universe. If the older traditions of religion attributed power to a divine being or beings, and if they feared, worshipped, and to a certain extent subdued such beings,the modern tendency is to claim power for one's self, inflate it,and magnify it with undue reverence. Most people today prefer power for themselves rather than a powerful God.

A related concept in the philosophy of religion is that of knowledge (*gnosis; scientia*). In the Judeo-Christian tradition God knows everything; therefore yielding to God's authority is for human beings the beginning of knowledge (Prov. 1:7), whereas, in most other religions, knowledge is a path to God. Hinduism, for example, underscores knowledge (*jnana* ) as a way of salvation. Knowledge in this instance is interpreted as spiritual illumination. This kind of knowledge presumably leads to absolute truth. The ancient Gnostics who sought secret wisdom were of a similar opinion. Researchers surmise that such religions are based on a certain doctrine of wisdom, "taught by sages and drawn from mystical experiences and esoteric sources not available to ordinary people."[16]

That God is present simultaneously everywhere is underscored in the statement about his omnipresence. God's ubiquitous quality suggests that he is present everywhere all the time. At the same time, God can also be present in a specific locale at a given time, Thus, for example, the Jews understand God as immanent for them in their assembly. [14] Christians believe that the incarnation of God in Jesus Christ and his presence in each believer and in the fellowship of believers are evidences of God's immanence.

That God is omnipotent and omniscient implies that God is a person. A person is known by his actions just as a tree is known by its fruits. For those who perceive God as a person of action, the other action-related expressions the Catechism uses to illustrate God (holy, meaning sinless and hating sin; just, meaning fair and impartial; faithful, meaning keeping promises; gracious, i.e., showing undeserved kindness, forgiving, etc.) will also help expand their grasp of the Divine.

The understanding of God as a person, however, has been losing its significance, especially among experts in comparative religions. According to them, those qualities deemed to be God's attributes are in themselves nomenclatures invoking tremendous mystery. Thus in the early part of our century professor Rudolf Otto spoke of "The Sacred" or the "Wholly Other."[15] Otto, like Luther, was dismayed by the terrible power of God's wrath on the unholy and the nonsacred. Accordingly, he understood God as distinct and distanced from the universe, belonging to a totally different order. More recently, while some philosophers of religion perceive what is commonly understood as God as being the ultimate reality, implying the limit beyond which it is impossible to go, others prefer "the term sacred reality to label this cross-culturally occurring common denominator, the religious source."[16]

Power and knowledge in themselves are mysteries of enormous proportions. Such phenomena exert a certain magnetic effect on people. In our age of knowledge expansion and information explosion, knowledge begets power. Knowledge will have served its ultimate purpose if it is capable of unlocking the real mystery of life. However, knowledge has left unanswered life's most important questions. Unanswered questions are the breeding ground for mysteries. Life's mysteries pave the way for subliminal thoughts. Subliminality leads to transcendence, and transcendence to the dream world of ubiquity.

The name of philosopher-theologian Paul Tillich is customarily associated with the interpretation of religion as man's "ultimate concern." In fact, the United States Supreme Court made use of Tillich's writings in support of its verdict that secular humanism is a religion. Nevertheless, Tillich's students argue that in arriving at this decision the Court misrepresented at least in part the Tillichian theory. According to them, Tillich interpreted religious symbols as having "a transcendent level which goes beyond the empirical reality we encounter," and since "secular humanism . . . specifically denies a transcendent or spiritual dimension, it should not be counted a religion."[17]

As McKenzie points out, "if the word 'religion' is to do any work, it should include reference to a transcendental power."[18] Transcendental power is implied, if not apparent, in the New Age thinking, when the followers of this movement strive to channel the spirits and their leaders claim to receive messages from the angels. A "world" that transcends the present is inbred in the philosophy of the New Age. That world may not be the abode of a god or gods, but that is precisely where the New Age differs from the world religions. New religions emerge and persist in the modern world although they may not be of the same pith and fiber of the older ones.

## The Psychology of Religion

When considering the psychology of religion one wonders if the theories set forth in this connection by the 19th-century Harvard professor William James (1842–1910) are rather more convincing today than, for example, those of the more modern depth-psychologists Sigmund Freud and Carl Jung. In fact, we owe the expression "psychology of religion" to William James. An established teacher of human physiology and psychology, James proposed the idea of a sound soul in a sound body. He believed that religion offered man assistance to accept himself as he is and his situation in life. Thus, religion served the purpose of maintaining a positive attitude towards life. Being himself an atheist of sorts, James dismissed the Christian interpretation of a soul sick with sin. His writings on the subject of religion were etched with a touch of optimism as well as mysticism. [19]

Against the positive influence of religion on man and his life that James saw, Sigmund Freud (1856–1939) viewed religion as a fading illusion. Of course, for Freud religion is a skyward reflection of the subconscious hatred people have for their physical fathers. The guilt originating from this aversion, Freud contended, causes people to project a greater father image in the heavens and call that image "god." Nevertheless Freud conceded that religion still has value (for want of a better system) in society insofar as it serves the purpose of preserving civilization. Furthermore, religion has a consolatory and wish-fulfilling power on those who are deeply troubled, and cannot cope with the problems in life.[20]

Carl Gustav Jung (1875–1961) maintained that religion is a peculiar attitude of the human mind. Religion has such a hold on human lives, said Jung, that it "seizes and controls the human subject which is always rather its victim than its creator."[21] In other words, the human mind is enslaved by the external phenomenon of religion because religion entails awesome, and at the same time threatening, intuitions about God, his laws, powers, spirits, demons and so on. Jung interpreted the mysterious presence of evil in the world as the "dark side" of God. Given this predicament, this Swiss psychotherapist considered his role in the world to be that of a healer of the psyche, the human soul.

Freud's and Jung's conceptions of religion may be viewed against the Marxist idea that religion is the most extreme form of human alienation and estrangement.[22] The Marxist dictum,"religion is the opiate of the people," is well known. "Religion is the sigh of the oppressed creature, the heart of a heartless world, just as it is the spirit of the spiritless situation," explained Karl Marx.[23]

Marx was disapproving a religion which, according to him, was far removed from the cause of common man. To be sure, the Germany of his time was influenced heavily by the dogma and piety of the Christian religion. Marx viewed religion as the privilege of the socially and politically elite. The ruling class in effect appropriated religion as a tool to exploit the masses and subjugate the poor and the less fortunate. Consequently the rich became richer, and the poor, poorer. The poor coped with the status quo, willingly serving their exploiters in the hope that their own reward was in heaven. On these and similar grounds, Marx asserted that religion had no place in society, for "Man makes religion, religion does not make man . . . . religion is the self-consciousness and self-feeling of man who has either not yet found himself or has already lost himself again."[4]

Marx evidently turned hostile toward the structuralism in the religion of his day. Nevertheless, one wonders if, for almost three quarters of a century, Marxism itself, and particularly its theory of dialectical materialism, was not the "opiate" of well over a third of the world's population. Although Marx pronounced his anathema on religion, others have aptly satirized Marxism itself as a quasi- or pseudo-religion. In fact, the Marxist ideology turned out to be a kind of religion from below: The proletariat was promised the utopia of heaven on earth. Terrestrial human beings replaced a transcendent God of traditional religions, and humanism drowned out theology. Communist (and, in China, Maoist) writings took the place of the Bible. The working class was the church, and the leaders themselves were the prophets, priests, saints, and demigods. Recent developments in Europe, in the former Soviet Union and in China, however, verify that Marxist theory has failed miserably to answer life's ultimate, if not basic questions.

Religion is a matter of the heart. Denying religion (and God) on psychological or psycho-political grounds does not altogether wreck the innate human desire to embrace a religion. While it is true that some people change their faith from one religion to another, others expect their religion to change. Yet others may be searching for new and different religions. But the legacy of religion will live on in the hearts of people.

In his introductory chapter on *The New Religions* Jacob Needleman drives home the point that the mushrooming today of the limitless number of new religions in the United States poses serious challenges to the modern European psychology, for example, of Freud and Jung.[25] Needleman relates that he was pleasantly surprised at the large number of psychiatrists and clinicians in San Francisco who listened to him speak on the new religions. These professionals assembled primarily because their younger patients were influenced by the literature of the new religions. Moreover, these experts themselves were struggling with questions which, to their knowledge, European psychology could not answer. "Was there something in the religions of the East, they asked, which could really call forth those human depths and heights which neither psychology nor Western religion seemed to be able to reach?"[26]

We will take cognizance here and in our next chapter of three observations from Needleman that illustrate how the New Age thinking, because of its proximity to the Hindu religion, may be calling forth those human depths and heights which Western thinking could not reach. The first has to do with "self-centeredness." That is, the goal of Eastern religions is always release from suffering—of the individual, along with the suffering of humanity (as opposed to individualism). Secondly, Western psychology views desires as needs and strives to *satisfy* them by means of offering love and recognition, whereas Eastern religions work toward the *tranformation of desire*. And, thirdly, the Eastern religions have a way of satisfying the "irrational" need in the psyche of all men (in contrast to Western rationalism).

# The Sociology of Religion

Sociologists have described religion as a shared experience. Religion undoubtedly is a *social* reality in human life. People of the same faith flock together for the sake of their own religion. Obviously, this kind of coming together offers them a sense of social identity unmatched by any other. And, if this tendency is strong enough to survive in our era, a person's religious bearings must be deeper and more vigorous than one's national (patriotic), linguistic, or even racial (caste, color, and ethnic origin) identity.

In the last century Ludwig Feuerbach dismissed religion as simply a projection of basic human relationships into a hypothetically heavenly realm with a God-image. Yet in human relationships he envisioned a new "true religion" without God, evidencing true love, compassion, self-sacrifice, and so on; all that because, for him, religion was a bond between people. However, the German socialist and Karl Marx's cohort Friedrich Engels sneered at this interpretation of religion as an "etymological trick" unbecoming of idealist philosophy.[27]

But how can we deny that true love, compassion, and self-sacrifice are inborn concepts with a certain religious dimension? Do they not blossom and produce the best fruits ideally in the context of religion and spirituality? Moreover, it is only fair to say that sociology, psychology, and related disciplines gradually bagged such and similar expressions for themselves from the religion glossary. Adversaries of religion may explain these virtues away as simply human or humanitarian. Nevertheless, the fact remains that religion first introduced humanity to this kind of thinking, and the purposes once accomplished alone by religion are now being patronized by those antireligious sentiments whose sole intent is to shove religion into oblivion. Do not even the most avid (and vivid) atheists experience a certain sense of religion as they gather to deny religion?

The qualities and attributes that bind people together are perfected in communities. Love and compassion, and even justice and peace, are relational virtues. When practiced in isolation they become selfish and egotistical and miss their intended purpose. Corporate life in communities therefore facilitates practice of virtues in the context of relationship and partnership. This does not mean that society is itself the source of all such virtues or that "the idea of society is the soul of religion," as for example, Durkheim claimed.[28]

The binding factors that truly yoke people together into durable societies are those of a transcendental nature. Communities that are not built and run on values of substance are torn apart gradually, if not abruptly, once their novel interests fade or their ideals prove to be far from practical. Transcendental values endure such testing merely because their source is above and beyond the human. These eternal principles are spiritual; therefore they are religious in form and in content. They are best understood and actualized in the context of religion.

Religion is still today the most significant link between people. This holds true in our world of rapid change, mobility, and cultural exchange. In the realm of change, flexibility rules. A fast moving society cannot stand up for lasting values, nor can it offer people permanent friendship and companionship. There are no absolutes in a society dominated by many "truths" and where relativism prevails.

Social solidarity with a religious inclination is inherent in human nature. This is apparent in spite of the mobility and flexibility of our time. While religion is a sensitive subject that more and more people avoid discussing in public, the issue of religion does surface during life's most important and auspicious occasions. More often than not, most people accomplish their social commitments in accordance with the statutes of a religion. Avoiding religious rites and ceremonies does not mean that these ceremonies are not real, or that they have lost their meaning. It only indicates that some show a preference to stay away from them.

Religious affiliation is the ultimate mark of homogeneity. The rising influx of new cultures and the subsequent demand on humans to alter their lifestyles do not summarily effect radical changes in peoples' religious orientations. Having been surrounded by an aura of change and uncertainty and obsessed with relativism, human beings are still inclined to look for absolute values and absolute norms that serve them as points of reference in establishing lasting relationships. These values and norms are for them nurtured and nourished in their own homogeneous groups.

Thus a person's religious identity is deeper and stronger than one's racial or linguistic identity. This is evident in the faith and practice of the world's major religions. Without a doubt, Christianity is a religion of community. Christian virtues are practiced best in the context of Christian fellowship. True Christian fellowship transcends all human barriers since Christians are bonded together with the Word of God and the sacraments. Christians also believe that the Spirit of God has created them anew as God's own family. When Christians move from one place to another, they also look for a new place of worship and fellowship. Community life is inherent in the Christian religion.

Perhaps the religion of Islam ranks on top in the matter of propagating and fostering a strong sense of community consciousness. The Islamic brotherhood has its roots deep in the faith and life of every Muslim. Converts to Islam from other faiths are bestowed a new identity that allows them to disregard their past and replenish life in a new, integrated family environment. In the end, there is one community and one brotherhood ruled by Islamic law.

Studies show that Asian Indians comprise approximately 0.3 percent of today's U. S. population. The vast majority of them come from a Hindu religious background, taking their religion along as they move. Although they adapt very well to the social and business lifestyle of the West, their own religious affirmations remain intact, preserved without stain or wrinkle.The undeniable Hindu presence in the U. S. is demonstrated by well over 100 temples spread over the nation and the circulation of more than 50 Hindu periodicals in the English language.[29]

Hindus preserve their faith and culture with strict orthodoxy. Their religion travels with them wherever they go. Of course, it is next to impossible to draw a fine line between Hindu faith and Hindu culture; for they are coexistent, and the one without the other is nonexistent. The Hindu way of life shows that there are needs and wants in life that only religion can satisfy.

Religion is, according to a recent broad, denotative definition,

> an institution with a complex of theoretical, practical, sociological and experimental dimensions, which is distinguished by characteristic objects (gods or sacred things),goals (salvation or ultimate good) and functions (giving an overall meaning to life or providing the identity or cohesion of a social group).

Our study will show that New Age thinking matches the above definition of religion with all its parenthetical details. Religion offers people a greater reason to come together than any other single sociological phenomenon. The New Age centers, most of them located in major cities of the West, offer their members a strong sense of unity and community that exceeds their own diverse generic backgrounds. Having defected themselves from the institutionalized religions, these New Agers are converted to a new religion that stands for its own dogma and fellowship. Surely, in the New Age thinking there is room for worshiping ghosts and spirits in the supernatural world. Perhaps what Eugene Nida said of religion in the modern scientific West is relevant also to the New Age: "Actually, however, it is God Himself who has been made to seem unnecessary and irrelevant, while belief in lesser spirits often continues."[31]

## The Theology of Religion

If, according to scholars of religion, *religion* is a difficult word to define, then a simple definition of theology is also absolutely beyond the reach of the best of theologians. As is readily seen, the expression *theology* is derived from a combination of two Greek words—*theos*, meaning god, and the other, *logos*, signifying science or understanding. Thus theology means the study of God.

However, just as scholars of religion prefer to operate with open definitions of religion, so theologians also do not purpose to confine their field of research to parameters set by preconceived etymological gimmicks. For they wish to operate on the meaning that the word *God* has acquired over the years. This tendency is true especially of most Christian theologians of our time. Over a period of half a century we have witnessed the budding (and sometimes shedding) of various new theologies such as those of the death of God, liberation, humanization, development, feminism, and deconstruction. By means of these and similar expressions, theologians have been trying to reach those minds that are haunted by emerging philosophies, with a view to offering them theological answers. Interestingly enough, this is done without the least mention of God, as they maintain that God is present *a priori* in all such contexts.

Thus in our endeavor to explain the theology of religion, we are battling two words that clandestinely elude normative definitions. And, there are ample reasons for this kind of struggle. For those who try to understand religion and theology today are hemmed in by a host of people-centered, people-directed, and people-dominated ideologies. Consequently we have lost the ancient art of letting God be God, and we refuse to surrender to mystery and transcendence. While denying the truth that God created us in God's own image, we make our gods in our own image, and we compose a religion in tune with our philosophy of life.

The God-question remains a philosophical question to the extent that we are preoccupied with a religion from below. In that event, the Marxist claim that man makes religion reigns unrefuted. In the absence of a revealed religion, man will make his own religion, for man can not live without religion. Several epochs in world history show that this is true.

Confucianism is a prime example of a religion from below. With little speculation about God, Confucius prescribed the ideals for a just and moral society built on human relationships. This Chinese sage preferred the word *heaven* to God as he said, "Heaven is the author of the virtue that is in me." His *Heaven* was further explained as a "consciousness of concern,"[32] which reminds us of Paul Tillich's "ultimate concern." Thus, if Confucianism is a religion, it is one from below. It promises a society whose moorings are fastened to the principle of filial piety. Filial piety permeates society in five different reciprocal relationships; between ruler and subject, father and son, husband and wife, elder brother and younger brother, and friend and friend. An endearing relationship well-maintained on all these levels will result in a society that can provide everything for all. Confucius left the God-question unanswered and nebulous, because his immediate concern was to wrestle with the issues of daily harmonious living.

In contrast to the "socialism" of Confucianism, Taoism is primarily a religion of transcendence. The Tao (or Dao) is the One, ultimate and metaphysical absolute. It is a reality that transcends definitions, for once it is defined, it is subjected to the limitations of that particular definition and hence loses its essence. A devout Taoist, because of his longing for immortality, anticipates his own entrance into that sphere where the Tao is, and there he shall be in virtue of his contemplation and meditation.

Buddhism can be understood as an atheistic religion, for the Buddha is believed to have said that if there were gods, they might be working out their own salvation. In the eyes of the West, a similar ambiguity also overshadows the Buddhist interpretation of the soul. While we are tempted to say that Buddhism defies the existence of an immortal soul, this "religion of transformation of consciousness" maintains that our true self is a combination of our human form, feelings, perceptions, impulses, and consciousness—all bundled up into one unit.[33] At death these components disintegrate into individual elements and come together again as one in the new incarnation. Thus, in the language of eternity, the self as well as the non-self are real. Gods are no better than humans.Therefore a Buddhist must work out his own salvation.

Hinduism is better known among its adherents as the Eternal Teaching (*Sanatha Darma*). Dharma is the cosmic order of disciplined behavior that is the destiny of each individual to obey in his or her lifetime. Conceivably, modern Hindu thinkers have shown a preference to describe this religion of India as a way of life.

If *dharma* represents teaching, *karma*, another important Sanskrit word, signifies work or action. Karma in the Hindu context represents *action* as well as its *consequence* which determines, for better or for worse, the doer's next sphere of existence. Their deeds shall indeed follow them in this religion. For, if in an earlier existence the soul was indulging in demeanors contrary to its own stipulated dharma, in its next state that soul will reincarnate into a lower form. Accumulation of good deeds will naturally reward a higher level of life. While this interpretation accounts for the social disparities in the Hindu society, it also counsels ways to release oneself from the fetters of bad karma: Do not deluge yourself in milk and become a cat in the next life (a cat steals milk). Do increase knowledge and know that you are god (knowledge begets power).

The God of philosophical Hinduism is more an *IT* than a *he* or *she*. "In it are to be found pure being (*sat*)) pure intelligence (*chit*) ; [and] pure delight (*ananda*). Brahman is the unknowable one."[34] There must be ways for finite human beings to comprehend this infinite (God). So the Hindu sages spoke of the various manifestations (incarnations) of God in conceptual, human, and even animal forms.[35]

Just as the God of Hinduism resists definitions, so also the world and humans are indefinable. God is the ultimate reality, the essence of all existence, and the rhythm of life. Or, perhaps the ultimate reality is God. Neither the universe nor human beings have beginning or end. These complete their cycles and then enter the next cycle *ad libitum* in accordance with the laws of karma and dharma. No other known religion can match the Hindu religion in its mystery and transcendence.

The Judeo-Christian God is very much mysterious and transcendent. The Bible is saturated with the mystery of God and his actions. Over the years, students of the Bible have spoken in endless detail about the *Deus Absconditus.* The story however does not end there. The Bible that deals with the mystery of God is also the Scripture that does not spare words to witness to the mighty ways in which he *reveals* himself. His final and ultimate revelation was in the person and work of Jesus Christ—according to the Christian religion. In Jesus Christ the mystery of God was finally revealed, and a transcendent God became immanent. The *Deus Absconditus* has been translated into the *Deus Revelatus.* The Christian religion is therefore a religion of revelation.

Of course, a revealed religion presupposes the revelation of mysteries. Both the Old and the New Testaments make the claim that God made himself known to everyone, including those who never asked for him.[36] The New Testament reassures us that God in Christ has taken residence in human hearts, and thus the mystery hidden for ages has now been disclosed.[37] Once God, the ultimate mystery, has been revealed, other related mysteries will be unfolded and drawn from Him. Our world ruled by science and logic looks for evidence. We are inclined to complete our search of one thing and then move on to other things (unless we choose to be nothing but Hegelians). From the Christian point of view, the God-question has been answered. Where does the New Age fit into all of this? To that question we shall now turn.

# 2

# The Religion of the New Age

The New Age is a syncretistic religion, a contemporary attempt to combine various opposing tenets and worldviews into a unified whole, appealing to the modern mind. There is, however, a tendency to downplay the religious nature of this new phenomenon. Many authorities have highlighted its sociological nature rising above all religious boundaries, while others have seen in it an impinging threat to existing religions. Among its leadership are social critics, visionaries, celebrities, natural scientists, and religious rebels. Among its teachings are concerns such as a profound social vision, environmental affairs, holistic health, human and humanitarian causes, spiritism, transcendence, and others. Our purpose in this chapter is to demonstrate that there is an overarching religious perspective to the New Age.

The religious nature of the New Age is clearly seen in its interests and practices such as channeling, meditation, occult, astrology, and divination, to name just a few. Again, some students are inclined to dismiss these traits as those of the least religious significance. However, our survey of certain other teachings of the New Age will illustrate the point that these too are religious renditions in keeping with the traditions and practices of the more ancient religions. Ashram, chakra, deva, dharma, guru, karma, kundalini, maya, panchakarma, sidhi, swami, yoga, and yogi are expressions loaded with religious substance in Hinduism. Equally religious are the ways in which these and similar expressions are understood and employed by those who embrace the New Age religion, as we shall see.

Historically, religious faiths have shaped cultures and traditions. In the present instance perhaps a cult and a culture show signs of turning into a religion. The New Age is the religion of like-minded people, a people who are obsessed with the modern heresy of deconstruction.[1] While they feel that God and religion are words that have lost their primary meaning in the contemporary society, to their dismay, they find themselves trapped in their own scheme as their mental impressions find expression largely in religious terms. What the Apostle Paul wrote concerning the law to the Christians in Rome could be said in our day about those who anticipate the demise of religion: When [those], who do not have [religion], do by nature things required by [religion] they are a [religion] for themselves, even though they do not [claim to] have [religion], since they show that the requirements of [religion] are written on their hearts.[2]

Much has been written on the subject of the New Age particularly since the 1980s. A significant number of books on the subject have been published by evangelical Christian scholars who perceive in the philosophy of the New Age a serious threat and a challenge to the Christian faith.[3] These publications in a systematic way help identify the leadership, teaching, and motif of this movement. The present writer is convinced that the Christian faith needs no human defense since it is not of human origin.[4] Nevertheless, it is our Christian duty to respond gently and respectfully to such challenges, because these are opportunities for us to give a reason for the hope we have in Christ (1 Pet. 3:15, 16).

Our task in the present chapter is to illustrate why we claim that the New Age is an emerging religion. We shall do so from two vantage points. First, we will examine the *modus operandi* of the New Age as it is popularized in the West. We will describe this as the method of indigenization, that is, the transplanting of foreign ideas and making them part and parcel of the native frame of reference. Second, we will show that the religious concepts of the New Age are notably Eastern, and fundamentally Hindu in terms of their origin.

# Indigenization

Without a doubt, the language of the Bible has infiltrated the English language. This is obvious when English speakers see "the handwriting on the wall" (as Daniel did) or as they "wash their hands of" a problem (as Pilate did). In a predominantly non-Christian culture, individuals like Mary and John may stand out as Christians simply because they are the proud carriers of biblical names. On the other hand, in the United States it is natural to meet a devout atheist Mary and an ardent secular humanist John. Several phrases and names from the Bible are indigenous to American culture today, and they do not necessarily reflect a particular religious identity anymore. While dictionaries list "the sacred book of Christianity" as the primary meaning of the word "Bible," the same word also stands for "an authoritative book in a particular field." (The *authority* part of the meaning is derived obviously from the hold the Bible has on Christians.) Thus, in popular book stores we encounter computer Bibles, *A Witches Bible Compleat*,[5] and *Powers of the Psalms*.[6] While *A Witches Bible Compleat* is prescribed as required reading for all witches, the Power of the Psalms boldly imitates the biblical Psalter numbering 150, and offering 325 purposes. Included in it are psalms designated to alleviate insomnia, bring customers to business, expand one's psychic abilities, and to protect one from insanity. This is indeed an example of indigenization with a deconstructionist twist.

Douglas Groothuis describes the spirituality of the New Age as a "hybrid spirituality" that "takes the essence of Eastern religions but retains some elements of the Western, Judeo-Christian worldview. What results is a mutation."[7] Such a mutation occurs as the New Age teachings exploit the Christian tutelage of the modern West by interpolating in it a distilled form of Eastern spirituality. The primary source of this Eastern spirituality undoubtedly is Hinduism, just as Judaism is the fountain from which Christianity, and later Islam, sprang. It is only proper to say that of all the better known religions of the East, Hinduism was the first to make its headway in the West.

If the New Age thinking is an amalgam of the Judeo-Christian and Eastern worldviews, to what extent is the Christian element retained in the philosophy of this new phenomenon? How are the familiar (Judeo)-Christian components themselves embellished with strange Eastern notions and commercialized into user-friendly terms? To answer these questions we will examine a random selection of concepts from the New Age glossary that we affirm to be of biblical and therefore of religious origin.

"But God is always present in the heart . . . . Look within. Seek the place where the Spirit is in hiding, cloaked in the love that is its substance and its action,"[8] writes Joan Borysenko, recollecting her own father's consoling response to her seven-year-old intellect, which was concerned and confused about a Sunday school picture of "a bearded, white-haired God peering out from behind the clouds."

The Bible cannot be faulted for a grandfather image of God, for it simply does not speak of God as an old man. The picture of God as "an old man who lives up in the clouds" was the creation of an artist whose generation really appreciated a father for a father and a grandfather for a grandfather. These generations saw in their parents themselves and in their lifestyles God's proximity to them. In the biblical records we also read about God delivering his people (from their enemies) with his mighty hand and outstretched arm (Deut. 5:15). Furthermore, as a spiritual song has it, "He's got the whole world in his hands." For a fact, the singers of this song are not lauding the legendary Atlas who holds the macrocosm in *his* hands! In spite of their vulnerability, human images of God are even today an effective medium to communicate to humans the things concerning God, granted that their thirst for him is not yet fully quenched, and their search not ended.

Let us return to Joan Borysenko's father's advice to his daughter to "look within" to see the god for whom she was searching. His counsel was soothing and refreshing to a

Jewish girl (Joan) who could not compromise with a god "who lived up in the clouds," where perchance "airplanes could zoom through his belly button." Again the fallacy of human language sets in here. Jewish theology does not regard God as a pie in the sky, to be sure. While recognizing God's handiwork in the mountains, skylines, constellations, and galaxies, Judaism looks beyond to the God who *made* the heavens and the earth, arrayed in majesty and glory.[9]

True, God is within us, but we are not God. God is everywhere; and yet everything and every place (including the sacred space) is not God. God is distinct and different from all that he is not. A coffee pot may contain coffee, and yet the pot is never coffee. Litmus paper may react with acidic substance, but the paper does not become acid.

God is within us and also without us. He exists independently of the universe. "His belly button" can therefore escape a billion-dollar zooming spacecraft headed towards outer space. And, why does an airplane fly *up* in the sky to go *around* the globe? When it comes to the God-question the sky is *not* the limit. God shall be even after "all the stars of the heavens will be dissolved and the sky rolled up like a scroll" (Is. 34:4). "Everything has a place and everything in its place," the sociologists say.

Jean K. Foster, author of the trilogy *Truth for the New Age,* in the first of her three books proposes "a God-mind plan for saving planet and man."[10] Foster envisions the God of the universe as man's "Teammate" involved in the process of saving planet earth from extinction. While discussing matters concerning God, she prefers the expression "God of the universe" to enable persons to think big. "The God concept must be expanded if it is to meet your expectations. The smaller the God concept, the smaller the expectations," she writes.[11]

Foster is a highly motivated writer. She understands her readership and sends them the clarion call to team up with her and God in order to spare the earth from impending catastrophe. Her authority to do so rests solely on the revelation she received from other "spirit entities," the spirits of those who departed this world in yesteryears and are now in a different plane. Saving and preserving planet earth then is a joint endeavor of the God (of the universe), of the spirits in the next plane, and of those today occupying the face of the earth. According to Foster, "When you say 'God,' you say the word that represents your concept of all that is good, perfect and powerful. God is that essence of perfection which is there to be used."[12]

On the face of it, there is little reason for anyone to dispute what has been said above concerning God. These specifications for God can easily match those of any of the world's major religions. God is great, majestic, and awesome. Indeed God is good, perfect, and powerful. It is only fair to say that, in a sense, God is the source of the essential goodness in all people. Christians can without reservations endorse all these statements.

On closer examination, however, this New Age understanding of God carries with it a strong element of synergism. Synergism is the idea that man (and, in the New Age thinking, also spirits from the next plane) cooperates with God to enhance and insure happiness and well being of all people on earth. What we encounter here is a kind of utilitarian philosophy with underpinnings of the popular notion that God helps those who help themselves. Your God is what you make of him. At the same time, Foster warns us that we will be the losers if we project a divinity that exercises power and authority over others. She says, "[But] if you perceive a God of vengeance, or a God who wants power over others, you retreat from the position of being able to use God's gifts."[13] In other words, what you want is what you get from this God of the New Age. Obviously, this is a dramatic shift from the way in which Christians perceive God as being equally just and gracious.

The New Age thinking decries the fact that the Christian religion stigmatizes all human beings as sinners. To call a person a sinner is itself a sin according to this view. Most Christians confess that they are by their very nature sinners, and that in their thoughts, words, and deeds they sin against

God and people. However, some popular versions of modern Christian theology no longer look at sin in its original, biblical sense.[14] Scholars who pursue this view emphasize the symptoms of sin while ignoring the cause. Sin has been described variously as capitalism or as communism. While some say sin is the shortage of the power of positive thinking, others say it is imposed on humans by an ecclesiastical hierarchy. If for some sin is exploiting nature and oppressing people, for others it is willingly submitting to exploitation and oppression. Sin is ignorance, inferiority complex, male chauvinism, and more. Perhaps these ideas may have served as the seed bed for the New Age notion that the very thought of sin needs to be erased from the human conscience.

The writings of Matthew Fox are widely quoted by many New Age writers. Fox's popularity among them makes sense as the subtitle of his recent book shows: *The Healing of Mother Earth* and the Birth of a Global Renaissance. [15] In that volume this Dominican priest raises the question, "Does the fact that the Christ became incarnate in Jesus exclude the Christ's becoming incarnate in others—Lao-tsu or Buddha or Moses or Sarah or Sojourner Truth or Gandhi or me or you?" Fox's own answer to this question, as he interprets Paul's letter to the Galatians, is negative. "The Cosmic Christ still needs to be born in all of us—no individual, race, religion, culture, or time is excluded. 'Christ' is a generic name. In that sense we are all 'other Christs,'" he writes.[16]

Before we respond to Father Fox's vision of the cosmic (and mystic) Christ, let us also become acquainted with a similar visualization by Gloria D. Karpinski. Karpinski is a professional teacher, counselor, and healer representing the "new breed of holistically oriented professionals." According to this itinerant lecturer, "The Universal Christ is represented not only by the historical figure we call Jesus. . . . Rather *it* (italics mine) is to be understood as the ultimate potential that exists in all beings. But it only comes into flower in one who has become fully self-realized."[17]

Great masters, those self-realized beings who live as manifestations of the Universal Christ, have appeared in many different traditions throughout history. They have demonstrated by their total beingness and their teachings the way to bridge humanness and Godness. That potential is present in every being. The Universal Christ is the means through which we reconnect with the Source. It is the saving grace that leads us out of ignorance and bondage on the wheel of rebirth. It is the Light of the World, which transforms lead into gold through the alchemy of pure love.[18]

Both Fox and Karpinski propose the need for a certain transformation in the living and thinking of the peoples of this world. Apparently both set Christ as the pattern after whom (which) others may model their existence, or as Fox sees it, they themselves become Christs. For Karpinski this is a process of self-realization, because she believes that the "Universal Christ" is already present in each individual. Evidently this kind of thinking explains the New Age phrase, "christic consciousness." Perhaps it is Matthew Fox's Christian upbringing and training that forces him to say that "the Cosmic Christ still needs to be born in all of us."

Before Christ is "formed" in any one Christ must be *in* that person. The Apostle Paul speaks of the situation in which people are "separated from Christ" (in fact, without Christ), and "without God."[19] The Paul who wrote to the Galatians was fully conscious of the time *before* Christ was "formed" in him. Not too long before, this same Paul was going around "breathing out murderous threats" against anyone who followed the way of the Christ. And then Paul was united[20]with Christ as the risen Jesus Christ met him on the road to Damascus. This is neither mutation nor the evolution of the self into a higher level, but a dramatic transformation in the thinking and acting of the person in whom the Christ takes residence. Its consequence is not a mystical union, but a communion with Christ in which the individual identities both of Christ and of the individual remain unaltered.

Fox writes that his book has to do with "*educing* what is already present in our midst: the image of God, the Cosmic Christ present in every individual. True empowerment happens when we *educe* the divine beauty and power from one another."[21] In these lines Fox is proposing a pedagogy for the New Age. Education has been, and will continue to be, on the forefront of any significant change in the life of individuals and communities everywhere. Nevertheless, our present age is living testimony to the fact that the "educed" themselves are yet searching for the ultimate meaning of their lives. If the Cosmic Christ is *already* present in each individual, why must the search continue? Why must we strive to become what we already are?

Perhaps Karpinski is more aware of the problem here than Fox, because she acknowledges that there is a need in every person "to bridge humanness and Godness." Obviously, a severing of the connection between the beings and their Source had occurred, and according to her, "the universal Christ is the means through which we reconnect with the Source." She confesses to a strong Christian influence as she states that the Universal Christ is "saving grace" and "the Light of the world," and we might add, the way, the truth, and the life. Karpinski catches the vision but again, like Fox, misses the point when she says that the potential to bridge humanness and Godness is present in every being.

We could easily avoid all these circumlocutions once we acknowledge the simple scriptural truth that human beings are sinners. To be sure, Augustine did not invent this idea on his own as Fox and Borysenko allege.[22] The youthful and successful king David, who preceded Augustine by well over a millennium, lamented that sin was his "star sign" as he said, "Surely I was sinful at birth, sinful from the time my mother conceived me" (Ps. 51:5). Few people in the world have known David and Augustine, and yet many know their own sin. Different communities and cultures may have labeled sin differently. Some ignore the issue of sin; others devise methods to get over sin and its consequences. Yet sin has been at the doorstep of everyone, a universally acknowledged phenomenon.

Christianity does not take pride or rejoice in branding everyone a sinner. It simply raises the human conscience and brings it to the floodlight of eternal justice. While exposing every spot and wrinkle of sin with the Law of God, this religion, where God truly meets man, gives freely and willingly everyone everywhere the healing and comforting power of the Gospel. In Christianity, the scope of sin, as well as the free *offer* of the way out of sin is universal. True, the Christian religion calls everyone to repentance. That call is not a threat, but a hearty invitation for everyone to return to the Source from which all have gone astray. There they shall be one with themselves and with others through Christ. The same Jesus Christ who once walked this earth will come once again to declare who is with him and who is not.[23]

Exactly a decade ago Matthew Fox declared that the Western Christian church was at fault for misleading a civilization into the notion of original sin. And consequently,

> Western civilization has preferred love of death to love of life to the very extent that its religious traditions have preferred redemption to creation, sin to ecstasy, and individual introspection to cosmic awareness and appreciation. Religion has failed people in the West as often as it has been silent about pleasure or about cosmic creation, about the ongoing power of the flowing energy of the Creator, about original blessing.[24]

Relating the human predicament to sin or to its derivatives is not exclusively a feature of the Christian religion. The Buddha, the Enlightened One (that is what the appellation means), by means of constant meditation received the enlightened understanding that, after all, suffering is the fact of life. The way out of suffering is to get rid of desire. Striving for bad things is evil. Equally bad is the craving to achieve good things through evil means. Desire therefore has to come to an end. For that the Buddha proposed the famous Eightfold Path.

A religion that does not acknowledge the basic sinful nature of mankind has no reason to claim a "Christ" of its own. In fact the Buddha never said that he was the Christ, nor did he claim that his purpose was to save others from their sins. But the Christ of the New Testament came to save sinners (1 Tim. 1:15). When Paul was faced with the dilemma that he could not on his own desire the right thing, in Jesus the Christ he also saw the lasting solution (Rom. 7:21–25).

Is the Christian understanding of creation pessimistic? By no means!—quite in contrast to the pessimism of other religions. According to many nonbiblical sources, the creation of human beings was itself the result of some type of warfare between the powers of good and evil. In the Babylonian creation story, man was created to aid the sea in its struggle against the gods that disturbed her. Zoroaster taught that the Good God created man to help him attack the forces of the Destructive Spirit. The *Rig Veda* of Hinduism explains that the world exists as a result of a primordial sacrifice in which the world-maker (Vishvakarman) sacrificed himself in order to bring the world into being. If the old Athenians conceived of *not* being born as the best thing for man, and death immediately after birth the next best thing, modern existentialists believe that they came into this world because of a biological accident.

The biblical picture of man appears to be more poignant here: God created man in his own image. The Lord God formed man from the dust of the ground (non-being), and breathed into his nostrils the breath of life (being), and the man became a living being. God created man and he saw it was very good. This is the original blessing.

The transformation from non-being to being makes humans what they are, namely, human beings. Human beings, according to the Bible, were created to rule and subdue the earth. The earth is not the gentle mother petting and cajoling her children, nor is it worthy of the worship of humans. The earth and the events taking place in it (what humans call natural disasters or the wrath of mother earth) continue to prove themselves to be out of human control. Interestingly enough, the same earth is crying out for its own salvation (Rom. 8:18–22). Thus we are stuck with a mother who can neither take care of herself nor offer us a better place to live. What better way to explain this than boldly acknowledge that all this is the result of original sin. And God said to Adam, "Cursed is the ground because of you" (Gen. 3:17).

There is room for ecstasy and cosmic awareness in Christianity in spite of its teaching regarding (original) sin. There is celebration in the Christian religion as it emphasizes creation as well as redemption. Earth, stars, the heavens and the firmament, as they declare the majesty and glory of the Lord their Maker, render humans speechless (ecstatic). Humans in turn are privileged to relish the song of the skies in honor of their God. Humans themselves are on top of the world, because God has crowned them with glory and honor (cosmic awareness).[25] Those that are redeemed, cleansed, and recreated by grace plead for the redemption of others in unspoken words and thoughts that surpass expression.

Nevertheless, there is no room in the Christian religion for venerating and worshipping created objects, including human beings. To God alone is due all praise and worship. Humans have but one life to live on this earth, at the summation of which they must depart this world, never to return. A second chance and another prospect is not in the destiny of any person. Both Jesus and the New Testament writers alert humans to the urgency of making the most of their only time on earth. They warn that soon the night in which no one can work will overshadow the universe. The world today is closer than ever to the point of no return. The only way to dodge this darkness is for humans to clothe themselves with the Lord Jesus, the Eternal Light.[26]

Once having established that New Age thinking follows the pattern of the Christian religion in a schematic fashion, it becomes easy to recognize Christian elements in the details of this new religion. To illustrate this point let us briefly review the New Age interpretation of some other Christian concepts.[27]

*Agape love* is a bonding expression in New Age thinking. This concept is interpreted as a "love that helps one another, not a love that encompasses a person with affection." Agape love is an abiding principle of the New Testament with far deeper meaning. The self-giving and self-sacrificing nature of this love was uniquely manifested in the incarnation of Jesus Christ. Jesus demonstrated the depth of this love by laying down his very life for others (John 15:13). It is this same agape love that holds all Christians together as a community in the strong bond of fellowship.

New Age writers make reference to some type of *automatic* writing. Such a procedure apparently empowers the writer to transcribe the "mind to mind communication" between the author and "the Brotherhood of God." For a Christian reader this quickly suggests a parallel to the concept of verbal inspiration. While Christians acknowledge the idea of God's involvement in the writing of the Scriptures, New Age writers claim that their source of inspiration is the "Brotherhood of God."

The *Brotherhood of God* links the New Agers with the spirit world, which according to them is "the next plane of life." This plane is allegedly the realm of the departed, "advanced spirits." These are the souls of the deceased who, instead of leaving the earth, linger in the air in order that they may assist those who are still on earth in their pursuit of truth. This notion is an indigenized version of the Mahayana Buddhist teaching according to which "the Bodhisattva postpones his goal of becoming a Buddha in order first to save as many others as possible."[28] However, one cannot lose sight also of the Christian nexus here when these spirits are contemplated as the "counselor, the comforter, [and] the teacher who work with those in the earth plane who open their minds to them." Needless to say, the parallel in the New Testament is that all these appellations are used to describe God the Holy Spirit.

The New Age religion claims that *Christ* is an idea that epitomizes the oneness of humans with God. "Each person can consider himself or herself the Christ in the sense of that oneness." The daintiness of Christ for the New Agers sets in here. Sadly, they see him only as "the lily of the valley" and "the fairest of ten thousands." While they would like to be Christlike, they ignore the Christ who takes away the sin of the world and who gives his life as a ransom for many. Undoubtedly this split vision of Christ was generated particularly by some Christian thinkers of the modern epoch.[29]

The New Agers contend that the Christian perception of God as Father and Judge is an expression of the limited way in which Christians are able to understand him. That is, the human descriptions of God represent only the extent to which people have been able to grasp the Divine. This is a compliment especially to Christians because they have come to know God not by means of human wisdom but through the Son of God. Christians believe that God is universally and eternally present, the beginning and the end, and that he is in all and fills all (Eph. 1:23). Undoubtedly, this is an all-encompassing and uncompromising picture of God.

An equally sensitive issue within the New Age philosophy is the problem of evil. In the Christian view, evil presents itself wherever morality and ethics are violated. Evil is innately present in each individual, not by design but by accident. God is not the source of evil, nor does he take pleasure in wickedness. Instead, God requires human beings to shun evil. Evil is the consequence of man letting the devil take control of his heart.

It is a blatant error on the part of any one to dismiss the fact of evil in the world. Evil is vibrant and abundant on planet earth. Evil operates consistently against the essential goodness with which God originally invested all of his creation. The effects of evil have brought destruction upon the cosmos; and hence the entire creation has been groaning as in the pains of childbirth (Rom. 8:22). The plight of planet earth is such that every human effort to save it from destruction, regardless of how sincere, is doomed to fail.

The followers of New Age ideology are forever conscious of the perilous situation on planet earth. In order to thwart this impending cataclysm and to enable both the earth and mankind to survive extinction, they persuade every human being to join forces with God "in a total team work." They seem to see the writing on the wall that "the time now appears on the horizon when the earth must reinstate purity into its being."

Why is it that (mother) earth is not pure today? To be sure, the earth has never been free from the threat of extinction since the fall of man. If it is the destiny of the human race, the custodians of planet earth, to hand over the torch of life from one generation to another, the earth, which is nothing but the temporary residence of humans cannot claim for itself any permanence. The old Epicureans, because they were aware of this impermanence, decided to eat drink and be merry. The modern existentialists also are conscious of this as they strive to live for the moment. Christians, while cognizant of their pleasant duty to work in the present earth and to take care of it, look forward to the coming of a *new heaven and the new earth* because they themselves are newly created in Jesus Christ.

What the West once considered pagan and uncivilized is today surprisingly neopagan and progressive thinking. What not too long ago was primitive and uninformed is now the symbol of wholeness and the pinnacle of erudition. What are the factors that caused such a dramatic shift in the Western view of life? Why is the West fascinated by the Eastern interpretations of life? We will answer these questions in the rest of this chapter.

# Monism

If there will ever be a "Who's Who" to raise the issue "What is truth?" Pontius Pilate will without a doubt top that list. Unlike everyone else, when Pilate asked that question, the very Truth was standing before his eyes in flesh and blood, according to the Bible. Perhaps confronting the Truth eye to eye caused such a psychedelic effect on this Roman governor that he was lost in that panorama of truth and found himself helpless to defend it.

Pilate joined the crowd, unable to stand up for truth. Truth was defeated momentarily, but not forever. Pilate had heard Jesus say to him, "Everyone on the side of truth listens to me" (John 18:37). Unwilling to heed that truth, people continue to claim, "What is true to you need not be true to me." Pilate must be "turning in his grave" as the search for truth continues even today.

If truth is hard to identify and define, harder yet is life, and its meaning. The book of Genesis indicates that God is the source of life. God formed man from the dust of the ground and breathed into his nostrils the breath of life, and the man became a living being (Gen. 2:7). The recorded words of Jesus say that he is the way, the truth, and the life (John 14:6). The book of Exodus recounts that the God of Israel revealed himself to Moses as the *I AM*, the God of Abraham, the God of Isaac, and the God of Jacob (Ex. 3:14–15). Jesus further illustrated that this God of the patriarchs is not the God of the dead but of the living (Matt. 22:32). Again, those who were privileged to hear, see, and touch Jesus say life appeared in him (1 John 1:1–2). In Jesus' own words, those who reject him will not see life (John 3:36).

The Christian religion distinguishes life (breath of life) from matter (dust of the ground). The dualism of Christianity makes a clear distinction between God the creator of all things and that which has been created. God, and everything God made are separate one from the other. As opposed to this idea of clear separation, monism represents the notion that all is one.

In Hinduism, in spite of the popular opinion that Hindus worship 330 million gods, the ultimate reality is one. That reality is the all-embracing, all-inclusive Brahman.[30] The Upanishads explain that the Brahman is *in* the wind, and the wind *is* him. He is unborn, limitless, everywhere, the brilliant light, and in the fire.

Later Upanishadic teaching noticed a distinct discrepancy in the understanding of the Brahman as a person. A person is subject to definition and to the limitations set by that definition. Whereas God, who cannot have limitations, must remain impersonal and without attributes, and therefore neuter (It). That *It* is the basis and source of all existence.

And yet, this unknowable needs to be understood. For this purpose the same unknowable and impersonal manifests itself in persons, places, and things. Thus, the Brahman (*world soul*) exists in a person as the unseen inner self (*atman*). Consequently, the true identity of an individual person and that of the cosmos is one and the same. The seeming separateness of the individual soul from the world soul is only a phenomenon. In other words, the so-called existence of the individual soul independently of the world soul is an illusion (*maya*). A celebrated illustration from the Chandogya Upanishad will help clarify this point.

The young and inquisitive Shvetaketu was searching for the meaning of life. Seeking an explanation of the mystery of life, Shvetaketu approached his father. "That which is the finest essence—this whole world has that as its soul. That is Reality. That is Atman. That you are, Shvetaketu," his father responded. Enthused about his father's response and yet baffled by it, Shvetaketu wanted his father to explain this idea to him further. By way of illustration, the father required the son to bring him a fig. As the fig was brought, the son was asked to divide it into small parts. Then the father asked the son to pick one very small part and again divide that part. The process went on, and finally Shvetaketu admitted that he could no longer see the parts, nor could he divide them.

"Certainly, my son, that purest essence that your eyes could not see—from that very essence the fig tree sprouts. Believe you me, my son. That which is the finest essence—this whole world has that as its soul. That is Reality. That is Atman. *That you are*, Shvetaketu." 31

By this parable Shvetaketu's father taught his son that there is ultimately no distinction between the world soul and the individual soul. Through the scenario of the object lesson the son had come to a point where he could no longer recognize the part of the seed, though it was present. Ultimately, reality is present in every minute and tiny detail of life even when the naked eye is unable to identify and appreciate it as it is.

Thus, in the monistic view, the ultimate reality is one, the indivisible One. It transcends definition and description. That One is in everyone and that One surrounds everyone. When the individual self (Atman) comes to the conscious awareness that it and the *It* (world soul) are one, there is celebration, ecstasy, liminality, and ultimate bliss. One has arrived. All is one. This is the essence of monism. Undoubtedly, monistic philosophy has been at the core of the Hindu view of life. It has been the religious source of comfort and hope for the Hindus, assuring them of the strength to continue through the rough and tumble of life. Monism offers people comfort amidst poverty, failure, sickness, and other setbacks as it reminds them that their true self is not themselves (the present existence is illusory and transitory). People also have hope in this religion because they know that soon they will come to the conscious awareness that they are one with the world soul (and that state will transcend the present social, caste, and economic disparities).

The principle of the Upanishadic teaching on monism was further explained in the eighth century of our era by the famous Hindu philosopher Sankara. The central teaching of Sankara's philosophy is identified as *advaita* or non-dualism. Following through on monistic philosophy, Sankara taught that the very existence of the Brahman, the world, and the individual is an unexplainable phenomenon. These entities do not exist independently of one another. At the same time they are not absolutely one either. Sankara therefore coined the expression *advaita,* which means *not two, not three or more.*

The puzzling human predicament of not being able to interpret life and its meaning obviously is not limited to Sankara alone.

Sankara's fascination for reality reveals itself in its numerous dimensions in other writings and speeches that pertain to the ultimate questions in life. For example, when we come across a piece of literature or an impressive discourse that deals with truth, justice, or love, we hear the authors telling us more about what these are *not* than what they really *are.* No two people seem to agree voluntarily and wholeheartedly on a principle that is clearly, solidly, and eternally true. Eternal principles therefore must be revealed from an eternal source, rather than discovered through human initiative and effort.

The Upanishadic concept of monism and Sankara's philosophy of non-dualism are based on the fundamental Hindu ideal that the very existence of everything is an illusion (maya). Although by the very nature of It the Brahman remains the absolute, unmanifest, and without attributes, through maya It becomes Ishvara and creates the universe. Thus what appears to our senses and experiences to be real within the created universe is not really real. In reality it is a phenomenon (illusion) caused by the "sport," "play," or "art" of the Brahman.[32]

The monistic view is so inherent in Hinduism that a creator/creation distinction similar to that in the Christian faith is impossible to make in this religion.[33] However, there is every indication that from time immemorial Hinduism understood the Divine as the source of life. Gods who generated life are also called upon to provide all that is necessary to maintain life on earth. Thus on a popular level, each local village appears to have its own particular deity or deities. For the purpose of stabilizing the supply of resources that are vital for the ongoing flow of life, villagers invoke gods and goddesses responsible for life, water, and fertility. Such gods are represented symbolically in icons of fertility, in the form of male and female sex organs. From a very practical point of view Hinduism preserves the idea of a mother earth and has traditionally maintained the notion of a matriarchal society.

The Vedas, the Hindu scriptures that preceded the Upanishads, made a distinction between spirit and matter, soul and substance. Accordingly, the created order came into being as the result of a cosmic sacrifice, a fission occurring in the world soul; for "there can be no life without sacrifice." Thus the cosmic body of the Brahman was divided into the four major classes of the Hindu society: the mouth becoming the priestly order (the Brahmins), the arms becoming the ruling class (the Kshatriyas), the thighs becoming the landowners, merchants, and bankers (the Vaishyas), and the feet becoming the workers, artisans, and serfs (the Shudras).[34]

Clearly evident in the matrix of the Indian society even today is the Hindu influence of the caste system. We cannot help noticing the difference in status of the various castes, once we recognize from the above mentioned illustration that the Brahmins and the Shudras evolved respectively from the mouth and the feet of the Brahman. While it is possible to claim a certain cosmic unity and harmony in the Hindu social structure (whether Brahmin or Shudra, all came out of the same world soul, the Brahman), it is equally reasonable to conclude that, whether for better or for worse, a person's social status is determined at birth (Shudras rank at the bottom of the social stratum). In a strictly parochial sense, this is in keeping with the laws of karma resulting in the cycle of birth, death, and rebirth, also known as *samsara* or reincarnation.[35]

Reincarnation is a very popular notion among the followers of the New Age. According to New Age theory, at death the soul of the deceased departs the body and takes residence in another, in a continuum, aspiring for perfection. This process continues until the individual soul attains *Nirvana* or eternal bliss.

David Christie-Murray has done an extensive study on the subject of reincarnation, which was published simultaneously in Europe, Australia, and the United States. The author cites numerous stories and confessions of individuals who claim to have lived different lives and played diverse roles on various continents. He notes that in modern times this belief is gaining more acceptance in the West than ever before. Christie-Murray concludes:

A certain archetypal theme runs through many creeds, for all their differences. We originate in some way from God; we descend into matter; we progress back to God. The purpose of the process is completely ethical and educational, to lead us by experience from innocence to so triumphantly victorious a morality that we are able and worthy to rejoin our Maker on—dare it be said?—

equal terms. Reincarnation is the tool by which our destiny is shaped.[36]

Studies in comparative religion have established that reincarnation or the belief in the transmigration of souls has been a commonplace doctrine in the creeds of many primal as well as several advanced religions. While ethical and instructional motifs are involved in this theory, it also suggests an evolutionary process by which finally humans will be able to return to their source.

The theory of reincarnation clearly states that something is fundamentally wrong with the human race and the space it occupies at the present time. This is the result of bad karma. As Christie-Murray has pointed out, those who believe in the reincarnation theory believe also in (some kind of) God. They maintain that the human race had its beginning in God; it plummeted into the material world (by accident, destiny, or divine design); and it strives to return to its Maker. This return (forever) will occur after the soul has gone through a series of recurring incarnations that presumably equip the individual self for its once-and-for-all entry into the point of no return (nirvana).

While it may be true that several world religions sustain a doctrine of reincarnation, only Hinduism draws a close link between it and the Law of Karma.[37] According to the Hindu tradition, "One's future existence is determined by the Law of Karma . . . . the law that one's thoughts, words, and deeds have an ethical consequence fixing one's lot in future existences. Viewed retrospectively, karma is the *cause* of what is happening in one's life now."[38]

The soul that is entangled in the whirlpool of the law of karma is usually in for more trouble, all but once when the good deeds of that soul are good enough for its emancipation from the cycle of birth and rebirth. Implied in the karmic theory is more bad news than good news. As one writer puts it, karma "hangs overhead like a thundercloud. Without warning, like a thunderbolt out of the blue, that karma descends on the doer at the proper time to effect its perfect retribution."[39] The world knows only one Buddha and perhaps a few Bodhisattvas for whom karma may have traced the road to freedom. For billions of other ordinary people this doctrine of retributive justice continues to spell perennial overcast skies and everlasting thunderbolts over them.

Critics of the New Age ideas of reincarnation and karma also have observed the close parallels between New Age teaching and Hinduism.[40] Obviously, this parallelism stems from the New Age's Hindu connection. Karma has been interpreted as "work, action; destiny (ineluctable consequence of acts performed in a previous existence); product, effect, etc."[41] It is true that on a popular level karma and reincarnation appear cynical and pessimistic. Nevertheless, in philosophical terms, these doctrines are encouraging and optimistic as well, when understood cosmically. Pain and suffering are the lot of everyone and everything that has assumed existence, including the gods. But "if the human condition is condemned to pain for all eternity . . . each individual who shares in it can pass beyond it, since each can annul the karmic forces by which it is governed."[42]

Perhaps the last mentioned point that *each individual can annul* the karmic forces is what makes karma, and its corollary reincarnation, fascinating and most appealing to the Western mind. The Western mind puts a heavy emphasis on the individual self and its independence. These two ingredients produce self-confidence. Self-confidence loves challenges. The greater the challenge the greater the desire to confront that challenge. If there is a will there is a way! There is always room for improvement in everything humans do. Ultimately humans can annul the karmic forces, so thinks the least religious follower of the New Age.

The theory of reincarnation is the fitting ancient antecedent to modern evolutionary science. Just as the theory of evolution deals with the so-called progression of life forms from lower to higher levels as a result of natural selection, reincarnation proposes the same evolutionary process for the soul. However, with the latter the process of elimination is so uncompromising that ultimately few make it to the eternal hall of fame (nirvana). Here too a kind of power-of-possibility thinking prevails. In spite of the fact that the odds of winning in this spiritual gambling are virtually nil, the New Age thinking infuses this notion with a certain spirit of sportsmanship.

The incorporation of monism, karma, and reincarnation into New Age thinking illustrates the fact that human beings are not willing, for any reason, to depart the present world, although they realize that it is the destiny of everyone to exit this planet sooner or later. Reincarnation is the tranquilizing rejoinder to the human failure to become modern Methuselahs (Gen. 5:27) and Ut-napishtims.[43]

According to Genesis, Methuselah was privileged to enjoy the greatest longevity on earth. Ut-napishtim is pictured in the Gilgamesh epic as the only man who was ever able to survive death. Having come to grips with the inevitability of death, King Gilgamesh set out in search of immortality. During his sojourn he was greeted by the immortal Ut-napishtim. To the king's dismay, the undying guru was confined to his bed, unable to move around or do anything because of his old age. The longest life span is not always the most covetable, the king reminisced! Unwilling to succumb to the reality of death and to the inevitable corrosion of the earth, the New Age philosophy presumes that it has the mandate to make the earth a better place to live. This ambitious goal of preserving planet earth from extinction is to be attained through synergistic means. That is, the god(s), the souls of those who have temporarily left the world, and the current residents of the earth together strive to bring heaven on earth. The earth is where everyone belongs, king or slave. After all, in the New Age ideology "there is no king who has not had a slave among his ancestors, and no slave who has not had a king among his."[44]

Those who uphold the monistic worldview cannot remain faithful to it unless they also follow its related doctrines of karma and rebirth. Those who subscribe to the laws of karma cannot indulge in any activity (not even in the spirit of a sportsman) and say, "To err is human."

Followers of the laws of karma will have to follow them all the way. They cannot get out of them until they have paid the last penny. How demanding is this law?

In consequence of many sinful acts committed with his body, a man becomes in the next birth something inanimate, in consequence of sins committed by speech, a bird, and in consequence of mental sins he is reborn in a lower caste. . . . Those who committed mortal sins, having passed during large numbers of years through dreadful hells, obtain, after the expiration of that term of punishment, the following births. The slayer of a Brahmin enters the womb of a dog, a pig, an ass, a camel, a cow, a goat, a sheep, a deer, a bird, a Kandala, and a Pukhasa. . . . A Brahmin who steals the gold of a Brahmin shall pass a thousand times through the bodies of spiders, snakes, lizards, of aquatic animals and of destructive Pukhasas. . . . Men who delight in doing hurt become carnivorous animals; those who eat forbidden food, worms; thieves, creatures consuming their own kind. . . . For stealing grain a man becomes a rat; . . . for stealing a horse, a tiger; for stealing fruits and roots, a monkey; for stealing a woman, a bear; for stealing cattle, a he-goat.[45]

If true, how can society expect men to do dishes and women to wash clothes and still look forward to reincarnation?

While considering the difficult question of the meaning of life, a Christian answer appears to be more convincing, and also perhaps the most comforting. Christianity (and other religions that are based on the Judeo-Christian worldview) maintains that human lives have their source in God. Every human being is created in God's own image. That means all individuals, regardless of their class, sex, color, race, and ethnic origin, are worthy of honor and respect. Each person is endowed with a unique identity. No modern champion of the human cause seems to have a problem with this idea.

If we take pride in the privilege that we are made in the image of God, we owe it to God to walk in his ways. Walking on this earth in God's ways is never easy for anyone, though God offers his Word to everyone as the lamp to their feet and the light for their path. In our failure to follow God's ways lies the cause of human misery and sorrow. Paul in the

New Testament spoke for all when he said that the good he wanted to do he was *unable* to do, and by his sinful nature he was led to do those things he always hated to do. (Augustine was not around at this time to brainwash Paul!) Paul was humble enough to acknowledge that sin was living *in* him causing him to will and to do evil. Paul also experienced the most convincing and the most comforting solution to this problem in God through Jesus Christ.[46]

The earth cannot plead exception to a law to which its rulers, human beings, are subject. The earth too suffers with mankind—frustrated, and anxiously looking for liberation and redemption. Not only the earth but the entire creation will be redeemed from bondage to decay (caused by human sin) in a way that is suitable for the new creation. The God who, without human assistance, designed the salvation of mankind also has his own ways of saving the universe.

What is "new" in the religion of the New Age but a modernization of old ideas—ideas that have withstood the test of time? If religions have a characteristic way of viewing God as separate from the universe, so in the New Age God, humans, and the dead work together.

If religions in general prepare humans for a good life here and a better life hereafter, the New Age aspires to make the earth itself the greatest place to live. It is to the earth that New Agers would like to return by way of reincarnation. While teaching others to free themselves from the sense of guilt, they hold their ancestors guilty of all that is wrong in today's world.[47]

In the New Age, earth is the Mother, and God is an energy Gestalt. There is no such thing as God and yet all is God. Channelers receive paranormal information from a certain spiritual entity, a monistic conglomeration of the so-called souls in the next plane. A consciousness revolution, they say, is inevitable for all to attain the awareness that God, mankind, and the earth are all one and the same. If there is one religion that can match all these goals, that fortunate one may be Hinduism. In the next chapter we will learn why this is so.

# 3

# Hindu Openness
# A Fascination
# for the West

Hinduism is a religion of the open book. It has been described as a way of life, giving its traditions as much validity as its scriptures. Unlike other major world religions, Hinduism has no founder and no specific creed. Hinduism is a growing tradition, always absorbing and assimilating new ideas, and always adjusting to new conditions. "Hinduism is therefore not a dogmatic creed, but a vast, complex, but subtly unified mass of spiritual thought and realization."[1]

It has been said that Hinduism, along with its branches Jainism and Buddhism, has supplied the raw materials for the religions of half the world.[2] Dr. S. Radhakrishnan, Hindu philosopher, statesman, and a former president of India, has remarked that the spiritual energies of much of the orient originated in India. The variety and diversity of Hinduism is its strength. It emphasizes the individual's intellectual acumen as well as emotional expression, its rationalism as well as mysticism. "While fixed intellectual beliefs mark off one religion from the other, Hinduism sets itself no such limits. Intellect is subordinated to intuition, dogma to experience, outer expression to inward realization."[3]

According to K. M. Sen, a scholar and researcher in Hindu philosophy and Indian folk culture, Hinduism is capable of meeting two fundamental religious needs of individuals. The Vedas, the Hindu scriptures that originated in the second millennium B.C., describe "the feeling of wonder and awe at the mystery of existence." Secondly, Hinduism has maintained a very strong "moral code of behavior." These two salient features have spilled over to Eastern and Far Eastern religions as well. Hinduism therefore is "more like a tree that has grown gradually than like a building that has been erected by some great architect at some definite point in time."[4]

Morality and mystery are two schools that will never suffer for low enrollment in the university of life and religion. While the biological sciences deal with observation and objective analysis of life, philosophy struggles with life's meaning. While scientific investigation cannot proceed without empirical evidence, philosophy can survive wherever there are inquisitive minds. Science has yet to discover the transformation from nonlife to life. The mystery of existence is therefore a mystery for science.

Not so with philosophy, whose purpose is to interpret life. Philosophy may add meaning to life, or it may cause humans to lose whatever meaning they once found in life. The claws of philosophy have a firm grip on every thinking organism. The moment people begin to deny that they have any grasp of philosophy, they themselves become philosophers! Philosophy inspires questions whose answers determine our destiny. Philosophy deals with the mystery of life (the source, force, and end of life) and what people do with it (morality, virtue, and discipline).

Hinduism employs a philosophical approach. It loves to play with the mystery. As we have seen, life itself is the *lila* (sport, play, or art) of the Brahman. In fact, the very Brahman is the *mysterium tremendum*, the unfathomable mystery. Hence this "Nameless and Formless is called by different names, and different forms are attributed to Him, but it is not forgotten that He is One."[5]

This is not just a philosophical proposition confined to the intellectually mature and socially elite. The illiterate and ordinary devout Hindus also believe that the Brahman is a mystery. The uninformed outsider who pays a visit to an Indian village may think that Hindus worship innumerable gods and their idols. Ask the village Hindus, and they will respond that "there are many gods. There is Siva here, and there is Vishnu, Ganesa, Hanuman, Ganga, Durga, and the others. But of course, there is really only one. These many are differences of name and form."[6]

Hinduism is an ever expanding, all-inclusive phenomenon. It accommodates everything it confronts. In it is a place for everything and everyone who comes near it.

> Suppose a Christian approaches a Hindu teacher for spiritual guidance, he would not ask his Christian pupil to discard his allegiance to Christ but would tell him that his idea of Christ was not adequate, and would lead him to a knowledge of the real Christ, the incorporate Supreme. Every God accepted by Hinduism is elevated and ultimately identified with the central Reality which is one with the deeper self of man. The addition of new gods to the Hindu pantheon does not endanger it.[7]

A popular south Indian song expresses the same spirit of the comprehensive nature of the Hindu concept of God and hence the openness of the Hindu religion:

> Into the bosom of the one great sea
> Flow streams that come from hills on every side,
> Their names are various as their springs,
> And thus in every land do men bow down
> To one great God, though known by many names.[8]

Hinduism is heaped with mystery in its faith and practice. It incorporates almost everything and leaves out next to nothing. Its openness fascinates both the insider and the outsider, the devout follower and the critical inquirer. David R. Kinsley compares Hinduism to an obsessive collector who gathers everything and throws away very little. "The Hindu religion has shown itself to be an incurable collector, and it contains in the nooks and crannies of its house many different things. Today this great collector may hold one or another thing in fashion and seem to be utterly fascinated by it. But very few things are ever discarded altogether."[9] These features portray the mystery of Hinduism.

Hinduism stresses a strong sense of morality among its followers. Moral law governs the entire structure of the

Hindu religion and society. Individuals have specific karmic responsibilities to fulfill in accordance with the nature of their position in society. Every action committed has its effect on the life of the person who performs it, determining that person's next realm of existence.

The moral law of Hinduism is well preserved as each individual diligently passes through the four stages of life. The ideal life for a Hindu begins with the study of the Vedas. For this purpose the student leaves his home and resides with the guru from whom he will appropriate knowledge through instruction as well as assimilation. Secondly, at the level of the householder, he marries from within his own caste and raises his own children. Having seen the first grandchild, or his own hair having begun to turn white, he enters the third stage of hermit. The hermit delves into the real meaning of life as he engages in purely spiritual and transcendental meditation. Finally he renounces the world and becomes a holy man (sanyasin) whose sole goal is to enter Nirvana.

This religion of mystery and morality has yet another aspect to it: a mysterious teaching about grace, which intrigues even a Christian and causes him to stop and think. The Hindu doctrine of grace has been described in the following comparison:

> A she-cat seizes the kitten and carries it where she wills. This involves a total passivity on the part of the kitten and . . . God's grace operates in the same way. All is effected by God, and man does nothing to achieve moksha. By contrast, the baby monkey clings to its mother. The mother monkey is responsible for the baby monkey's continuance of life and movement, yet there is no total passivity . . . . We cling to God, and God effects our salvation.[10]

Hinduism leaves out hardly anything that could go into a definition of religion. It offers everything to everyone who embraces it: mystery, morality, self-confidence, and divine grace. In Hinduism grace abounds in spite of human sin and malfunction. Divine providence fastens the individual soul safely and securely to the bosom of the divine, just as the mother cat seizes the kitten. The kitten remains utterly passive in this process.

The baby monkey-mother monkey illustration may suggest synergism, the idea that humans work with God to bring about their salvation. The mother makes sure that the baby has all that it needs; the mother monkey watches over the youngster and provides security and protection to it; but the baby monkey clings to its mother, forever faithful and forever passive.

Hinduism is a religion of transcendence. As such it appeals to the conscience of many. Unlike Christianity, where the person of God transcends the idea of God, in Hinduism the ultimate focus is on the nonpersonal and the limitless idea of God.[11] Because this ultimate reality is unlimited, the same reality may be found within one's own self. An acknowledged Hindu way of "discovering" the God within the self is to utilize the power of the mantras. Mantras are words or phrases with magical power that enable the worshipper to rise above earthly surroundings and become immersed in the world of the Brahman. Mantras elevate the meditating soul from the world of sound and fury to the sphere of silence and serenity.

The most popular and perhaps the most original of all mantras is the OM, (or AUM). OM is the Brahman in the form of sound. OM in itself is a contrast to the Brahman: it is emptiness as well as fullness. "The recitation of OM, on the one hand, reduces all beings into the nothing of OM, 'the image of the supreme reality.' On the other hand, the recitation makes OM itself meaningful without, however, identifying it with any particular being."[12]

OM is the beginning and the end of everything. It is the Alpha and the Omega. This mysterious sound of eternity is the "Amen" of Hinduism. Every hymn, every prayer, the reading of every sacred text, and every religious rite begins and ends with OM. The Upanishads describe AUM as the four stages of consciousness: A represents waking state, U stands for dream, and M symbolizes deep sleep. The three together constitute the transcendent state.

OM—this syllable is the whole world. Its further explanation is: the past, the present and the future—everything is just the word OM. And whatever else that transcends threefold time—that too is just the word OM . . . .OM is the atman.[13]

Yoga is another mesmerizing and mystifying Hindu idea that has become extremely popular in the West. Many in the Western world regard yoga simply as a discipline that strengthens the mind's power to concentrate and renders relaxation and quietness to the soul. To be sure, yogic practices do calm the storm of the mind and let the soul relax and renew itself. However, in the context of Hinduism (the source from which yoga evolved) yoga is a means by which the individual strives for personal salvation. Yogic exercises reach their climax as the soul enters a trance in which it becomes one with the Brahman. Thus the Atman-Brahman dualism is transcended and all streams of the individual soul are merged into the deep sea of the Brahman.

The ultimate goal of yoga is to attain for the human soul its definitive union with the world soul. Etymologically yoga means *to yoke, to join,* or *to unite* (with the Brahman). A yogi therefore is someone who is well advanced in the various techniques of this discipline. Yoga cannot be self-taught; it needs to be taught by a guru. Yoga is markedly initiatory in character, as Eliade points out. "For, as in other religious initiations, the yogin begins by forsaking the profane world (family, society) and, guided by his guru, applies himself to passing successively beyond the behavior patterns and values proper to the human condition."[14] It is as if the individual is now dead to this world and reborn for the next.

According to Eliade, Indian spirituality consists of four interdependent concepts, the study of any one of which will inevitably lead to the other three. These four are karma (the law of universal causality), maya (cosmic illusion), nirvana (immortality) and yoga.[15] After extensive historical study of the subject, this scholar is convinced that "the absence of the Yoga complex from other Indo-European groups confirms the supposition that this technique is a creation of the Asian continent, of the Indian soil."[16] If Eliade's conclusion is correct, the New Age owes the supply of all these religious ideas to its Indian precursor, Hinduism.

Yoga techniques suggest eight stages for attaining perfect control of the body: restraint against harming living creatures; self discipline involving internal control and calmness; body postures that facilitate concentration of the mind; regulation of breath; control of the senses to shut out the outside world; focused concentration on a single object; meditation; and the final trance in which the yogi becomes one with the Brahman.

Hinduism suggests three very practical ways for individual souls to become united with the Brahman. These three ways underscore the openness of Hinduism, offering a space for every creature somewhere in the Hindu way of life. Each individual, according to ability, may pursue any one of these ways to enter Nirvana.

# The Way of Knowledge

"Knowledge puffs up, but love builds up" (1 Cor. 8:1) may be an appropriate verse for understanding the Hindu idea that knowledge is a way of salvation. Some Christians in the church at Corinth boldly ate meat offered on pagan altars (some of which was then sold in the open market). They did this because their faith told them that Christians do not have to follow dietary regulations. But Paul admonished them not to indulge in such freedom for the sake of other believers who were endowed with a weak conscience. Paul was concerned for the weaklings who would misinterpret the action of the strong as a breach of the Christian faith.

To avoid misunderstanding, and to warn those who put their trust in their own knowledge, Paul wrote that the man who thinks he knows something does not yet know as he ought to know. But the man who loves God is known by God.[17] Contrary to the Christian doctrine of being known by God, Hinduism suggests that the individual can reach God through knowledge. If knowledge is a way to nirvana, what kind of knowledge does it take for one to get there?

Hinduism is a religion of wisdom. The root word of the word *Vedas* (the Hindu Scriptures) is *vid*, which means *wit* or wisdom. In contrast to rational or empirical knowledge, knowledge in the present instance means *absolute, intuitive,* or *esoteric wisdom.* Simple commonplace pedagogy is not the appropriate means to impart this kind of wisdom. The Hindu way of wisdom that makes people "wise unto salvation" can be transmitted "only in the living relations of minds, one mind prepared to teach and the other prepared to receive."[18] Neither the written word nor the spoken word is the source of this wisdom. True knowledge is basically an intuition, a context in which the pupil (*shishya*), equipped by the master (*guru*), is able to accumulate enough wisdom that leads to self-awareness. The pupil-master connection therefore is as important, if not more so, than the husband-wife relationship.

The ultimate goal of self-awareness is the knowledge of one's own oneness with the Brahman. Awareness of becoming one with the Brahman calls for experiential knowledge. Experience of this kind must evolve from within the individual soul. The teacher, the scriptures, and everything that surrounds the individual may in their own right facilitate this process for the person seeking union with the world soul. The final goal, however, has to be reached by each one individually.

Knowledge is the gateway to freedom from the present existence. That belief stems from the notion that humans are stuck with this world of misery and sorrow because of their lack of knowledge (*avidya*) of who they really are. Human beings are prone to think that they are independent entities by themselves. That is wrong. Those who think that way do not have the right information about themselves. They must be able to think of themselves as part of the whole, because they themselves are whole.

The Upanishads use different kinds of analogies to explain the oneness of the Brahman and the Atman. Rivers lose their individual names and forms as they flow into the same ocean. In this instance the rivers are the individual souls and the sea is the Brahman. Souls rise from the world soul as waves from the sea and sink again back to their source, like waves dropping down into the sea. If we should see a drop of sea water flying across the sea, what we see is not a drop but the sea in the sky.[19]

The transition from the present world of ignorance to that of true knowledge of the self obviously is exhausting. It is a demanding exercise because the uninitiated human mind is unable to discredit as unreal (maya) all the forms of appearance that surround it. Difficult and demanding as the process is, the Upanishads enumerate four steps for attaining this ambitious goal.[20]

The first step is being "awake." At this level the individual soul is open to sense perception and rational thought. The mind is conscious of the environment, open to the "reality" that surrounds it. The person is still rational and follows the laws governing the universe.

The second is the "dreaming state." At this level the spirit is able to transcend the laws of the physical world. Because the spirit can now exceed space and time, it wanders unbound and creates a world of its own. Thus the spirit has isolated itself from all physical boundaries.

The next level is that of a profound and dreamless sleep, called the "blissful state." Obviously, this is a step higher than the dreaming state. Here, as in deep sleep, there is no recollection of anything—fission or fusion, separation or assimilation. The spirit rests at ease because at this level there is no conscious awareness of either loss or gain.

The final state is that of "ultimate freedom." Ultimate freedom is indefinable. Freedom, like truth, once defined is no longer freedom:

> [I]t is perception of neither external nor internal objects, neither knowledge nor ignorance; it is without describable qualities; it is supreme consciousness of consciousness, a cessation of all movement and all multiplicity, complete freedom. It is the self; and it is the knowledge of the self, which is the same, because the self . . . is pure knowledge, being, bliss.[21]

Perfect knowledge transcends definition and description. A condition is best defined by a person who has comprehended it and possibly experienced it firsthand. In the case of nirvana, however, we are groping to define an existence that defies explanation. An eyewitness testimony to nirvana, though most covetable, is all but incomprehensible because those who have entered that state obviously are at the point of no return. They do not return to the "living" and therefore are unable to explain bliss to those who have not entered it. Nirvana achieved by way of knowledge, doubtless, is a kind of enlightenment. Consequently, philosophical Hinduism prescribes four general qualifications for those who seek salvation through the way of knowledge.[22]

First and foremost, those who pursue the path of knowledge must have the innate ability to distinguish the real from the seemingly real, the spiritual from the superficial. Secondly, they must willingly and wholeheartedly renounce all desires and sensual pleasures because these often hinder the pursuit of unimpeded knowledge. Thirdly, they must practice a self-control that will produce a dispassionate mind, inner tranquility, endurance, and faith. And finally, aspirants must always maintain a positive longing for freedom.

In Hinduism, knowledge that leads to ultimate freedom is "reflexive knowledge of the soul itself."[23] Individuals must arrive at this definitive goal on their own, without seeking help from others. The means to achieve this end is *intro-*

71

*spection.* This is the process of self-examination or soul-searching that enables a person to look within. Those who look for true meaning elsewhere (from without), other than in themselves (from within), do not achieve their goal because what they see around them is not real, but only a phenomenon. That which is real is within the soul. That soul in its essence is the world soul.

Ours is the age of knowledge explosion. We are tempted to value knowledge as the most prized possession. Rekindling and fostering self-awareness (knowledge from within) in individuals is an important purpose of education. Increased knowledge truly expands the mind's horizon, opening the mind's eye to endless possibilities. Unfortunately, knowledge of this kind also could "puff up" and lead inadvertently to a certain flagrant self-esteem that refuses to acknowledge the limitations of human knowledge.[24]

New Age thinking is entangled in the negative use of knowledge. Looking within, New Agers claim to see "the God within." They translate the old Hindu metaphysics of knowledge into modern existentialist language. In the New Age religion, heaven is the earth and the earth is heaven. Earth is as good as heaven. Though death causes people to exit the world momentarily, reincarnation enables them to return to earth in due course.

## The Way of Works

An open religion that is all-inclusive, all-encompass-ing, and all-embracing must have in it a place for all kinds of people. In all fairness to the Hindu religion, we should say that the way of knowledge was considered feasible primarily for the members of the "twice born" castes,[25] the intellectu-ally and socially elite in the community. The way of knowledge had merit for the well-to-do and the intelligent who could afford time and energy to immerse themselves in the study of the various philosophical systems of Hinduism.

But Hinduism offers other ways for those who are unable to pursue the path of knowledge. One is the way of works. This requires individuals to adhere strictly to the rules of their own caste as stipulated in the laws of karma. This path is open to all classes of people.

The way of works is the way to please by means of righteous deeds those celestial beings who control the destiny of humanity. In a sense this is the world-affirming aspect of the Hindu religion. Here willingly and actively serving the needs of other humans, animals, and nature is considered a worthy way of seeking God and attaining deliverance from the misery and sorrow of the present existence. "Active material service is as much part of Hindu life as contemplation and spirituality."[26]

The way of works "promises bliss and wealth and a sojourn in *svarga*, a heaven with earthly pleasure, as the highest goal after death."[27] With this incentive, people strive diligently to fulfill their duties in keeping with their position in society. Following the way of works entails privileges and responsibilities. It is a privilege for individuals to serve nature and society through selfless love and compassion. It involves obligation, because deeds done in the present life determine the soul's next sphere of existence.

The way of works unquestionably reinforces the teaching of reincarnation. Reincarnation presents itself as the worthy corollary of the principle of karma. The individual soul is caught in the wheel of birth and rebirth until the karmic forces are totally and fully exhausted. Each birth therefore is indeed a "rebirth," for

karma determines both the fact of another incarnation and the nature of that incarnation. It fixes the thatness and the whatness of incarnations. "Obtaining the end of his action, whatever he does in this world, he comes again from that world to this world of action." "[The soul] being overcome by the bright or dark fruits of action, enters a good or an evil womb." Transmigration continues. [28]

The way of works "is meant for those who have given up all worldly liabilities, with interests that go beyond spouse and children, house and property, business and entertainment."[29]

Humans cannot evade the moral and ethical responsibilities entrusted to them. They are bound to abide by certain designated duties appropriate to their particular position and status in life. Constantly remaining faithful to such stipulations gradually enables them in the end to find their way out of this world of misery and sorrow.

Karma is an action word. A person's position in life entails duty. There is work to be done in the present existence, and there are obligations to be fulfilled. Action therefore is greater than inaction. Only through responsible execution of action can humans achieve release from this illusory world.

Responsible action in Hinduism is better represented by another word, *dharma*. Dharma motivates the doer to engage in righteous behavior without concern for the results of the action. In this sense dharma is a matter of the human conscience. It is selfless duty, and hence results in unselfish, goal-directed behavior. That this path assures release even to ordinary human beings makes it a favored route for all to pursue. Dharma outlasts the usual stimulus-response scenario and outweighs any and all emotions and sentiments, as the following incident in the *Gita* illustrates.

The *Bhagavat Gita* is perhaps the most popular and powerful of all Hindu writings. It is part of the *Mahabharata*, the longest epic poem in the world, with 100,000 verses in the Sanskrit language. The plot of this dramatic composition is the battle between two royal families, the five sons of Pandu fighting against their cousins, the one hundred sons of Kuru. In this struggle of moral and theological proportions, Krishna, an *avatar* (manifestation) of Vishnu the second person of the Hindu triad, assists the righteous ones to discharge their dharma against the evils of their own cousins, the unrighteous ones.

Arjuna, the lead fighter of the Pandu brothers, is faced with a moral dilemma. He is a member of the warrior class. As such his dharma requires that he fight. Nevertheless, he is called upon to confront in battle his own kith and kin. In his emotional and spiritual struggle Arjuna conjectures that he will corrupt his soul, should he fight his cousins. To the soul of Arjuna, deranged and perplexed between duty and filial piety, Krishna speaks.

First, Arjuna must remember that only the body is killed in battle. The *Atman*, the inmost identity of the individual, is imperishable. Earthly warfare for a right cause does not destroy the souls of those being killed. Secondly, warrior Arjuna is overly concerned about the physical death of his relatives by his own sword. He must remember that death is the lot of every man, sooner or later. Should he kill his cousins in the battle for justice, he is not in any way annulling their fate. Doubtless, in the course of time death will take its toll on them too by some other means. And thirdly, Arjuna cannot forget his dharma as a warrior. A warrior is born to fight. By involving himself in the present combat, Arjuna's destiny is clear. This is his opportunity to escape the world and misfortune. Nirvana awaits him inasmuch as he does what his dharma demands.[30]

The way of action must be carried out with an attitude of detachment and indifference. "People generally act with attachment, that is, with desire and fear—desire for a certain result and fear that this result will not be obtained."[31] Actions performed with fears and expectations do not qualify for eternal release. Instead they bind humans to the phenomenal world, demanding more action. Actions that warrant the individual soul's final exit from this world are those performed without fear and without desire. "This is the way of holy indifference and nonattachment, where persons offer everything they do as a symbol of devotion to duty."[32]

Krishna, the manifestation who equipped Arjuna to perform his karma, is the favored god of the Hare Krishna movement.[33] This movement, which first evolved in Bengal, India in the 16th century, regards Krishna as the supreme, personal god. Krishna, to them, is not just an incarnation of the absolute reality; but he is the eternal and the absolute. "We should perform all our actions as offerings to Krishna and do nothing for our own sense gratification,"[34] declares their position statement. That the Hare Krishna movement is welcomed in the American Academy of Religion and that reputed religion scholars rise to its defense against all possible misgivings demonstrate this movement's favored position among many American intellectuals.

Krishna's qualities and subsequently many of the practices of the devotees of Krishna, the Vaishnavites, could easily find their counterparts in the New Age religion. Vishnu (of whom Krishna is the eighth incarnation) descends from heaven in bodily form to restore justice and rescue the just. "He who meditates upon the god Vishnu, who is all-pervading, a whole without parts, indestructible and unchangeable, who frees a man from old age and death, is free from misery," it is said.[35] The concepts of reincarnation and meditation are repeated in the Vaishnavite religion. The devotees of Vishnu are known to be vegetarians. A popular name of Krishna is *Govinda*, which means "Cowherd." The stories of his childhood and youth have to do with milk, butter, and cattle barns. At times he is domestic, at times he is erotic. Among his consorts are the goddesses of Fortune and the Earth.[36] He is a god deserving undivided devotion.

## The Way of Devotion

Not everyone knows enough to understand that he or she is god. Not everyone does enough good works to merit his or her release from the cycle of birth, death and rebirth. For those who do not qualify either for the way of knowledge or for the way of works, Hinduism offers another way, the way of devotion.

Devotion (*Bhakti*) involves the body, mind, and spirit. It is the way of engaging the total person in intrinsic, and mystical concentration on something (persons, places, things, or concepts) beyond one's own self. Obviously, devotion consists of worship and adoration. Worship is an attitude. Objects worthy of adoration may be worshipped in private (in the bottom of one's own heart) or in public (in the presence of—and in the company of—other worshippers).

We have said that faith influences culture. Culture too leaves its imprint on faith. Read any book on world religions. Before describing a particular religion, they try to familiarize us with the geography, topography, and demography of the land in which that religion is practiced. We cannot know India until we understand Hinduism. Nor can we appreciate Hinduism until we have grasped India.

The way of devotion follows the ways of nature. Nature itself is worthy of worship in the Hindu religion. From the Himalayas in the North to Cape Comarin tapering into the Indian Ocean in the South, India is adorned with every object that fascinates a nature worshipper—mountains, hills, valleys, animals, reptiles, shrines, places of pilgrimage, bodies of water. Rain and storm, heat and cold, flooding, and earthquakes are no strangers to this land renowned for its variety. Here nature manifests its power. Power induces fear, wonder, and love. To Indians no love is greater than motherly love. Mother nature is as much worthy of worship as one's own mother.

The natural panorama of India is very deserving of adoration. To those who believe that nature is god, India presents itself as the domicile of mysterious nature gods worthy of worship. The Himalayas are the abode of Shiva. There he sits in meditation. Through yoga the immortal Shiva keeps on storing his energies. He releases his energies periodically into the world to invigorate the cosmos.[37] The world needs that kind of energy to go on. The Himalayas were indeed a mystery to every human being until 1963 when Edmund Hilary and Tenzing Norkay subdued its highest peak, the Everest.

The spiritual might of the River Ganges reigns superior to that of the Nile, the Rhine, or the Yellow River. The Ganges, to the Hindus, is "Mother Ganaga" and the holiest of all rivers. Tributaries from the Himalayas, the very dwelling of Shiva, give rise to the Ganges. According to Hindu mythology, the Ganges is dispensed from the feet of Vishnu, the source of divine manifestations. From there it falls upon Shiva's head and subsequently flows out of his hair. The Ganges' place of origin, its junction with the River Jamuna, and its mouths that empty into the Bay of Bengal are all holy and sacred places for Hindus.

Legend has it that an ancient Indian king through meditation brought the Ganges down from heaven to save his nation from drought and famine. Every drop of Ganges water is holy. The sacred waters of the Ganges have the power to heal. No pilgrimage is ever complete until it culminates on the banks of the Ganges. Every devout Hindu dreams of taking his last breath by the waters of the Ganges. "For whoever dies upon that sacred soil, especially if his feet be immersed in the sacred river and his body cremated with due ritual on a burning ghat, goes to Shiva's heaven of unending light."[38]

The city of Varanasi (Benares) by the Ganges is the most holy city for Hindus. Those that are privileged to die in or near the Ganges at Varanasi are approximating nirvana for themselves. From dawn to dusk visitors to Benares are greeted by an assortment of funeral pyres burning relentlessly. No other place in the world is living testimony to the biblical remark, "Dust you are, and to dust you shall return." Conscientious Hindus who have realized that their earthly sojourn is soon to be over choose to make one last trip to the banks of the sacred river. There they shall breathe their last. There, as their bodies turn to ashes in the consuming fire, their souls run their last lap to be one with the world soul.

Not every Hindu is capable of bringing his pilgrimage to its blessed end by the waters of the Ganges or to Kailas in the Himalayas, the residence of Shiva. However, India, as vast a geographical entity as it is, offers a wide variety of sacred places for all to bring their spiritual sojourns to a blessed culmination. Almost every mountain in India is reminiscent of a certain event in Hindu mythology. As such, these hills turn out to be sanctuaries where the gods meet humans. Holy hills offer pilgrims who arrive there a top-of-the-world feeling.

Devotees who set their feet on holy places do so with due reverence. These landmarks are easily identified from a distance as their temple towers jut up into the skyline. Sojourners are overwhelmed and overjoyed by the simple fact that, as they mount those final steps, their lifelong ambitions are realized. They see in their mind's eye the very presence of their favorite god.

Each pilgrimage is the concluding stage of a long and enduring soul-searching and soul-cleansing process. It emerges from a concerted effort on the part of the individual, involving weeks (and sometimes months) of introspection, self-examination, and confession of sins. Pilgrims consider themselves prospective and often cryptic swamis or holy men, those who have arrived at the fourth level of the Hindu way of life. With that in mind, they stay away from the mainstream, normal life of the society and family, though for a limited period of time. All pilgrims refrain from eating any meat or fat food. They pommel their bodies and control their desires. They are intent on yielding themselves to a complete spiritual overhaul, as it were, eagerly longing for renewal and refreshment.

Sages, having travelled long distances from far away places, leave their vehicles miles away from the sanctuary. Then they proceed to the holy place barefoot with their hands raised, symbolizing veneration of, and total submission to, the god they favor the most. They carry on their heads little bags containing representative offerings in kind that are the most delightful to their favorite god. At the top of their voices they chant in unending sequence prayers and praises to their god. From a distance they prostrate themselves toward the deity's temple. They shower on their heads and bodies the dust of the holy ground as a token of their total resignation and humiliation. Rain or shine, hot or cold, rituals and ceremonies continue to the end until devotees are content with the vision of the sacred.

Renewed and rejuvenated, their past sins having been forgiven, devotees descend the holy hills to return to normal life. Life will go on with its struggles and strains. Every devout Hindu is willing and anxious to swim against the current of unending struggles. Hinduism is a religion of endurance. There is no such thing as a "free lunch" in this religion. Individuals pay for their sins individually. Thus uncertainty prevails in every spiritual act. Has one known enough to understand that he or she is god? Has one done enough good deeds to earn Nirvana? Has one clung closely enough to god in pursuing the path of devotion?

Restless as it is, the soul tries to do everything it can to reassure its eternal salvation. As a part of this strenuous process, those who are alive venerate and worship the spirits of their ancestors. The spirits of the departed linger in the air. They remain ghosts forever unless the last rites (*sraddha*) for them are properly performed following their death. Ghosts that are not cared for will haunt their living relatives in many ways. The spirits of the departed therefore are worthy of worship, and those whose last rites are suitably fulfilled will shower their blessings on their descendants.[39]

Obeisance to the deceased begins at the time of their physical death. After the corpse is cleaned it is wrapped in a brand new cloth. The corpse then is decked with flowers, and a religious mark with holy ashes is placed on its forehead. Normally the eldest son, (in the absence of a son, the next of kin who qualifies to take that place) leads all the rituals and ceremonies that follow. After the body is brought to the cremation grounds, the officiant sprinkles water on it. With an iron rod he draws three lines on the floor, one each for the three gods of cremation, time, and death. Several minor rituals follow involving the wife of the deceased (if the deceased was a married man) and other members of the immediate family. Then the eldest son lights the funeral pyre. While the fire is still on, various gods are invoked to give the departed a favorable place among the ancestors.[40]

Exactly ten days after the cremation, the officiant visits the graveyard and there offers a ball of rice. This is food for the ghost of the deceased. It is required that crows come and peck at these rice balls. If by any chance crows do not arrive, the relatives conclude that the one who died left this world with unfulfilled wishes. So they make every effort to attract the crows, even if it means long hours of waiting for the birds. A person for whom death ceremonies are not properly performed will remain forever an evil ghost. [41] For the sake of the deceased then, in some traditions, every year at the dawn of the new-moon day in August-September the relatives perform a special ceremony by the nearest body of running water (preferably the sea, if accessible). Friends and family may have departed this world in the physical sense, but they are not really forever gone. They are around as spirits, now appearing in various life forms and now disappearing.

Worshipping God as the spirit(s) and venerating the spirits of the deceased may account for the transcendental nature of Hinduism. Hindu worship can nevertheless be simple and down to earth. For a devout Hindu God is where life is. God manifests Itself in various forms of life. God's presence in the world is to be sensed and felt by everyone everywhere through tangible and visible means. One popular object in Hinduism for acknowledging and experiencing God's presence with people is the sacred cow.

For the orthodox Hindu, the cow is the most sacred animal in the world. The cow is the saintly symbol of Mother Earth and of the entire animal kingdom. In certain parts of India cows are let loose (even on a busy street) with the idea that in cows the gods meet mankind. On certain festive seasons "garlands are placed around their necks, oil is poured on their foreheads and water at their feet, while tears of affection and gratitude start into the eyes of bystanders." [42]

In the opinion of Mahatma Gandhi the father of modern independent India, the sacred cow is "the central fact of Hinduism, the one concrete belief common to all Hindus." Gandhiji wrote:

Cow-protection to me is one of the most wonderful phenomena in human evolution. It takes the human being beyond his species. The cow to me means the entire subhuman world. Man through the cow is enjoined to realize his identity with all that lives . . . . She is the mother to millions of Indian mankind. The cow is a poem of pity. Protection of the cow means protection of the whole dumb creation of God.[43]

Consequently for every Hindu both cow dung and cow urine alike are pure, with the power to purify everything these cow excretions come into contact. Cow excretion as well as cow milk are used to purify those who, for example, become ceremonially unclean by breaking the caste taboo. Feeding and taking care of the cow is in itself an act of worship. In honoring the cow people are honoring all other lower forms of life.

The cow is also the living symbol of Mother Earth. Earth provides all that is necessary for the sustenance and the ongoing flow of life. Earth is itself addressed by Hindus as *Bhudevi*, a goddess deserving worship and adoration. A Vedic hymn declares the splendor of Mother Earth in this way:

Let your hills, your snowy mountains, your jungleland be pleasant, O earth. The brown, dark, red, many-colored, firm, broad earth, guarded by Indra, upon this earth I have settled, unconquered, unsmitten, unwounded. Your middle earth, and your navel, and the nourishments that have sprung up from your body, in them set us; purify yourself for us; earth is my mother, I am earth's son.[44]

Equally appealing to the modern mind is the following extract from "Mother Earth," first presented as part of a felicitation address for Jawaharlal Nehru, the first prime minister of India. In that essay V. S. Agrawala wrote,

Mother Earth is the deity of the new age . . . . The modern age offers its salutations to Mother Earth whom it adores as the super-goddess . . . . Mother Earth is born of contemplation. Let the people devote themselves truthfully to the Mother Land whose legacy they have received from their ancients. Each one of us has to seek refuge with her. Mother Earth is the presiding deity of the age, let us worship her. Mother Earth lives by the achievements of her distinguished sons.[45]

The above statement about Mother Earth, when it first appeared in India almost 45 years ago, obviously had nothing to do then with what is now known in the West as the New Age. However, there is no better way of paraphrasing the New Age understanding of Mother Earth than what is described above. Mother Earth indeed is the presiding deity of the New Age. The earth is certainly saluted as the supergoddess of this new religion. And the New Age religion is no stranger to achievements and distinctions because it has become the way of life of many an accomplished member of modern society.

The idea of describing God as Mother is fashionable in theology today. Only God knows what will become of God in theology in the days and years to come. The current notion of interpreting God in feminine terms, we are told, is partly because of the feminist movement in our time. At the same time, theological scholarship today perceives a strong Hindu connection in this kind of jargon inasmuch as it has chosen to draw the feminist inspiration from various forms of Devi and her worship in Hinduism.[46]

If the emphasis on a female God (or the feminine nature of God) is a sign of progress in religion today, we must acknowledge that Hinduism was endowed with this "advanced" concept already at the time of its inception—this in spite of the popular opinion that women in India are not given the honor and respect due them. In the Hindu religion the gods of wisdom, good fortune, as well as judgment are females.[47] Sarasvathi, the goddess of wisdom, education, and truth is the consort of Brahma, the Creator God. Lakshmi, the goddess of beauty, fame, and good fortune, the consort of Vishnu the preserver of the universe, assumes various manifestations. Kali (also known as Durga) represents death and judgment because she is the wife of Shiva. Her job it is to destroy life and to recreate it.

The great Hindu philosopher Sri Aurobindo Ghose was convinced that in the Hindu religion the idea of the Mother preceded all other more familiar ideas about God. He wrote, "The Mother is the consciousness and force of the Divine."[48] The Mother is the power (*Sakti*) behind and beside the Lord of the Universe, said Aurobindo. Accordingly at the popular level, "for millions of Hindus Devi, the Great Mother, is all that the word God can express," and "all the other great gods are merely her instruments and servants."[49]

Older Hindu traditions saw The Mother as the source, the guardian, and the summation of the cosmos. She was knowledge and illusion alike. The Mother was great power, memory, and delusion. She was the primordial matter, that which was from the beginning. She was the goddess of good fortune, modesty, knowledge, bashfulness, nourishment, contentment, and forbearance. The Mother was at the same time exceedingly beautiful and terribly vicious as she was armed with swords, spears, clubs, arrows and other deadly weapons. She was power. She was the supreme Mistress. The Mother was the soul of everything. And she gave form to the Hindu Triad: Brahma, Vishnu, and Shiva.[50]

To be sure, by trying to reinvent feminist principles through the New Age Movement, today's society has moved a step closer to ancient Hinduism. The New Agers, perhaps unwittingly, may have absorbed from Hinduism those essentials of womanhood that are practical and applicable to the modern era, ignoring the seemingly outdated and the mundane. Essential Hinduism places the woman (The Mother) on a pedestal and holds her in high honor and adoration. A woman achieves her ideal selfhood by becoming a mother. Mothers are visible symbols of love, security, and authority in the family as well as in society.

The way of devotion is the way of absolute trust and faith. It admits that humans are unable to measure up to the standards set by the Divine. The Divine itself is unapproachable and beyond human comprehension. Its presence, however, is to be known and felt in the simple and complex objects of nature. The souls of the departed, the powers of nature, animals—all represent in some form or another the one and only eternal truth—the World Soul. Clinging to their sacredness is to claim recovery from the present, transitory world.

Thus there is in Hinduism a place for every one who struggles to find meaning in life either through excessive escalation of one's own self-knowledge or by means of giving oneself up to the services and well being of others. Those who would like to become Hindus may take with them their own gods and their own self-understanding. Unfulfilled and imperfect as they are, they will find their fulfillment and perfection in this religion.

Hinduism can be intellectually highly overwhelming and at the same time simple and down to earth. True knowledge enables us to realize that what we see around us, including ourselves, is not real but only a shadow. The world and all its vain glory fades away swiftly and abruptly. The soul remains and that soul, once purged and released from the present, will merge with the world soul. There is no beginning and there is no end.

Bad deeds will have to be paid for, but good works will pay off. It is possible for humans to work their way up from pain and sorrow to comfort and joy. God takes sides with those who try their best and works with them to do good. There is always a second chance and a third chance. At death we depart this world only to come back to it at a later time. There is always room for progress, growth, and improvement.

There is no limit to the potential within man. Man, after all, is God in miniature form. What is God other than that reality within each human being? Through self-discipline human beings can conquer anything that stands in their way to self-realization. All that needs to be done is to tune up the mind with the World Soul through concentration and in meditation. Hinduism underscores many things that the

West considers vital for a successful life. As one writer put it, "All of us may be already much more Hindu than we think."[51]

# 4
# Philosophical Hinduism and Its Resurgence

Hinduism, as a world religion, has been a growing tradition. Throughout its known history Hinduism has permitted kindred faiths to emerge and flourish on its own native soil. It has welcomed other religions into its household and let them thrive in their own ways as well. In keeping with Hinduism's inherent belief in the one world soul, Hinduism has been tolerant of other religions because it sees every religion as a different way leading to the same ultimate reality.

Hinduism is to Jainism, Buddhism, and Sikhism what Judaism is to Christianity and Islam. In the sixth century B. C. Jainism emerged as a religion and presently has a membership of approximately three million people. Vardhamana Mahavira, after 13 years of rigorous wandering, search, and fasting, attained enlightenment at the age of 40. His followers acclaim him as the Great Hero (that is what Mahavira means) who was finally able to perfect his own soul. Mahavira attained a kind of godlike knowledge that qualified him to transcend the cycle of rebirth and enter nirvana. He thus became the conqueror (*jina*, and hence the name Jainism) of the wheel of life.

Jainism views life as warfare between two equally powerful forces, those of good and evil. Both the soul and matter are eternal in an unending dualism that avoids the need for a creator god. All elements in the world are either soul or matter. The individual is a soul trapped in the flesh. Flesh, as matter, needs to be subdued and defeated so that the soul can be released from the clutches of matter (flesh). Each individual must go at this struggle alone without any outside help. The Mahavira himself set the pattern for others to follow.

Perhaps the greatest contribution of Jainism to the world is its teaching about reverence for all life. Out of respect for life Jains remain vegetarians and avoid such jobs as soldiers, butchers, and others that require either hurting or taking the lives of humans and animals. Needless to say, the Jain emphasis on asceticism and nonviolence (*ahimsa*) later became an accepted pattern of religious discipline in the Hindu way of life. In fact, the Jain philosophy of life shaped Mahatma Gandhi's policy of nonviolence as a strategy to force a foreign intruder to retreat from Indian soil.

Gautama Buddha, another sixth-century Indian holy man, launched his pilgrimage in search of the true meaning of life. Having been raised a prince, Gautama was no stranger to the pleasures and comforts of pompous living. By design of his father, this heir apparent to the royal throne was sheltered from poverty, sickness, old age, and death. At age 19 Gautama married his cousin, and later they became the proud parents of a son.

Within a decade, Gautama came face to face with the realities of life. At last his eyes were opened to the very things his father wanted him never to see. Almost as though a planned sequence of events, Gautama encountered a rotting dead body, a wrinkled and crippled old man, another with a despicable disease, and, lastly, a serene and peaceful monk. At his birth it had been predicted that Gautama would become a monk, should he ever encounter any of these sights of human misery and sorrow. Against his father's wish, the prince pursued the path of a monk, leaving behind his own family and the crown.

Gautama followed the path of knowledge as the answer to his struggles. But he discarded that method because it failed to satisfy his soul. He then immersed himself in a severe form of asceticism. He truly pommeled his body and suppressed his feelings to the extent that, according to legend, he limited his food to just one grain of rice a day. Gautama's rigorous spiritual exercises made his body "so thin that when he grasped his stomach he touched his backbone." Among other things "he sat on thorns for a time and slept in a graveyard among the rotten flesh of corpses."[1] Through all these strenuous efforts, however, he failed to reach his goal.

An exhausted and worn out Gautama finally found the road to freedom. It came with a splash of cold water on his face one day when he fainted and fell into a river. He arose, came to his senses, and on second thought ate a good meal and proceeded to the shade of a tree under which he could sit down and meditate. His meditations led him to a kind of enlightenment that helped him formulate the four noble truths of Buddhism. According to the Buddha (the title Gautama merited because he received enlightenment), suffering is the reality of life. Suffering is caused by desire. The way to end suffering is to work for the cessation of all desires, for which the Buddha suggested an eightfold path.

The eightfold path has been condensed to three categories for a well balanced life: morality, spiritual discipline, and insight. Morality consists of right speech, right action, and right occupation.[2] Spiritual discipline requires right effort, right mindfulness, and right composure. Insight is gained through right knowledge and right attitude. This then is the path to Nirvana, the state of eternal happiness and bliss, forever free from pain, sickness, and sorrow. The Buddha's discovery has been considered a well-balanced middle way between the extreme forms of asceticism and a luxuriating life style. Later Buddhism spread to the far East but remained a minority in India because Hinduism was able to absorb most of its teachings.

Jainism and Buddhism grew from within the indigenous Hindu matrix. But Sikhism, which developed into a religion in the 16th century A.D., was largely the result of a cross fertilization of certain religious ideas of Hinduism and Islam. In fact, its founder, Guru Nanak (1469–1539), held that there is no Hindu and no Muslim. Sikhism continues to be the faith of almost 18 million Sikhs today, dispersed all over the world, with roughly 250,000 of them residing in the United States.

Guru Nanak was born and reared in a Hindu family in Punjab. Very early in life he displayed a special interest in both poetry and religion. He was schooled under a Muslim teacher who also influenced his thinking. At age 19 he was married and raised his family with two children according to the Hindu tradition. However, almost like the Buddha, at about the age of 30 Nanak received a revelation that he was to be a prophet of a new religion. As part of his search for the ultimate reality of life, Nanak even made a pilgrimage to Mecca, the most sacred pilgrimage spot for Muslims.

The Islamic presence had been in India for well over a thousand years. Already in the eighth century, Muslims from Turkey and Afghanistan had moved to parts of northwest India. The religious influence of Islam on this part of the Indian subcontinent later in 1947 gave birth to a separate nation of Pakistan at the time of India's independence.

As a result of centuries of Muslim rule, Islamic art also left its imprint on India, for example, in the famous Red Fort in Delhi and the Taj Mahal in Agra. The state of Punjab, the home of Sikhism, located in the northwestern part of India, is a natural place for the blending of Hindu and Muslim ideals.

The Sikh religion is noted for its deep-rooted mysticism and devotion. Following the example of their founder, each morning the Sikhs confess God as *the True Name*, an expression of their faith in one God. A mystical element is added to this confession as they gather in congregational worship accompanied by hymn singing and meditation. Singing is meant to be the way for human hearts to reach God and to feel the divine presence within the self.

Guru Nanak's teaching is a synthesis of selected ideals from both Hinduism and Islam. To demonstrate this, it is said that Nanak's own attire was comprised of fragments of typical Hindu and Muslim dress. Nanak is the Guru (teacher) and his followers are the Sikhs (the Punjabi expression for disciple). Nanak combined the strict monotheism of Islam with the One ultimate reality of Hinduism and called it the

True Name. Rejecting the caste hierarchy of Hinduism, Nanak gave preference to the (Islamic) brotherhood of all believers, regardless of their caste origin. Perhaps influenced by Islamic teaching, Nanak taught that human beings are God's supreme creation. While endorsing the Hindu doctrine of reincarnation, he rejected the Hindu notion of *ahimsa* (non-violence) and vegetarianism. Using the cycle of birth and rebirth, Sikhs reinforce the idea of karma, much like the corresponding doctrine in Hinduism. In fact, Sikhs maintain that "the spirit of Nanak was reincarnated in the bodies of those gurus who succeeded him as the leaders of Sikhism."[3]

Sikhism has always remained a separate religion, distinguishing itself from the Hindu mainstream. The Sikhs do not, however, deny that their ideals are derived from the inspired writings of both Hindu and Muslim holy men. The Sikh alliance with the Hindu faith is further evidenced by the fact that Guru Gobind Singh, the tenth guru, promoted among Sikhs the worship of Durga, the Hindu goddess who symbolizes judgment and death. Nevertheless, the Sikhs continue to strive as a community to manifest its faith in the absolute oneness of God with a steadfast desire to promote equality, justice, and peace for all.

While the Hindu religion set the stage for new religions to emerge, Hinduism itself did not forever remain still or stagnant. Rethinking as well as resurgence was taking place within the Hindu way of life, especially when it was encountering challenges from other religions. It was capable of withstanding the innovations of both Christianity and Islam. Historically, Hinduism has not denied others the freedom to pursue individual paths of spiritual fulfillment. Though initially some reform movements within Hinduism posed challenges to the already existing Hindu systems, in the long run they were absorbed into the main frame of Hinduism. Let us now examine some selected examples of Hindu resurgence.

# Vedanta

The word Vedanta means literally "the end of the Vedas," the more than 200 produced during the period ending the revelations contained in the Vedas, the most ancient Hindu scriptures. The Vedanta writings date back to the time between 800 and 400 B. C. The Vedanta are the wise words of those who retired to the forest at the fourth stage of life of a Hindu gentleman. Some of these sages, after deep contemplation and meditation, composed their discourses for others still seeking the meaning of life. These wise sayings are believed to have been first delivered to those disciples (*shishya*) who came seeking superior wisdom from the sages (*rishi*). The seekers sat (*shad*) down (*ni*) near (*upa*) the rishis and listened closely to their words of secret wisdom. Hence the collection of these sayings is known also as the *Upanishads*. The Upanishads for the first time identify the individual soul with the Brahman, the ultimate reality in Hinduism. They also suggest different ways which, when strictly followed, enable the individual soul to realize its oneness with the Brahman.

Modern students of Hindu philosophy therefore maintain that Vedanta is the most appropriate way of describing what is commonly implied in the modern umbrella term "Hinduism." According to them, Vedanta fittingly represents the comprehensive nature of the Hindu religion, supplying that way of life with its well deserved breadth and depth. As one writer explains, "Hinduism is a modern word. Vedanta is the best among numerous names given to the religious faith of the Hindus. He who professes and practices Vedanta is a Vedantin."[4]

Students of resurgent Hinduism also alert us to the depth of several Hindu teachings that are commonly misunderstood, and hence misinterpreted by non-Hindus, especially those trained in the European system of education.[5] According to this view, those who interpret Hinduism as either pantheistic or polytheistic are not being fair to its authentic teaching.

To be sure, Hindus have a great regard for nature and all the powers therein because for them these are different manifestations of the one divine power. The objects of nature are for the Hindus powerful means to achieve depth of knowledge and greater appreciation for the force behind them. Thus, while showing reverence to the natural phenomena, true worshippers are actually lifting their souls to the ultimate source of all things. It is as if the worshipper is acknowledging the Unknown by means of demonstrating reverence to the known. The ultimate reality, however, transcends all that is visible, tangible, and audible. As the great Hindu philosopher Shankara confessed while praying to Shiva,

> Forgive me, O Shiva, my three great sins. I came on a pilgrimage to Kashi forgetting that you are omnipresent; in thinking about you I forget that you are beyond thought; in praying to you I forget that you are beyond words.[6]

Shankara distinguished between the "higher" and the "lower" levels of knowledge. Knowledge that is attained by means of the five senses and the sense organs of the body has its limitations because it is conditioned by space, time, change, and cause-and-effect relationship. According to Shankara, this kind of knowledge is at the lower or secondary level.[7] The vast majority of human beings are at this level with reference to their knowledge of the Divine. They need to be assisted constantly with discourses, meditations, prayers, and pilgrimages as they struggle to perfect their knowledge to the higher or primary level.

The higher level of knowledge, according to Shankara, is attained through direct insight. It transcends all limitations of the human intellect, and hence it is capable of realizing that the ultimate reality is one integrated whole. Incidentally, the Sanskrit equivalent of the word *philosophy* (love of knowledge) is *darsana* which means *seeing*. True knowledge must therefore enable the individual soul to meet with the world soul and fuse with it. No communication is now necessary, because the union of the two has taken place. Thus the dualism of the individual soul and the world soul ceases, and monism prevails.

Hindu philosophers frown on the Platonic way of searching for reality on a purely intellectual level. They ask, "What is the use of philosophy if it does not enable a man to commune with reality? And has one who communes with reality any further need of philosophy?"[8] For them knowledge at its highest level is a spiritual discipline that defies description and definition because it goes beyond the boundaries of human language. It is the ultimate state of bliss because through it the individual self rises to the level of being able to commune with the True, Real, Self whose very nature is pure intelligence.[9]

Modern teachers of Hinduism would like their students to avoid another misconception about the Hindu religion, that is, the way in which the concept of *karma* is interpreted. Karma is the moral law of cause and effect—that actions performed in the present life determine the soul's next form and sphere of existence. Properly understood, the law of Karma "is the application in the moral sphere of the law of conservation of energy."[10] No cause goes without generating its corresponding effect. "The effect lies inherent in the cause, as the tree lies potentially encased in the seed. If water is exposed to the sun, it cannot avoid being dried up. The effect automatically follows."[11] In the same way laws of karma govern the realm of the spirit. Though the physical body disintegrates at death, the eternal laws of karma operate beyond death as long as the individual soul exists independently of the world soul.

Yet Karma cannot be dismissed as the Hindu perception of fatalism. A fatalism that accepts one's own destiny with a sense of Stoic lethargy, Hindus maintain, is an indication of antiquated Western paganism. Conversely, the Hindu term for fate is *vidhi*, which means law. Vidhi reminds everyone that every action is bound to generate its own outcome. Thus, there is no point in performing an act, even though done unintentionally, and then expecting to undo the effects of that action, however gruesome and unpleasant those effects may be. Natural consequences must follow every act that has been performed, whether it was generated as a thought, word or deed. The one who performs an act must therefore expect nothing but the natural consequence of that action.[12]

Vedanta philosophy emphasizes that human beings are capable of exercising their free will. The Upanishadic narratives demonstrate that human beings can entertain voluntary attitudes and engage in voluntary activities, for better or for worse. Such an approach to life would not have been possible had karma been taken to mean fatalism in the literal sense of the word. Instead, "according to the doctrine of karma, there are necessary and sufficient conditions which account for the fortunes and misfortunes in the life of every living being. The individual reaps only what he sows, no more and no less."[13]

Karma, for modern Hindus, is the wake up call to assume individual responsibility. Karma determines the vocation of every person in accordance with station in life. It is also the most appropriate way for God to dispense justice for people all over the world according to his will. As the fountain and preserver of the law of karma, God entertains no favorites and shows no favoritism. God does not trap anyone into the jaws of karma, nor does he promise to deliver anyone from its grip. For, as Radhakrishnan says,

> If we fall into error, no supernatural deliverer will come to our rescue. There is no forgiveness for a broken law. No single word can be unspoken, no single step retracted. The past is determined, however free the future may be.[14]

This is precisely how the Hindu idea of karma appeals to the fancy of modern times, especially to those who embrace the New Age lifestyle. Shedding its negative subtleties as the law of destiny echoing terror and trembling, karma now assumes a new and promising role appealing to those who want to work their way through without seeking assistance elsewhere. It holds a person responsible for his actions, demanding that the individual be his best at all times. It whispers in the individual's ear that self help is always the best help.

Hinduism views all creation as the sport (*lila*) of God. Out of his free and dispassionate will, *Brahma*, the creator god, brought the world into being. Brahma created the world by exercising his creative power and with a certain sportsman-like spirit. His energy is the source and ground of all existence. The universe is the instinctive expression of the Brahma's creative spirit. In creating the universe, Brahma completed a magnificent piece of art work as it were, leaving it to run on its own. Since then he has had no further dealings with creation. Hence he is perhaps the least remembered, if not the almost forgotten god of Hinduism.

Consequently, those humans who are left on the face of the earth are also on their own to shape their future. They need to run their course well, following the laws of karma. They need to be masters of their own destiny and work their way to return to their source. In fact, the god who brought them into this world has left them forever. As the one without attributes (*Nirguna Brahman*), the impersonal, the unmanifested, and the unknowable, god cannot be interested in the welfare of people.

That God is remote and far removed from the created universe is only a partial explanation of the Hindu under-standing of the Divine. Obviously such reasoning implies the transcendence of God. At the same time, the Upanishads describe the immanence of God as well. The Hindu scrip-tures depict a Brahma *with* personal attributes (*Saguna Brahman*). While the Brahman without attributes is mysterious and unknowable, the *One* with attributes can be known and described. While the Brahman without attributes remains abstract and non-personal (It), the *One* with attributes (person) is known through his actions. While Brahman is beyond all the heavenly bodies, forces of nature, and the elements of the earth, he is also the inner con-sciousness, the reasoning, and the feeling of every individual human being. The Upanishads decipher the tussle between the formless and the formed Brahman in the following way:

> There are, assuredly, two forms of Brahman: the formed and the formless. Now that which is formed is unreal [or not fully real]; that which is formless is real [i.e., ultimately real].[15]

Brahman is very much involved in the affairs of the natural world. That (aspect of the) Brahman who is involved in the creation and since then in the preservation of the world is known as *Ishvara*, Ishvara is the creative spirit that pervades the entire cosmos. How can a god who created the universe and distanced himself from it since then still be involved in the world's affairs? The seventh-century Hindu philosopher Shankara addressed this. He discovered from the Upanishads that the creation of the universe was the result of the Brahman's own desire to multiply. "Would that I were many! Let me procreate myself," the Brahman wished for once.[16] Once again, creation is the result of a divine sporting event.

That the universe came into being as the result of the One's (Ultimate Reality's) desire to increase in number—and that the world is the arena of the same One's sport (*lila*)—implies that the diverse forms of the present existence are just a phenomenon or *maya*. The Western world has always been tempted to translate the Hindu concept of maya into illusion, because "*lila* is related to the Latin *ludere* (to play), from which the English term 'illusion' comes."[17] Nevertheless, this is yet another misconception about Hinduism that resurgent Hindu scholars would want Westerners to avoid. For they contend that *maya* in Hinduism is not illusion, but on the contrary, the manifestation of the (essentially) spiritual in the material world. These manifestations serve as helpful tools for the wise to become wiser, although it is sad to note that the intellectually less mature are constantly being deceived by the lure of these appearances.

Maya is Brahman's game plan for this phenomenal world. To be sure, Brahman has let the world to run on its own. However, as Ishvara, he is still at work in the present world. In this context, Vedanta philosophy teaches that the concept of maya serves a very pragmatic purpose. It prepares people to divert their attention from the fake nature of things that surround them and focus purely on lasting values of eternal significance. Maya thus compels humans to be involved in righteous and fair action. If, as common knowledge, maya is interpreted simply as illusion, the Hindu law of karma would easily lose ground. There would be no incentive for people to engage in righteous acts of charity and good will, and hence karma would forfeit its relevance.

One writer uses the analogy of the football and the air that inflates it to illustrate the interconnection between the world and the Brahman. This is helpful also to understand how Hindus view God's involvement in the natural world as his sport. Sri. Chakravarti Rajagopalachari writes,

> It is the air in the football that jumps and functions in all manner of ways when the ball is knocked about in the field. Yet we forget the air, and we look on the ball as the thing we play with, not the air. What is all-pervasive and invisible is lost in the obvious tangible hard reality, the ball.[18]

Modern students are able to project positive elements in the philosophical concepts of the Hindu religion that outsiders deem controversial and more pessimistic. Against the criticism that Hinduism promotes the idea of fate, Hindus would say fate is no more than assuming karmic responsibility for one's own actions. To the challenge that the creator God is far removed from his creation, devout Hindus would respond that God, though distanced from the created order, is present everywhere and anywhere. To answer the charge that God is not at all interested in the affairs of people, Hindus would say that the very idea of karma is God's design that leaves endless possibilities for individuals to excel in their endeavors without depending on another's helping hand. Hindus would quickly endorse the view that God helps those who help themselves, because they see all humans as having their own part in God's game plan.

The underlying principle that consolidates these diverse ideas into a unified whole is monism. Experts on the religion and culture of India speculate that the typical Indian mind is endowed with a unique disposition to search for the unity and cohesion of the events and things surrounding it. In contrast to the Western tendency to analyze everything empirically, the Indian mind struggles to discover the rudimentary principles that harmonize seemingly independent and even conflicting entities. To the great majority of Indians, reality is one, and plurality is just a phenomenon. Persons and things do not exist independently of one another. Instead, they coexist and complement each other on account of their inner cohesion. Harmony is not something to be discovered but to be realized.

The idea of a certain cosmic unity that undergirds the Indian mind is a fascinating mystery for those who are used to Western ways of thinking. Indians do not seem to draw a line between mind and spirit. For them religion and religious beliefs are very much a part of daily living. Faith is never apart from culture (believing that all Indians are Hindus), or perhaps faith transforms itself into culture. There is no dualism as such. God is everywhere and everything *is* God. As Robert Hume observed,

If there is one intellectual tenet which, explicitly or implicitly, is held by the people of India, furnishing a fundamental presupposition of all their thinking, it is this doctrine of universal immanence, of an intelligent monism.[19]

In all fairness it may be said that the Indian mind owes its monist disposition to the great Indian philosopher Shankara (788–820). Shankara was born a miracle baby in answer to the prayers of a South Indian Brahmin couple who remained childless for a long time. They had been praying to Lord

Shiva, the re-creator of new life, to recover them from their barrenness. Their prayers were answered, and, at Shankara's birth Shiva himself assumed human form, so it was believed. Interestingly enough, from childhood on Shankara showed little interest in worldly life and was determined to become a mendicant. His father died when he was eight years old.

Though Shankara's mother placed her hopes for the family's future on her only child, his desire to renounce the world only grew stronger. And, as legend has it, one day the moment of decision arrived. While the young lad was bathing in a river, he suddenly was caught off guard by an alligator. In his battle for life, Shankara shouted to his mother one last time, earnestly pleading that she would let him become a monk. Caught in such a precarious dilemma, the mother granted her son permission to lead the life he always coveted. In an instant the beast released the boy from its clutches. Shankara was now on his way to freedom.

Shankara traveled north and received further instruction on the Vedanta from the experts of his time. He mastered the art of interpreting the Upanishads in a manner so far unfamiliar among Hindu sages. Shankara found his new home in Varanasi, the threshold of Hindu spirituality. His message would soon spread to the four corners of India. Although Shankara would die at age 32, his enchanting legacy would live on as monism (advaita).

Troy Wilson Organ, in a rather convincing fashion, explains the different levels of the evolutionary process in the Hindu religion which effected the transformation of its inherent polytheism into the new monism.[20] The thought of a certain cosmic unity was at the heart of this venture. The Vedic religion had been accustomed to the way of worshipping a conglomeration of gods (devas). As it is the practice among all polytheistic religions, people sought help from a particular god in order to meet a specific need. As the first step towards the formation of monistic thought, these multitudes of gods were consolidated into major groups according to the nature of these gods. Thus, for example, various gods of nature such as the wind, fire, and light were classified as the gods of natural phenomena. These could be identified easily as they had the prefix "vas" attached to their names. Accordingly the sun, the god of light, received the name Vasudeva.

The second level of integrating various gods of Hinduism led to a certain henotheistic thinking. Henotheism is the belief that one can choose to worship one god without necessarily denying the existence of other gods. It is an attitude worshippers have towards their god. In contrast to the way of the polytheists, henotheists call on the same deity as *the* god worthy of worship, and bring all their needs to him. The henotheistic tendency in Hinduism came about, for example, when *Agni* (life force), *Mitra* (the guardian of the law of karma) and *Indra* (sky god) were all considered one and the same, as this prayer suggests: "Thou at thy birth, O Agni, art Varuna; when kindled thou becomest Mitra; in thee, O son of might, all gods are centered; thou art Indra to the worshipper."[21] This development, Morgan points out, was another step toward monism.

A further movement toward monistic philosophy was evidenced when the Hindu religion began to identify God as the creator. The One, Creator God was mighty in power, spirit and intelligence. This god was the first cause of the universe. Having assumed various names for himself, he was considered the name-giver of other deities. He possessed the knowledge other deities were still seeking. He made the world, and sustained everything in it. It was impossible to know him for any one and still exist in human form.

The concept of *Rita* was yet another way in which Hindu teachings progressed towards the monistic level. At first it signified the appropriate way in which sacrifices were offered. Then it was understood that that which maintained the order of the universe was rita. Absence of rita brought about chaos and decomposition. Rita transcended the devas and existed independently of them. In fact, as the cosmic order, even the gods could not transgress rita. Rita controlled times and seasons. Rita also had moral implications as it helped maintain the rhythm of life, distinguishing between good and evil.

Hindu thought was now ready to reach the acme of its philosophical expression as it began to nurse the idea of God as an impersonal reality. Studies show that Vedic literature contains phrases, if not verses, which exhibit monistic tendencies. References in the Vedas to the ultimate reality as "That," "That One," "Being," "The One God," and so on leave the impression that a striking tendency towards the perception of God as One was already in process. Descriptions of God as "the sole lord of created beings," "the giver of soul," and "whose shadow is immortality" further support this point of view. Later, in the Upanishadic period, God would be understood in one of three ways: the One impersonal, the One impersonal but not abstract, and the One impersonal and abstract.

Monistic teachings became an accepted system of thought in Hinduism about the beginning of the Christian era. It is believed that Badarayana, an eminent teacher who lived in the first century before Christ, delivered a series of monistic aphorisms based on the Upanishds, which were later compiled to form the *Vedanta Sutra*. Badarayana's profound reflections were beyond the grasp of the ordinary mind. They were so profound that when they were first uttered "his own oral commentary was necessary to render them intelligible."[22]

These developments within Hinduism and the later contributions of Shankara, Ramanuja, and Madhava gave rise to three systems within Vedanta philosophy. Of the three, Shankara's philosophy has had a tremendous influence on all later rethinking and reformation in Hinduism. Shankara's views on the *advaita* serve as the canon of resurgent Hinduism. Advaita hinges on the simple claim that, after all, the ultimate reality is one and there is only one reality. And Brahman is that reality.

The *Brihad-Aranyaka* Upanishad narrates an incident in which a disciple approached Yagnavalkya, the most important *rishi*, with the difficult question, "How many gods are there?" Yagnavalkya responded that there were as many gods as were mentioned in the hymns of the gods, 3,306. The disciple asked again, "How many gods are there really?" "Thirty-three," the rishi responded. The story goes on that each time the confused pupil repeated the question the uneasy rishi kept reducing the number of gods to six, three, and one-and-a-half. Finally the rishi conceded that there was, after all, only One [god]. In this way "the One as a unitary principle became the cornerstone of the dominant philosophy of India," namely, monism.[23]

Shankara, with his advaita philosophy, argued for the same principle. With his depth of knowledge and strong command of the Upanishads, Shankara claimed that there was only one reality. That reality is the Brahman. Everything else that catches the human eye—every object, every experience, every thought, every relationship—is *maya*. Maya prevents human beings from perceiving things as they really are. Consequently, Brahman, the ultimate reality, appears as an "outsider" to those minds that are distracted by the luring power of the maya. This happens because ordinary humans are not capable of realizing that in the present form of existence the Brahman is "superimposed" by the transitory ideas generated by human fantasies.

Shankara used the famous illustration of a man who mistook a piece of rope for a snake to substantiate the claim that the maya of Hindu thought is not unreal but an illusion. A man was out one moonlight night walking on a village pathway. From a distance he saw something long swirling and moving ahead in his way. For a moment he thought he saw a snake, and in fear he jumped and turned around. But on second thought he went ahead and took a closer look at the object. To his dismay he realized that it was just a piece of rope. His own eyes had deceived him as he was looking at the rope from afar, shining in the enchanting moonlight. Relying on his own preconceptions, he was superimposing a snake (maya) on the rope (real).

Such is the "truth" of the things that surround us in our present existence, Shankara claimed.

That the world in the Hindu view is just a shadow of the real is further seen in the following prayer from the *Rig Veda*, which appeals for the soul's release from the present.

> From the unreal lead me to the real!
> From darkness lead me to light!
> From death lead me to immortality!

As expected, the transfer from the unreal to the real is easier prayed for than realized. It is one thing by reason of intellect to accept a proposal as true. But it is yet another to subject one's feelings, emotions, desires, and pains and to balance and control them so that, pressured by such vagaries, reason does not lose sight of the eternal truth. Enlightenment is necessary for everyone to distinguish the essentially real from the unreal. It is as if the unenlightened is captured by the things that it seemingly "sees" and loses its focus on the sunlight that causes the objects to be seen.

> The sunlight that shines and spreads equally in all directions has no shape. But shadows have shape. The rays of light that make everything else visible are themselves completely invisible. . . . The individual souls are like shadows caused by the infinite light of the supreme being. . . . Karma causes what corresponds to the shadow, i.e., births and lives. . . . The shadow that is caused by the light of the sun is by no means an unreality. The shadow is as true as the light, although it is the light that makes the changing and diverse shadows.[24]

## Modern Hinduism

Hinduism has always maintained its ability to become all things to all people. As we observed earlier, it has never claimed a single individual as its founder. Nor has it ever met in councils to define its doctrinal position or to act on the question of heresy. Nevertheless, over the years many reformers have emerged within Hinduism. Though some of them may have created tidal waves when their ideas first surfaced, they have been respected and put on a par with the rishis of yesteryears. The diverse and complex nature of this religion has been a conundrum for devout Hindus themselves.

There was no need for any Hindu apologetic until India came under the influence of other major world religions like Christianity and Islam. These two religions, with their respective emphases on monotheism, posed serious challenges to the Hindu religion, monistic at heart, but at the popular level polytheistic in faith and practice.

Many Indians view both Islam and Christianity as religions of the oppressors. Islamic influence in India was strongly felt especially after the Mughal emperors came to power in the 16th century. Since then Islamic art and architecture have played a decisive role in the Indian milieu. As mentioned previously, the Red Fort in Delhi and the Taj Mahal in Agra are timeless examples of that Islamic influence. Theological as well as cultural differences between Hinduism and Islam caused much tension between the ruling Muslim emperors and the native Indian Hindus who were subjected to foreign rule.[25]

The Christian presence in India took on national proportions chiefly after the 17th century with the arrival of the British East India Company. Britain invaded India primarily for business and political reasons. However, Christianity traveled along with the English, who carried out various missionary enterprises. Later, Christian missionaries flocked to India from other European nations and North America. Christianity did not limit its mission to just preaching and teaching. It entered the bone and marrow of the Indian society with the introduction of English-style education, hospitals, and other institutions of charity.

The simple and universal nature of Islam attracted millions of Indians to that new religion. Islamic brotherhood transcended all caste and class distinctions, to the detriment of the built-in Hindu caste system. Moreover, Christianity with its emphasis on charity and love opened the doors of self-worth and freedom to a large segment of the Indian population, because early Christian missionary activities centered mainly on the less privileged people from the lower stratum of Indian society.

Earlier, Shankara had announced that a Hindu had to be born a brahmin before he could pursue the path to nirvana. We have noted that brahmins were among the few "twice-born" castes whose chances of leaving the cycle of death and rebirth had greatly improved. In this sense, Hindu philosophy had been conservative and fundamentalistic. Caste segregations were reflected heavily in public life. There was very little interaction between high caste people and those from the lower classes, some of whom were stigmatized as "untouchables."[26] Caste taboos virtually denied these folks access to the holy shrines and sacred places of Hinduism.

Mass conversions occurred mainly among the lower class Indians, to both Islam and Christianity, giving them a new identity and sense of community. Such new developments within Indian society forced the Hindu leadership to reconsider its views on authentic human existence. Consequently, independent India by virtue of its constitution opened the gates of Hindu temples to those who until now were considered untouchable. Large-scale conversions, especially to Christianity, were thus reduced to a minimum. Many communities that became Christian for purely sociological reasons reverted to their original spiritual heritage which they had received from their fathers.

Hinduism's encounter with Christianity resulted in the formation of several reform movements within Hinduism. Christian influence on the Indian lifestyle became a factor to reckon with, especially for those who lived in the cities and urban neighborhoods. Hindus educated in Christian day schools of the English pattern began to cast doubt on the propriety of child marriages and *suttee*, which, according to Hindu practice, strongly encouraged the surviving widow of the deceased to end her life by jumping live into her husband's funeral pyre.

One of the earliest pioneer Hindu reformers was Raja Rammohan Roy (1774–1833). Rammohan Roy gained popular respect as "the prophet of Indian nationalism and the pioneer of liberal reform in Hindu religion and society."[27] Roy was brought up in the strong tradition of Vaishnavism and Shaivism. He was a linguist of sorts, through advanced education exposed to Zoroastrianism, Buddhism, Islam, and Christianity. He came to believe that the fundamental principles of the Christian religion were already present in Hinduism. Thus "his own creed grew out of the conviction that the truth underlying all religions is the unity, personality, and spirituality of God."[28]

To promote his new message, in 1828 Rammohan Roy founded an organization in Calcutta called the *Brahmo Samaj* (The Society of God). Known in English under different names as *One God Society* or *The Theistic Church of India*, the Brahmo Samaj was dedicated to the worship of "the One Eternal, Unsearchable and Immutable Being, who is the Author and Preserver of the Universe, but not under or by another name, designation or title." Roy found it difficult to rationalize the worshipping of numerous gods and their idols as it was practiced in popular Hinduism. By introducing this new approach Rammohan Roy hoped to revive the worship of one God. For this purpose he continued his search of the Hindu scriptures and gleaned from them those passages that most likely had references to ethical monotheism.

Rammohan Roy's exposure to other world religions and his constant encounter with Christian missionaries enabled him to promote a new religion among his countrymen. According to M. M. Thomas, Rammoham Roy's new creed contained three important doctrines. First, Roy was very emphatic about the unity of God, thus denying any reason for worshiping various gods and goddesses. Secondly, he promoted the idea that the true essence of religion was morality. He launched an attack against polytheism, contending that the worship of many gods and idols was the cause of moral degradation in society. Thirdly, he stressed the importance of rationalism in religion. Roy maintained that religion should promote only such things as are appealing to human reason which will help it stay clear of unnecessary fairy tales and superstition.[29]

For Rammohan Roy reforming religion was the way to reform society. His antagonism against the unpleasant practices in the name of religion came to a head when he happened to witness the forced immolation of his sister-in-law at her husband's funeral. After that he worked for lifting up women by supporting better opportunities for their education and urging marriage only after they came of age. He was vehemently opposed to tantrism,[30] a form of religious sexuality. He also spoke against the sacrifice of animals in the name of religion, and the worship of a form of Kali as the spreader of disease, decked with a necklace of skulls.

Neither was Rammohan Roy positive about everything Christianity had to offer. He rejected the Christian doctrine of the Trinity but acknowledged Jesus as a great guide and teacher of morality, peace, and happiness. Jesus was not God but an ascetic. He opposed the many denominational differences within Christianity. His goal was to revive the primitive mode of Hinduism and fashion it in such a way that it would appeal to the modern mind. As a representative spokesperson for Indians, Rammohan Roy traveled to Europe. He died in Bristol, England, in 1833.

Reformation within Hinduism continued under the auspices of another Bengali Brahmin, Sri Ramakrishna (1836–1886).[31] Ramakrishna did not receive formal education. From childhood he was exposed to a series of religious experiences. Music and poetry were his first love. His formal religious life began humbly as a priest in a temple dedicated to Kali, a manifestation of the Divine Mother. Deeper knowledge of the divine was given him, it is said, through direct revelation. As his job required, Ramakrishna spent much of his time in close proximity to the image of the

Divine Mother. He began to concentrate on the image with his heart, soul, and mind, convinced that what was before him was not just an idol but the actual incarnation of God. His spiritual experience grew deeper and stronger. His spirit was transformed into a mood of ecstasy, and in a trance he received repeated visions of the image drawing ever closer to him and then moving away.

From then on Ramakrishna embarked on a spiritual journey. His religious search opened up new horizons for him. During the next 12 years he gained deeper knowledge of the Vedanta and wrestled with the many ways to spiritual fulfillment suggested in Hinduism. He received revelations of God as the Divine Mother, as Rama, Krishna, and Sita, Rama's faithful spouse. Ramakrishna went on testing his religious experiences against the teachings of other religions. He pursued the paths of Jainism as well as Buddhism. Muhammad and Jesus Christ seemed to him to be true manifestations of God, like any god of Hinduism. In all truth and sincerity he tried to live both as a Muslim and a Christian, as he understood those religions. "All religions were to him different ways to God, and all creatures were God in so many different forms."[32] For Ramakrishna all religions are bearers of the same universal truth.

Ramakrishna's devotional encounter with an object usually led him to a momentary trance (*samadhi*) with that particular object. He let go of the surroundings as he himself became immersed in the divine mystery represented in the individual object. For him, every thought, every expression, and every lifestyle was the reflection of a mental attitude. It is said of a vision of Christ that he had,

> Christ emerged in Ramakrishna, who forthwith lost his outward consciousness and became completely absorbed in the *savikalpa samadhi* in which he released his union with Brahman with attributes. After this experience Ramakrishna remained firm in his conviction up to the last days of his life that Jesus was an Incarnation of God.[33]

Ramakrishna did his best to put into practice all that he amassed from his exposure to various religious experiences. He won the hearts of multitudes through his unique stories and parables. His heart went out to the poor, the needy, and the sick. Perhaps distressed by the traditional Hindu concept of karma (their deeds shall follow them), Ramakrishna insisted that true acts of charity must leap forth from an attitude of selfless love. In every person he met, he saw God himself. Lending a helping hand through an act of mercy was to him the true worship of God.

Ramakrishna's teachings gained further acceptance and wider popularity through the efforts of his faithful disciple Narendranatha Datta whom the world knows as Swami Vivekananda (1863–1902). Vivekananda grew up in Calcutta as a member of a wealthy and liberal Brahmin family. He was a highly successful university graduate, demonstrating extraordinary skills in the academy, music and athletics. With all these credentials as a backdrop, the youth was aroused by the teachings of Ramakrishna, who gladly and gradually cast on him the mantle of leadership.

Upon the demise of Ramakrishna, Vivekananda committed himself to fostering and promoting the spiritual insights of his master. To equip himself for this giant task, he set out on a pilgrimage from the Himalayas to the Tri-seas in the South. In Kanyakumari he secluded himself on a lonely rock jutting out in the ocean, within swimming distance from the shore. From there his mind's eye beheld the multitude of fellow Indians and the misery they suffered. The moment of meditation was transformed into a moment of action. Renewed and refreshed, he returned to Calcutta to give voice to his enlightenment and popularize it.

Vivekananda's quiver was filled with arrows of wisdom he acquired through intense study of the Vedanta. He became the first Indian intellectual to introduce the West to the universal scope and relevance of philosophical Hinduism. He proudly represented his Indian heritage at the World Parliament of Religions in Chicago in 1893. While interpreting Vedanta for the whole world, Vivekananda emphasized the need for the followers of each religion to respect the teaching of others and to learn from one another.

Alerting the assembly to the urgency of a worldwide spiritual awakening he exhorted, "Come up, O lions, and shake off the delusion that you are sheep; you are souls immortal, spirits free, blest and eternal; ye are not matter, ye are not bodies; matter is your servant, not you the servant of matter."[34] Vivekananda's message was widely received in the West as he went around speaking at different conferences and convocations. Within a year the Vedanta Society was founded in New York.

Vivekananda returned to India and established the Ramakrishna Mission in honor of his guru. He expanded on the vision of his master, aided by generous support from those in the West who were anxious to promote a just cause. The enterprise grew in size and in service to humanity in a few short years. The membership of monks and disciples in the society kept increasing. The principles of the new movement permeated Indian society by means of educational institutions, hospitals, primary health centers, orphanages and other institutions of charity and good will. Vivekananda's short span of life awakened the Indian mind to balance properly a profound spiritual vision with the basic needs of the human body.

Vivekananda's philosophy was dominated by a combination of monism and theism, the two fundamental categories of Hindu thought. Religion students prefer to describe his view as "panentheism," that is, everything is within God, as evidenced by the following: "He is in everything; he is everything. Every man and woman is the palpable, blissful, living God. Who says God is unknown? Who says he is to be searched after? We have found God eternally. We have been living in him eternally."[35] Vivekananda taught that there was unlimited divine power encased in each individual, and people could release that power for positive purposes if only they realized what was contained in them.

Perhaps these were the ideas that fascinated the West as they listened to the vigorous, intelligent, and compassionate spirit of Vivekananda. His new approach to religion and humanity was very appealing to intellectuals who were in the pursuit of the absolute. He opened their eyes to see the reality within each individual. This idea became the basis for a large-scale Hindu renaissance that continues even today. India today discovers the potential in its population and puts it to right and proper use, a remarkable shift from the traditional Indian notion of floating along with the passage of time.

The idea that, after all, all religions are the same is obviously music to the ears of many. Apparently this is the premise on which leaders of religion enter into dialogue with one another. History shows that such meetings often bring out major disagreements among religions rather than help them discover any solid common ground. Striving for a common ground for all religions, (and ultimately working for one universal religion) though reasonable and logical, is practically impossible in spite of good intentions. Religions of man, by their very nature, cannot become unified because all religions do not maintain the same perspective of life and its meaning.

Vivekananda was wise enough to perceive this. He never said that all religions are the same. In the Parliament of World Religions he did not promote a world religion. He only encouraged people to follow faithfully their own religions without converting from one to another. In essence he was promoting the peaceful coexistence of all religions. But he never hesitated to show his disagreement with other religions. For example, Vivekananda maintained that it was a big mistake to label a person a sinner. Nor did he believe that Jesus Christ came to take away the sin of the world as John the Baptist witnessed (John 1:29). According to him, "'Taketh away the sin of the world' means that Christ would show us the way to become perfect. God became Christ to show man his true nature, that we too are God."[36]

For Vivekananda, Jesus was another guru, a yogi, who reached his own self-awareness that he is God. Jesus came to teach others the same method of self-awareness when he said,"The kingdom of heaven is within you" and "I and the Father are one." He viewed Jesus as a mystic, not even as a teacher of righteousness. Because Christ was God incarnate, the Jews could not kill him. What hung on the cross was just a phantom in his place, a mirage.[37]

From our perspective the New Age philosophy has not created anything new in terms of its interpretation of man and his goal in life, but it faithfully follows the vision of Vivekananda. Vivekananda could not let go of his monistic and deistic frame of reference even when he was trying to grasp Jesus' elementary teaching that man is a sinner and cannot save himself from the curse of sin. Vivekananda interpreted Jesus' direct references to sin as *avidya* (lack of self-understanding), an idea Hinduism views as the cause of human misery. He avoided the biblical concept of sin and therefore did not have to acknowledge Jesus as the savior from sin.

Undoubtedly the giant who successfully expanded Hinduism's broad social and political dimensions was Mahatma (the great soul) Gandhi (1869–1948). Gandhiji grew up in a traditional Hindu home. He studied law in England and practiced law in South Africa, representing the Indian community there. The unpleasant experiences he encountered in that country (clear signs of racism, the white population treating others as second-class citizens) alerted him to the situation in his own homeland then under British rule. Gandhiji returned to India to join and bolster the movement that was already in progress for the independence of India.

Gandhiji employed a strategy of nonviolence and noncooperation to fight the national enemy, a scheme that had never before been tested anywhere as a political weapon. He was convinced that it was wrong to take the life of another, even if the other person was the enemy and the epitome of evil. He considered the struggle for freedom to be a spiritual war. He advised those who rallied around him not to resort to arms. Such an approach required a certain emotional and spiritual maturity, a product of spiritual discipline.

Gandhiji's tactic against British rule was shaped by his religious convictions. He was a faithful student of the Bhagavat Gita and the New Testament, especially of Jesus' Sermon on the Mount. His method of nonviolence (*ahimsa*) was the large scale political application of the Jain ideal of respect for all life. Gandhiji believed that strict adherence to the principle of nonviolence was necessary to achieve justifiable, laudable, and truthful ends. His personality was an unusual combination of tolerance, patience, endurance, and resistance. For Gandhiji, Truth was God and the pursuit of Truth was religion. Satyagraha (exercising the power of Truth) was his method of actualizing his goals. He was determined to tame the enemies and compel them to accept defeat.

According to M. M. Thomas, three important concepts constitute the fundamentals of Gandhiji's philosophy and creed: Truth (*satya*), non-violence (*ahimsa* ), and service to the immediate neighborhood (*swadeshi*).[38] As his autobiography explains, Gandhiji was dedicated to truth, and he would not oblige to none but truth. For him truth was God, and God was not a person. Truth and non-violence go hand in hand. They cannot be separated one from the other. *Ahimsa* is what makes man a true human being. "*Ahimsa* is the Supreme Law or *dharma*, " and "there is no other Law or *dharma* than Truth."[39]

From Gandhiji's point of view, *ahimsa* represents absolute and unconditional selflessness. It is an attitude that frees the individual self (*atman*) from thinking about itself, which flows into a lifestyle of care and concern for others. Gandhiji leaned on the Hindu sages to prove that "if man desired to realize his self, i.e. truth, he could do so only by being completely detached from the body, i.e., by making all other beings feel safe from him. That is the way of *ahimsa*."[40]

The practice of truth and non-violence, therefore, was religious activity for Mahatma Gandhi. "My life is my message," Gandhiji claimed. As the fighter for freedom for his homeland, he applied these spiritual principles at the practical level during each encounter he had with the foreign powers. This was where the concept of swadeshi also came in handy for him. The word *swadeshi* signified making the most use of the resources that are locally available whether they were in the sphere of economics, society, or religion. Our interests concern Gandhiji's vision of the religion of India, namely, Hinduism.

Gandhiji maintained that people must remain faithful to the religious surroundings and traditions into which they are born. Should they find their native religion defective in any respect, they must strive to purge it, instead of deserting their own religious heritage and embracing another. He was strongly convinced of the connection between religion and culture. It is as if by divine design people are born into a particular religion. Just as we are unable to choose our parents, our ancestry, or our place of birth, so also religion is not a matter of our own choosing. We are bound to the religious environment and traditions of our ancestors and our culture. Gandhiji said that his position was in accordance with the doctrine of dharma as explained in the Bhagavat Gita.[41]

Nevertheless, Gandhiji kept an open mind to the fascinating ideas of the Christian religion. He was greatly attracted to the exemplary life of Jesus who taught others through his life to walk with another the extra mile, share the extra garment with the needy, and to lay down one's own life for others. In his life Jesus demonstrated the law of love as he taught it in his Sermon on the Mount.

Gandhiji fell in love with the ethical teachings of Jesus rather than with the historical person of Jesus Christ. For him the Sermon on the Mount summarized the entire message of Jesus. Gandhiji understood that the Sermon on the Mount and the Gita (which he called "the Light of Asia") spelled the same message, that of renunciation, that is, world-negation. Should he by any chance be deprived of the Gita and for some reason forget all its contents, he would still feel happy and content if he had a copy of the Sermon on the Mount.[42]

Jesus Christ for Gandhiji was more a principle than a person. He was least interested in the historicity of Jesus. Questions concerning the historical Jesus lose their relevance once people adhere to his unique message. Gandhiji's impressions of the teachings of Christ would still be the same even if some day someone would prove beyond all doubt that the historical Jesus never existed. Jesus on the cross became the supreme example of sacrifice and martyrdom for all. And, "if Jesus represents not a person but the principle of non-violence, India has accepted its protecting power."[43]

Not surprisingly, Gandhiji rejected the idea of God becoming man to "take away the sin of the world." He could not see how the sacrificial death of Jesus could atone for the sins of all mankind. Even his own fellow countrymen from the Hindu elite who had embraced the Christian faith could not convince him on this point. He was rather offended by those Christians who claimed that they were saved by faith in Jesus Christ but who never cared to mend their lives in a Christ-like manner. He posed the following challenge to Christians:

> God did not bear the Cross only nineteen hundred years ago, but He bears it today, and He dies and is resurrected from day to day. It would be poor comfort to the world, if it had to depend upon a historical God who died two thousand years ago. Do not then preach the God of history but show Him as he lives today through you.[44]

Gandhiji wanted everyone to imitate Christ and emulate his principles. There was nothing in the life of Jesus that other humans could not do. From his birth, Jesus had the ability not to sin. As a human being Jesus was just like any other person confined to the limitations of flesh and blood. Jesus had to work his way to perfection. Gandhiji was opposed to the Christian doctrine of the person and work of Christ:

It was more than I could believe that Jesus was the only incarnate Son of God and that only he who believed in him would have everlasting life. If God could have sons, all of us were his sons. If Jesus was like God, or God himself, then all men were like God and could be God Himself.[45]

Gandhiji's opinion of Jesus is virtually the same as the majority of non-Christians. It does not go beyond the general view that Jesus was an exemplary man, a superman who practiced what he preached. Like the other modern Hindu reformers who preceded him, Gandhiji ignored the most important purpose of Jesus' incarnation—atoning for the sins of mankind through his sacrificial death on the cross. His mind rejected the free offer of forgiveness through faith in Jesus Christ, although he put his heart and soul into practicing the ethical teachings of the New Testament in their literal sense. Commenting on this attitude of the Mahatma, R. C. Zaehner wrote, "Mahatma Gandhi was no Christian, and the Christians were amazed that this should be so, for never in modern times had they seen any man tread more faithfully in the footsteps of Christ."[46]

Gandhiji was neither a philosopher nor founder of a religion. He benefited from a blend of ideals from the religions and philosophies to which he was exposed. He viewed these principles against the crises of his own people, the population of the Indian nation. He adhered to the principle of fostering indigenous methods to meet the basic needs of people, including their religious needs. On cultural and religious grounds he justified the traditions of Hinduism such as the caste system, the teaching of karma, cow worship, and transmigration. Working with the poor for their welfare and advancement was at the core of his social and political agenda. In the poor and downtrodden he saw God himself. Gandhiji perhaps was trying to practice the philosophical ideal of Hindu monism.

Dr. S. Radhakrishnan (1888–1976) was a well known philosopher, Hindu theologian and statesman, and a former President of India. Radhakrishnan's family background gave him his own Hindu religious heritage, while his education under Christian missionary teachers exposed him to Christianity. As a professor he taught at Oxford as well as at various universities in India. He wrote extensively on philosophy and religion. His writings have been reviewed by Christians in India and elsewhere, including Hendrick Kraemer, C. E. M. Joad, and Albert Schweitzer.[47]

Radhakrishnan defended Hinduism as the world's greatest religion. Against the critics, he interpreted Hindu concepts as world affirming and spiritually uplifting, following the Vedanta philosophy and in line with the pragmatism of Vivekananda and Gandhiji. He is regarded as the champion of neo-Hinduism and Hindu humanism. In his own words, "Hindu religion, like all true religion, is essentially 'other-worldly.' It pictures the world as a mere vestibule and training ground for another in which alone life is real, rich and abiding; yet it moves men to the most impressive and sustained demonstrations of human courage, power, and persistence and has woven for itself a secular vesture."[48]

Undoubtedly, Radhakrishnan's goal was to discover a renewed relevance of Hinduism in today's world. He saw mysticism as the essence of all religions. In his own scholarly way, he found support in the words of Jesus and early and modern Christian writers that this is true even of the Christian religion.[49] At the same time, perhaps overpowered by the language of the Sermon on the Mount, Radhakrishnan (unlike Mahatma Gandhi) reacted that "the only ethic that Jesus can preach is a negative one, to enable man to free himself from the world and fit himself for the Kingdom. It is a penitential discipline and not a humanist ethic."[50]

Yet, his spiritual struggle was shaped by a strong sense of individual responsibility, as the Hindu law of karma demanded. For him life was a game of chance, as if humans stood under the ever-alert scrutiny of eternal justice. There was no way to undo the things a person did in the past. There is no pardon and forgiveness of any kind because there is no supernatural deliverer who would condescend to remedy the fault of others. Radhakrishnan wrote, "Life is like a game of bridge. The cards in the game are given to us. We do not select them. They are traced to past *karma* but we are free to make any call as we think fit and lead any suit. Only we are limited by the rules of the game."[51]

Radhakrishnan's philosophy has been described as having three basic principles, that is, non-duality of the Godhead, the divinity of the soul, and the unity of existence.[52] These three fundamentals he saw as the criteria for a harmony of all religions. As a scholar who benefited from the knowledge of philosophy and religion from the East and the West, Radhakrishnan restructured his own heritage in a way that is appealing to many who search for their own identity. Perhaps the most appealing of all is his version of the unity of all existence, which is the essence of monism.

# 5
# The Hindu–Christian Connection

India is renowned for the variety and diversity of its faiths and cultures. Among the nations of the world, India stands unmatched with its assortment of distinct cultures, races, languages, and religions. It includes Aryan, Dravidian, and Mongolian races. India's ethnic diversity is further seen in its 15 different official languages and almost 300 different dialects. Yet this nation has no equal as the prime example of unity in diversity. India, the world's largest democracy, is the home of slightly less than a fifth of the world's population, ranking only next to China. Compared to the United States, India is roughly a third in size, with almost four times as many people.

To separate the faith of India from its culture is more than a struggle. Indians are known to be inordinately religious people. Other than its own well-known distinctive attribute as the land of the Hindus, India has been the home also of Buddhism, the major religion of much of the Orient. Juxtaposed to its inherently religious nature, India remains a secular state by virtue of its constitution. It promises equality of status and opportunity for all her people and assures their dignity and liberty in the context of the nation's unity.

Modern India has been the testing ground for various religious adventures, political philosophies, and ideologies. In 1948, the major Protestant Christian denominations joined to form the Church of South India.[1] A similar attempt in the north resulted in the Church of North India in 1970. Some parts of independent India favored the assimilation of Communist principles, perhaps as a viable means in the peoples' struggle against poverty and social inequality. In fact, the Communist party has been able to win elections through the democratic process and assume power in certain states of the Indian Republic.[2] India continues to be the land of religious pluralism and multiculturalism, never closing its doors against theism, atheism, or secular humanism.

The Christian religion in India has succeeded in the struggle to establish and maintain its own Indian identity. In view of the inimical belief that Christianity was imported to India by Western colonialists to maintain their vested interests, as well as government aversion to outsiders, devout Christian missionaries as well as their Indian counterparts have attempted to indigenize the Christian Gospel to fit the patterns of Indian faith and culture.

Our purpose in this chapter is not to be critical of the different ways in which Christian thinkers, many of them converts themselves to Christianity from the orthodox Hindu way of life, struggled to communicate the Gospel of Jesus Christ to the typical Indian mind. Daring as these ventures have been, we need to acknowledge that the sole intent of all such struggle has been somehow to relate the distinctive truth claims of Christianity to the cultural and spiritual context of India.

## Indianization

Father Robert de Nobili, an Italian Jesuit priest who arrived in Tamil Nadu, South India, in 1605, is perhaps the first foreign missionary who dared to interpret Christianity in terms of the faith and culture of India.[3]    Interestingly enough, Jesuit missionaries were accorded a warm reception by the Mogul emperor Akbar (1556–1605) who, though a Muslim by birth, readily kept an open mind for assimilating ideas from the generic Indian religions as well as from Christianity.

Jesuit missionaries from Goa promptly arrived at Akbar's palace at his own invitation with the hope that the doors of India would  open wide to Christianity, should the emperor himself embrace the new faith. However, this was not to be. Akbar, out of dislike for Islam, incorporated the ideals of the religions he chanced to know about, then forming a new religion (the *Din Ilahi*), positioning himself as its head.

Father de Nobili felt that his mission was to reach the noble men and the high class people of India with the message of Jesus Christ. He settled in Madura, a city in South India, a center of learning for Hindu philosophy and science. He knew about the elevated position of Brahmins in the Hindu community and the authority they held in society by virtue of their priestly office. He also surmised that the best way to win converts to the Christian faith was for himself to assume a role similar to that of a Hindu holy man (*sanyasi*).

De Nobili was determined to reach the people of India on their own terms. He claimed that his Italian origins were equal in status to the Kshatriyas of India. He exchanged the traditional black cassock of the Jesuit monk for the saffron garb of the typical Hindu priest. He isolated himself from other Jesuits and lived in a simple, cheap dwelling attached to a chapel. He hired Brahmin cooks and lived on a modest vegetarian diet consisting of rice, vegetables, fruits, and milk. He also acquired expertise in Tamil, the local vernacular, and later in Sanskrit, having been tutored by Brahmin school masters. Assuming the position of a Christian guru, this Jesuit priest gained courage to engage in philosophical and religious dialogue with Hindus.

The results of this totally new approach to missions were breathtaking, though only momentarily. Within two years, more than 60 people converted to Christianity, many of them from the Brahmin caste, including the one who taught de Nobili the Vedic scriptures. De Nobili was convinced that it was not necessary for people to abandon their social, cultural, and racial identities, once they embraced the Christian faith. He administered water baptism to the new Christians in the name of the Triune God, strictly admonishing them to discontinue idolatry and to carry out their lives as natives, conforming to the traditions, customs, and practices of their respective societies.[4]

Apart from believing in Jesus Christ there was nothing foreign in de Nobili's religion. Christian prayers were said in worship services in place of the Hindu *mantras*. Separate communities were established for new believers according to the respective castes in which they were born and raised. Worship was held for different caste Christians at different times. Later on separate missionaries were commissioned to take care of the spiritual needs of people according to their castes. However, as the mission expanded and different caste Hindus became Christians, problems within the church also increased. Criticism rose from within the Jesuit mission, maintaining that the taboos of caste were not in keeping with the principles of the Christian faith. Thus, after a period of almost a half century of experimentation, de Nobili's adventures became less appealing and also more strained in relation to the true spirit of the Gospel.

Perhaps there is no single successful method for relating the Gospel of Jesus Christ to any particular people or culture. The history of Indian Christianity shows that many who once professed the Christian faith have, in the course of time, for various reasons, chosen to return to the religion of their fathers. This was true even in the case of de Nobili's own Tamil teacher. In several instances peoples' attraction to Christianity was short-lived—in some cases until the missionary who first brought them the Gospel left for another station, in others, when the fringe benefits that accompanied the new faith ceased. Yet, churches were strengthened in the faith and the number of believers increased.

The end of the 19th century marked also the end of mass conversions to Christianity, especially as the grand scale missionary movement was slowly winding down and as the spirit of nationalism was steadily gathering momentum in India. On the one hand, sages like Vivekananda projected Hinduism as a global religion and instilled in every Hindu a certain pride and self-esteem. On the other hand, the converts from Hinduism to Christianity struggled to translate to their fellow nationals the essence of Christianity in the familiar language of authentic Hinduism.

We have noted earlier that the Hindu religion suggests three paths of spirituality, that is, the ways of devotion, works, and knowledge. Contemporary attempts on the part of many leading Indian Christian thinkers to present the Christian faith to the people of India may also be broadly classified under the above three categories.[5] We will briefly examine how this has been done.

Religion is an attitude of the spirit, the inner being of human beings. Religion lets the human spirit wander into those mysterious avenues of human life where the rational mind hesitates to tread. Religions may not always have a reason to posit what they uphold to be genuine and ultimate. In religious matters faith and devotion are said to transcend reason and cognizance. Faith loves mystery, for faith itself is a mystery (Heb. 11:1). Faith acknowledges that the ultimate questions in life are beyond the grasp of human wisdom, and as such, they are answered better by means of revelation than by reason.

The Hindu way of devotion is grounded in the mystery and transcendence of God. Devotion entails a certain dedication to, and fervent love of, God as a person. It zealously seeks a sincere faith in God and reflects itself in piety and charity. The way of devotion has God as its focus, and it strives to view the entire universe as dependent on, and strikingly manifesting, the goodness of God. It elevates the human soul from the mundane and this worldly to the celestial and the other worldly. Religious people therefore strive for spiritual depth and devotion in their lifestyle because, according to one Indian definition, "religion is the soul's attitude, response, and adjustment in the presence of the supreme realities of the transcendent order."[6]

It may be said that Christianity first attracted a cross section of modern India primarily because many saw in this new religion an abundance of mystery and transcendence. Many well educated and highly accomplished Hindus discovered in both the very words of Jesus and the writings of the apostle Paul evidences of piety, mystery, and even ecstasy. Examining the life and teachings of Jesus from their vantage point, these well meaning scholars identified in the ancient scriptures of Hinduism vestiges of a savior figure comparable to the Jesus of Nazareth. They became bold enough to replace the Hebrew Old Testament with the Hindu scriptures and interpret the person and work of Christ to suit Indian patterns of spirituality and devotion.

In this connection Robin Boyd has suggested that two major strands have emerged in Indian Christianity in keeping with its strong affinity to Hinduism.[7] The first has been an attempt to interpret the Christian faith in the language of Hindu monistic philosophy. Monism, as we have seen, is the purest form of philosophical Hinduism, which advocates the oneness of all forms of existence with God, the world soul. Theologians who build their system on monistic philosophy evade the issue of creation and redemption, two fundamentals of theology. They also do not distinguish the Creator from the created order; nor do they regard sin as the human act of disobedience to God and the resultant state of alienation from him.

The second strand of Indian theology, according to Boyd, emerged from the interpretation of God as a person in a very peculiar sense. It views God as separate from the universe, just as each individual soul is separate from the individual body. This separation, however, is not the same as dualism which distinguishes clearly the spirit from matter. Hinduism has preferred the expression *modified non-dualism* to explain this phenomenon. Instead of assuming the soul's identity with God, this modified version of monism makes the claim that God dwells in the individual self as the transcendent reality. This approach enables humans to worship God and accordingly lead a life of devotion (*bhakti*). We shall see how some Indian theologians struggled to apply this principle to Christianity.

Christian missionaries who were rethinking an effective strategy for mission in India, as well as many early converts from Hinduism, were of the opinion that interpreting the Christian Gospel in monistic terms was the most successful way to appeal to the Hindu mind. Christian missionary activities in India reached their peak while the British controlled much of the Indian subcontinent, although it is true that most European nations which entered into trade relations with India were the least interested in the missionary enterprise.[8] Unfortunately, most Indians failed to recognize the difference between what is European and what is genuinely Christian in spite of the fact that the Christian religion had its humble origins in Asia. As a result, they easily dismissed the basic teachings of the Christian faith as interpolations from the West. What was left, therefore, was an image of Christ who was able to arrive at his own existential self-awareness, who set a pattern for others to emulate. Suddenly there was a great regard for Jesus when his teachings and work were being interpreted in Indian terms.

Evidence of the Christian way of devotion was amply supported by the variety of Christian literature that was made available in the various vernaculars of those communities in which the Gospel was able to penetrate. Following the native writing styles, pieces of Christian poetry and lyrics were composed to suit the simple and the most popular patterns of Indian music. Christian story telling, patterned after the traditional style of narrating an event accompanied by music to a larger audience, was adopted as an effective tool for communicating the Gospel. An extraordinarily talented Christian poet in South India produced, among other things, an epic inspired by, and faithfully following, John Bunyan's *The Pilgrim's Progress*.[9]

Apart from the Christians of the Syrian and the Orthodox traditions, much of modern Christianity in India is the product of the modern missionary movements. Since these movements flourished at a time when India was part of the British Commonwealth, many Indian intellectuals welcomed Christ with a deep sense of devotion to him, although they were constantly opposed to the European missionaries who introduced them to the Christian faith. The Hindu response to the missionary enterprise was two-fold: While many of these thinkers perceived in the new faith the fulfillment of the Hindu faith, others revitalized Hinduism to resist the innovations of a foreign religion.[10]

Particularly throughout the 19th century India witnessed the mushrooming of a number of indigenous Christian organizations. Many of them operated on a transdenominational basis, in the long run preparing a solid base for unity among the Christians of India. All Christians who subscribed to the Apostles' Creed were welcomed into this new venture. Several new associations emerged, many of them matching a similar establishment in the Hindu religion. Indian Christians emphasized the dire need to distinguish between what they termed substantive Christianity and adjunctive Christianity.[11]

"What is the sine qua non of the Christian religion?" they asked. It can be defined in no better way than in the Apostles' Creed. Substantive Christianity hinges on the simple faith that Jesus Christ, the Son of God, was born a human being, who lived, died, and rose again for the salvation of mankind. This is the unalterable and universal truth and foundation of the Christian faith. Adjunctive Christianity, on the other hand, is the result of the church's struggle to foster and preserve the faith. Auxiliary formulations of Christianity differ according to the culture and the milieu in which the Christian faith takes root. These differences are genuine expressions of the same faith that is confessed by people living in diverse cultural contexts.

This approach obviously is a very positive way to introduce the Christian faith to people of a different culture. Nevertheless, the fact remains that in most traditional communities like India it is impossible to draw the fine line between faith and culture, precisely because in these communities faith dominates culture. There is hardly a society whose historic origins are not in some way shaded or conditioned by one or more religions. There is hardly a person whose culture has remained the same even after he or she has embraced a new faith. As is well known, almost every nation that was ever open to Christianity has been attracted by the Christian culture, though it may not have welcomed the new faith with open arms.

Some Christian theologians have argued that God's revelation in Jesus Christ must be translated into the cultural language of other religions in order to communicate the Christian message to non-Christians effectively. They, like other students of comparative religion, claim that what the world knows today as Christianity is nothing but a skillful blending of the teachings of Jesus and the tenets of Western civilization. If in ages past the West had the privilege of combining its civilization with the Christian religion, any culture with which Christianity makes fresh encounters must also be given *carte blanche* to make its own experiments with a new faith. These explorations should naturally incorporate factors from other religions that are part of that culture as well—so the argument goes.[12]

# Sundar Singh

For our purposes we will consider some examples from India where sincere attempts have been made to interpret the Christian faith according to the way of devotion. Some adaptations, in some respects, were orthodox. Others, like the current New Age efforts to harmonize Christianity with New Age notions, distorted or actually undermined the basic biblical teachings. Sadhu Sundar Singh (1889–1929) was an outstanding Indian Christian who, without the luxury of any formal theological training "was steeped in the teaching of the New Testament and had an instinctive, or perhaps rather inspired, understanding of the nature of theological thinking."[13] Though born into a family of Sikhs, Sundar Singh's mother reared him in the *bhakti* tradition. As a boy he grew up very knowledgeable about both Sikhism and Hinduism, learning the Bhagavat Gita by heart.

Sundar Singh, like most modern Indian sages and leaders, was educated in a Christian mission school. As expected, he was exposed to the Bible and the teachings of Christianity.

An unhappy and angry Sundar Singh rejected the new religion and gave vent to his emotions by burning a copy of the Bible. However, his search continued. His search of the Hindu scriptures, rigorous yoga practices, and even the reading of the Koran could not offer him the peace he was constantly seeking. Then one night, at the early age of fifteen, he was determined that, if he could not find the peace he longed for, he would end his life on the railroad tracks the following morning. Before dawn, to his great surprise, he had a vision of a glorious Jesus arrayed in majesty and beauty, commanding his absolute obedience. Sundar Singh yielded. He tasted peace at last, "a peace which made him constantly assert that he was living in heaven upon the earth."[14]

Sundar Singh was baptized into the Christian faith after almost a year of instruction. He entered the divinity school at the behest of missionaries and friends, but academic study of theology did not interest him. In a year he chose to leave St. John's Divinity College in Lahore to become an itinerant preacher, wandering all over India and into Tibet. The New Testament was his constant companion, which drew him ever closer to the Lord, even in times of trouble and distress.

Sundar Singh's life of witnessing is shrouded with mystery. Some of his testimonies gained for him, though momentarily, the reputation of an impostor who made up heroic stories about himself to impress people. His own humble and simple lifestyle, however, proved his critics wrong. This new convert to Christianity related a series of events in which Jesus Christ appeared to him, not in dreams or hallucinations, but conversing with him in person. He narrated incidents about his miraculous escape from the jaws of death as he sojourned barefoot in the Himalayas. He spoke about his encounter with a three-century-old Christian sage who lived in the icy mountains. In Tibet his enemies threw him into a dry well filled with carcasses. But he was rescued without any visible human intervention. Sundar Singh's testimonies were well received in America, Australia, and Europe. From all over the world he drew people to the foot of the cross. A final journey to Tibet is the last known account about this "apostle of the bleeding feet."

As a first generation Christian, Sundar Singh developed his own deep appreciation of Christ and his suffering for the human race. Like his Lord and Savior, he spoke in parables as he related his own religious experience to his listeners. He compared Christian suffering to a doctor hitting a weak newborn baby to make it cry so that the breathing process can begin. "Through suffering God strikes us in love. The Cross is the key of heaven. . . . The Cross will bear those who bear the Cross, until it bears them up to heaven, into the actual Presence of the glorious Redeemer."[15]

Although he spoke about ecstasy and mysticism in his faith-union with Jesus, the greatest religious experience for Sundar Singh was being in the presence of God. Unlike the followers of the Hindu *bhakti* tradition whose goal is a certain mystical union with the absolute, Sundar Singh spoke of the communion and fellowship with God. He understood Christian prayer as communication between God and man which demonstrates the free intercourse between the human and the divine. He explained: "If we want to rejoice in God we must be different from Him; the tongue could taste no sweetness if there were no difference between it and that which it tastes."[16]

A deep appreciation for faith-union with Jesus was possible for Sundar Singh because he was always conscious of sin as a human predicament. According to him, those who deny the fact of sin do so because they are overcome by the power of sin. In a sin-filled world it is impossible for people to feel the burden of sin because, in fact, they are ruled and governed by it. To be aware of one's own sin is in itself a great blessing. To ignore sin is perhaps the most dangerous of human situations. Concerning the loathsome control of sin over human life, Sundar Singheristic style:

It is a healthy sign to feel that we are sinners. It is dangerous when we do not feel it. Once while bathing in the river Sutlej I sank into deep water. Above my head were tons of water and yet

130

I did not feel the burden at all. When I came to the bank, I lifted a pot filled with water and found it very heavy. As long as I was in the water, I did not feel the weight. Similarly a sinner does not feel that he is a sinner as long as he lives in sin.[17]

Sundar Singh rejected the notion of salvation by works. He stressed Christ's atoning death on the cross as the only means of salvation. He illustrated this through stories from human life as well as from nature. Christ's substitutionary death on the cross was like a man who dug a tunnel under a mountain in order to connect two villages with a road; the man himself died in the very act of constructing the underpass, a task he willingly undertook to establish the link between two communities.

Christ's redeeming love for mankind is like a father who freely offers his own blood for a transfusion to save his son from a fatal injury. The father dies in the process of saving his son's life. Christ's self-giving love is like a mother bird who chooses to die with her young on a tree that is set on fire. The mother's love for the young bird is so intense that she stays there with her young with no thought of saving her own life.[18]

Sundar Singh had a strong view of sin and its grave consequences. We must remember that his religious background before his encounter with Christ was heavily marked by a strong sense of morality and work righteousness. Naturally he linked sin with the concept of karma. Sundar Singh called sin "a state of mind" or "a disposition." Sin to him was a power humans are unable to resist or subdue. Contrary to God's will, sin is powerful enough to drag the human soul into the never-ending misery of hell. "God has never sent anyone to hell. . . . It is sin which drives souls into hell," he said.[19]

Equally powerful was his vision about those who have experienced the joy of salvation in Jesus Christ. Salvation was brought about by Christ's sacrificial death on the cross. Christians need to reflect that salvation to the world by leading a life of sanctification. Christians, by righteous acts, must demonstrate to the world that they are the redeemed children of God. Salvation entails deliverance from the power of sin. "Perfect salvation," in Singh's own words, "is freedom from sin, and not merely forgiveness of sins. Jesus Christ came not only to forgive sin, but to make us free from sin. We receive from Christ a new vital power which releases us from sin. . . . To be saved by Christ is to receive new life from Him, to become a new creature."[20]

Even though he appreciated the Hindu scriptures and respected all faithful seekers of truth, Sundar Singh realized that God's revelation in Jesus Christ was unique. He believed that the true revelation of God is given through Jesus Christ and the Holy Spirit even when it is given to non-Christians, although they may not realize it.[21] His true adherence to the Christian faith was evident in his rejection of all the ways of salvation, including yoga, suggested by Hinduism.

## Modified Nondualism

We have noted earlier that some Hindu philosophers saw how difficult it was to maintain total adherence to monism especially at the popular level. Monist philosophy is idealist philosophy which stands for the oneness of all things, and as such it does not allow room for relationship or fellowship with the ultimate. Monism can only raise the soul to an existential self-awareness that ultimately it is itself the world soul. To overcome this struggle Ramanuja, a 10th-century Hindu philosopher, proposed a new system that came to be known as *modified non-dualism.*

According to modified nondualism, the world soul and the individual soul, although ultimately one, are distinct from each other. Just as the soul is different from the body, so God is different from the created order. The individual soul needs to be released from its present form of existence. Unconditional surrender to God by way of devotion is the means to achieve this end. The way of devotion requires an

132

unselfish, pure heart which whispers to the soul that the one thing that is truly real is the world soul. Bishop Appasamy followed this route in order to develop a Christian theology for India.

# A. J. Appasamy

A. J. Appasamy, a Christian writer, teacher, and later bishop in South India, developed his theology following the bhakti tradition of Hinduism. Appasamy grew up in a Christian family. His father converted from Hindu piety to Christianity. Appasamy received an advanced education, studying for several years in the United States and England, where he was influenced by Von Hugel, Heiler, Otto, and Eckhart, and was exposed to a variety of literature on Western mysticism. He also came across the many ways in which Western scholars had interpreted the gospel of John by using the language of mysticism. In Oxford, he wrote his doctoral dissertation on *The mysticism of the Fourth Gospel in its Relation to Hindu Bhakti Literature.* Sadhu Sundar Singh, whom he met in Oxford, also had a tremendous influence on Appasamy's Christian spiritual formation. Appasamy was convinced that the people of India would better appreciate the Christian faith if it were presented as a way of devotion.

With few exceptions, among the books of the Bible the gospel of John appears to be the most attractive piece of Christian literature for the people of India. Somehow the mission and ministry of Jesus Christ as narrated by the apostle John communicates well to those who are preoccupied with religious mystery and mysticism. Appasamy endeavored to find in Hinduism parallels to the philosophical language of John's gospel.

Two statements from the Johannine writings are fundamental to Appasamy's theology. These are the words uttered by Jesus himself: "I and my Father are one," and "Abide in me."[22] Commenting on the former, Appasamy said that by those words Jesus was not referring to a kind of monistic fusion of himself into the Father, but a fellowship between the two, because Jesus also said, "The Father is greater than I." Jesus' relationship with God the Father is further evidenced in his high priestly prayer where he prayed "that all of them may be one, Father, just as you are in me and I am in you" (John 17:21).

Contrary to the monistic notion of absorption into the ultimate, Appasamy described Christian salvation as an everlasting fellowship with God in Christ. Salvation is something that can be experienced at the present as implied in Jesus' call to abide in him. Christians lead a life of salvation in response to God's love in Christ for them. Parallels to this experience may be found even in the Hindu interpretation of *Moksha*.

> Cursed be that knowledge which makes me one with Thee. . . . I am thy servant, Thou art my Lord. . . . Water cannot taste itself nor trees their own fruit; the worshiper must be separate, thus alone pleasure arises from distinction.[23]

However, Indian Christian writers have made generous use of numerous religious expressions from Hinduism in appealing to the people of India with the Gospel—either by identifying Hindu idioms that may have parallels in Christianity or by injecting Christian meaning into already popular Hindu phrases.[24] For example, songs of praise were composed for the Christian Trinity using the imagery of the *Saccidananda* (pure being, intelligence, and bliss). And God was venerated as the supreme example of motherhood bestowing all good gifts.

Christ has been described as "the river of life from heaven and the mountain of salvation, the ocean of bliss, the cloud that showers the rain of grace, life-giving medicine [and] the gem of gems. He is the heavenly Ganges that takes away sin."[25] This was a way for Indian Christians to say that human beings are sinners and cannot save themselves. One poet compared salvation by works to the futile effort of "building a bridge of butter over a river of fire." They were agreed that there is no other name under heaven given among men by which we can be saved (Acts 4:12). They worshipped Jesus as their Lord, King, Guru, Swami, Mother, Father, Ocean of Mercy, Avatar (incarnation), and the Moon that came down by the stairway of its rays. They understood the Holy Spirit as "a flood of joy, medicine for the heart, the key to heaven, the stream of oil of happiness and sacred milk."[26] They in fact gave Christianity a familiar face in India.

Salvation by grace through faith for Christ's sake was well received in Indian Christian theology as long as the Gospel was communicated as a way of devotion. The missionary challenge, however, became rather acute and intense when the good news was interpreted according to the Hindu pattern of the way of knowledge and of works.

Appasamy, himself an admirer and faithful student of John's gospel, identified a strong connection between the Johannine use of the *Logos* and the Hindu idea of God as the *Antaryamin* (indweller). John wrote that the *Logos* (Jesus) "was in the world, and though the world was made through him, the world did not recognize him" (John 1:10). Appasamy claimed that there was a close Hindu parallel to this Logos description of Jesus because Appasamy interpreted in his own way a text from the Upanishads on the "indweller," which said that "having created that, He then entered the same."[27] Traditionally this Johannine text is understood as referring to the incarnation of Jesus and his rejection by the people of his day. Contrary to that position, Appasamy took those words to mean the immanence of God in the world even before he was incarnated in the person of Jesus Christ. As the indweller (antaryamin), God was already present in all people, Jews and non-Jews alike. Claiming that the incarnation of God in Christ was another visible way of restating the same truth, he wrote,

Because men have not understood Him, even though He is immanent in them, He has "become flesh." The incarnation is a more effective means of showing God than mere immanence.[28]

God as the indweller is an important concept in Hinduism. It emphasizes the nearness of God to all people. It also means that God as the spirit is always present everywhere in the universe. We are startled and amazed that there is no human thought, word, or deed that can be or is hidden from God, because God lives deep down in our own inner being. Humans can neither escape him nor deny his presence anywhere (Ps. 139:1–10).

As Appasamy constructed the above correlation, he went through the struggle that most students of comparative religion have. That is clear when he says that the *Word,* as it existed *before* its incarnation in Jesus, is already present in and among all people, exhilarating and inspiring all human hearts. The same Word, however, was incarnated in Jesus Christ so that people may understand him better and more clearly. In Jesus Christ the incarnation of the indweller was fully and finally perfected. Though the light from above is shining on everyone everywhere, through many and various ways it focuses as the floodlight in Jesus Christ. "Though the Logos has been quickening men's hearts everywhere in the world, he is fully embodied in Jesus."[29]

The parameters for our present study do not let us highlight the various ways in which Indian Christians have worked hard and still do so in order to make the Gospel of Jesus Christ effective and easily understandable to the people of India. Most of these thinkers have held that using Western frames of reference to interpret the Christian message is the greatest hindrance to the spread of the Christian message to other parts of the world. They maintain that Christianity will fare well in other nations and cultures if it is clearly separated from Western philosophy and worship styles.

Philosophy or not, when the simple claims of the Christian faith are reformulated in the systems of another religion and into an altogether different form of spirituality, the task of communicating the message becomes ever more complicated and in that process faces the danger of diverging from authentic truth. Of course, it is necessary to employ the thought patterns and phrases of a different language and religion for effectively communicating the Christian message to the people of that culture and religion. In doing so, care must be taken not to lose and let go of the distinctiveness of the Christian message.

For example, the Christian religion speaks well to the people of India about Jesus Christ as the incarnation of God. Naturally this is a very meaningful way of sharing the Christian faith with a community that is familiar with the concept of God manifested in various forms. According to Hindu belief, Vishnu, the second entity of the Hindu triad, entered the world in ten different incarnations. Most of these are relatively less significant when compared to those manifestations of God in Rama and Krishna. And Krishna ranks on top as the highest and the greatest of them all. Again, Hinduism has not hesitated to regard saints and entities of other religions as worthy of worship, also as incarnations of the same God. In fact, the Buddha is considered an incarnation of Vishnu. In this context then, when Christians speak of Jesus Christ's incarnation, they must give specific Christian content to that expression in order not to give the impression that Jesus is only one of many incarnations of God, a common misunderstanding among most people of India.

Other Indian Christian theologians have attempted to interpret the Christian faith in monistic terms.[30] They do not agree with those who strive to relate Christ to the Indian context in incarnational terms, because in Hinduism the god who is manifested in the flesh is *Ishwara*, one who is lower than the Ultimate (*Brahman*). Thus if we would say, following the precepts of the Hindu religion, that Jesus is God *incarnate*, we would be acknowledging that Jesus was revealed in human form as only a lesser deity. However, the Christian position is that "in Christ *all* the fullness of the Deity lives in bodily form" (Col. 2:9; italics added).

Furthermore, monistic thinking allows no room for a savior figure in any way, shape, or form. A God who graciously redeems mankind from sin and its consequences cannot be part of the monistic vocabulary. Those who tend to apply monistic philosophy to the Christian faith and attempt to interpret the Christian faith in monistic terms unfortunately are making a new religion of their own by trespassing biblical boundaries.

In this connection, Stanley Samartha, a leading advocate of what may be called "Christian monism," maintains that Christian theology in India today faces the challenge of Indianizing itself in order to accomplish its mission in the modern world. According to Samartha, Christians today must enter into dialogue with those who follow the Hindu way of life and must discover the common ground between the two religions. The most effective way to communicate the Christian message to the Hindus is to interpret it in monistic terms because Indian thinking is deeply rooted in monistic philosophy. Samartha does not believe that Indian Christianity must retain its Hebrew or Semitic heritage. If Origen exercised freedom and followed Platonic philosophy and if Aquinas utilized Aristotelian thought patterns to formulate their respective theologies, the church in India ought still be allowed to interpret the Gospel in monistic terms as stipulated by the Indian philosopher Shankara.[31]

The Indian mind has a variety of ways of expressing itself religiously. The various ways (to salvation) in Hinduism are an example of this peculiar luxury enjoyed by most Indians. Needless to say, interpreters of the Christian faith for India have utilized all these Hindu religious expressions in their endeavor to apply the Christian faith meaningfully in the Indian context. For example, India endows with respect those sages who receive special revelations (*darshanas*) from God. Sunder Singh's testimony that he received a series of revelations from the risen Christ therefore would be credible in that context. Indian tradition also highly prizes direct religious experience. Bishop Appasamy's emphasis on experiencing (*anubhava*) Christ would be an example. Many in India claim to have experienced God through visions and ecstasies. Numerous Indians who became Christians also claim to have had such experiences. In the Christian context, these incidents are believed to occur as individuals encounter the Word of God (Rom. 10:17).

Christianity in India also has been interpreted as a way of action. One of the leading champions of this is Dr. M. M. Thomas who, in his major contribution to Indian Christian theology in *The Acknowledged Christ of the Indian Renaissance,* provided examples to show how Christianity permeated modern India and transformed its social life and thought and brought about a renaissance. The leaders of these reforms, though many of them never made public confession of their faith in Jesus as Lord and Savior, demonstrated through their actions that the message of Christ has had a transforming influence on them. Thomas, himself a member of the Mar Thoma Church, was convinced that Christ was and is at work in India especially through the efforts of the great reformers.

After extensive research on the topic, Thomas arrived at the conclusion that most Indian intellectuals who first encountered the Christian message made a clear distinction between Jesus Christ and the Christian religion as it was presented to them by the Westerners. While the people of India developed a great appreciation for the message of Jesus Christ, they found it difficult to go along with the Western interpretations of that message. Instead, they interpreted Christ in terms of the religious, philosophical, and social rhetoric with which they were most familiar. What we see in these instances is a kind of Christ who becomes all things to all men.

In order to present his study in the context of the various ways in which Christ has been acknowledged in India, Thomas suggested that Christ has been at work already among the people of India, although many of them do not confess him in the Western sense of that word. Reinforcing the message of Christ to the Indians by the West has, nevertheless, resulted in a dynamic renaissance in India, "the Christ in the Western culture awakening the Christ in the Indian culture and preparing India for the new life and the Gospel of Jesus Christ."[32]

Thomas makes his case by citing examples from Indians who dedicated their lives for nation building, particularly because they gained inspiration to engage in such activities from the moral and ethical teachings of Jesus.[33]

What we have pointed out are representative ways in which the Christian faith has been interpreted in India by using Hindu categories of thought. This is perhaps typical of the struggle Christianity experiences whenever it strives to permeate another culture. Unfortunately, much of India has embraced all that Christianity has to offer except "the one thing needful" (Luke 10:42).

The interconnection between Hinduism and traditional Indian culture is so strong that it is almost impossible to separate the two. Consequently every attempt to interpret the Christian faith in terms of Hinduism has resulted in some form of syncretism because "for the modern educated man in India religion is philosophy or it is nothing."[34] Most Indians today acknowledge Jesus as an eminent moral teacher, a famous reformer, and a great revolutionary—everything except who he really is, namely, "Christ, Son of the living God." This is precisely what C. S. Lewis called the "patronizing nonsense" which every one must take heed to avoid.[35]

# The Great Reversal

Christianity is often considered the religion of the poor, at least when it is newly introduced to a nation or community. Ever since its inception, this religion of pure grace has targeted the so-called socially unacceptable and economically poorer levels of people. The majority of Christians seem to have been those who were less privileged and unable to measure up to socially approved standards and norms.

The numerical "success" of Christianity in India has been for the most part with the economically less fortunate and the socially underprivileged. It is true that many first generation converts to the Christian faith received generous support for their bodily and material needs from those who brought them the Gospel. History bears out that the faith that was generated in them continues to live on even after the material emoluments discontinued. Obviously, for the vast majority of them, Christianity is still answering the ultimate questions in their lives.

While Christianity was making strides in various communities in India, some serious rethinking began to take place in the very fabric of Hinduism, particularly in its approach to social and humanitarian issues. Religious Hinduism has always emphasized a spiritual and devotional lifestyle, mainly anticipating a better and improved form of future existence for the soul. The future in this case, of course, is conditioned by life performance in the present. Imperfections in the present life are to be remedied by countering them with good and sincere efforts to lead an honorable and righteous life. Focusing primarily on life after death, popular Hinduism has coped with the sorrow and suffering of daily living.

Proof of a strong Christian presence in India is seen in the multitude of Christian schools, hospitals, orphanages and other institutions of charity—highly disproportionate to the number of Christians in India—and to the number of Christian churches and other purely religious institutions. Not a few of the local and national leaders of India were influenced by Christian ideals because they were schooled in a Christian environment. Christian acts of charity and good will began to permeate many communities that were in the grip of poverty, ill health, and depravity. Christians in this land may be the salt and the leaven, and their presence cannot be ignored or easily dismissed (less than 2.5% of today's more than 900 million).

As a reaction, as it were, to the Christian invasion of India, Hinduism also began to go through a process of rethinking and reformation. Hindu ideals were now interpreted in more practical ways, in which they too could raise people's spirits to respond to the needs of the present and make the present existence meaningful and worth living. Compared with a metaphysical hope of a better existence in the future based on the idea of the transmigration of the soul, the current needs of both the soul and the body began to gain special attention in Hinduism. Institutions of education, hygiene, and charity were no longer the distinctive hallmark of Christianity. The doors of Hindu temples, which used to remain closed to everyone except high caste Hindus, were now open to all, regardless of caste. Hindu sacred writings, many of which were first translated into European languages by Christian missionaries, now became the tool to relate the Hindu message to Christians and to the people of the West. Modern Hinduism developed its own study circles and sent out its own missionaries. The religion of India was now fully prepared to make its way to those peoples and nations that first brought the message of Christ to India.

As never before, 20th-century Christians are constantly rewriting their mission statement in a variety of new forms and shapes. Unfortunately, good intentions do not necessarily produce good results. Christian theology today, unlike other world religions, has the tendency promptly to modify its message to the world in order to keep pace with fast changing worldviews. In that process, Christians are tempted to overlook their mandate to proclaim to the world the great news that God reconciled the world to himself in Christ. Thus, in our day Christian presence overrides Christian preaching. In the end people ask, "What difference does it make whether you are a Christian or not?" To be sure, Christianity today continues to permeate the world as the catalyst for social change and the stimulus for humanitarian endeavors, pleading the case of the poor, the oppressed, and the socially unacceptable. But at the same time many Christians, not being nourished by good Gospel preaching, are leaving their home base and pursuing other paths, in search of a better way and a deeper and more intimate sense of spiritual fulfillment. Modern Hinduism is marching forward into those very areas of human spirituality from which modern Christianity has been consistently marching away.

The Hindu ethos continues to spread throughout the world with extraordinary success, albeit without any specific mission strategy. Hindu ideals have the innate ability to permeate a society without leaving visible imprints of their religious implications. Unlike Christianity, Hinduism does not require trained personnel and able bodied leadership. Not having been confined to the limitations of specific creeds and confessions, Hinduism is able to spread its tentacles over other religions and philosophies and bring them all into one monistic whole. Hinduism itself has always claimed to be universalistic, while it accuses Christianity of being particularistic and exclusivistic.

For example, yoga was first introduced to the West as a form of physical exercise that lets the mind take control of the body, although it is, in its purest form, "an all-embracing search for enlightenment."[36] Yoga is "more intuitive than reasonable, more experimental than formalistic, more other-worldly than of this world, and more akin to art than to science."[37] The roots of yoga have been traced back to the pre-Vedic times of Indian civilization. However, the channel through which the world became familiar with yoga practices is obviously Hinduism.

In its religious sense, yoga is a Hindu way of union with God. Shiva, the symbol of life and vitality in Hinduism, is also the patron god of ascetics and holy men. Shiva also appears in yoga poses, himself indulging in deep meditation. As Eliade points out, "all Indian spiritual techniques shared in Yoga to some degree. Among the populace, the yogins have always been regarded as redoubtable magicians, gifted with superhuman powers."[38] Early Hindu reformers have argued that yoga is not the road to ultimate freedom, although such techniques are helpful for preparing the soul to attain metaphysical knowledge that alone can guarantee nirvana.

Yoga is one of the six systems of classical Hindu philosophy. It is a spiritual exercise designed to experience the clear distinction between *Purusha* (the pure, free, eternal, and unchangeable spirit) and *Prakriti* (the cause and the energy of the material universe).  As an integrated system, yoga puts forward an eightfold disciplinary path for the soul to overcome all worldly distractions.  This path, when followed successfully and systematically, will enable the soul to be totally in control of the self and the senses, and it will sharpen the skills to focus on one object.  This kind of exercise lets go of the self, and through meditation it ultimately empowers the soul to enter a state of superconsciousness.

Yoga is closely linked with meditation.  Meditation techniques have certain mysterious powers and those who practice meditation are able to achieve whatever their hearts desire.  He who meditates on the ultimate reality, and on ultimate freedom, must therefore "'dismiss everything perishable from his thoughts and meditate upon what is imperishable only.  There is nothing imperishable except Purusha.  Having become united with him (through constant meditation), he obtains final liberation.' But this is precisely the counsel of the *Yoga-sutras*."[39]

Yoga techniques were popularized in the West on a large scale particularly by Maharishi Mahesh Yogi, the founder of Transcendental Meditation.  The Yogi, in his best seller *Science of Being and Art of Living*, has offered Americans a technique that "eliminates stress and fatigue, improves health, increases energy and well being, and expands mental potential."[40]

We have seen how Anna Riva, in her *Powers of the Psalms*, suggested 375 ways of using the Psalms to eliminate stress, alleviate insomnia, improve financial stability, and so on.

Here is an instance where an ancient religious concept (yogi is a holy man who has reached enlightenment through yogic practices) is presented to modern audiences in palpable and attractive fashion.  It encourages us to believe that the above and similar modern religious movements can provide the people of our generation cures, comforts, and conveniences that modern disciplines of medicine, psychology, and psychiatry cannot guarantee. Yoga and meditation techniques assure their practitioners that no one in the world, including those who live to be very old, dies (has ever died) a natural death. People die of disease, they say, of heart attack, of pneumonia, etc. Humans can avoid this predicament by practicing yoga and meditation. Obviously, Eastern thinking has certain things in it that can fascinate even the scientist, the humanist, and the theologian.

That yoga, apart from being a thoroughly tested and proven disciplinary exercise, is still a religious ritual is seen in the way in which it is worked out in Transcendental Meditation groups. In the *puja* (worship) ceremony, the names of the creator, the redeemer, and the emancipator are invoked. The creator is identified as the lotus-born Brahma, and the redeemer as Krishna. Reference is made also to Vyasa, to Shankaracharya, and to other great gurus of the Hindu religion. Furthermore, cloth, rice, flowers, incense, light, water, fruits, betel leaves, coconut, and camphor light are offered to "the lotus feet of Shri Guru Dev."[41] Such attention to details gives us a cue that special religious meanings are attached to these offerings, especially because betel leaves, coconuts, and camphor lights (relatively rare commodities in the West) are required even when the ceremonies are observed, for example, in the United States.

Similarly, *kundalini* and *tantrism* are religious rites akin to yoga practices. When kundalini energy (serpent power) is awakened, it illuminates the individual conscience and facilitates its union with the world soul, resulting in an experience of union and liberation. This process is understood as a reenactment of the original sexual union of Shiva with Shakti. Tantrism is another religious ritual that expedites the soul's direct encounter with the eternal soul resulting from enlightenment. Tantric realization is attained by exercising a variety of methods such as visual images, repetition of sounds (mantras), breath control, and other rituals involving sacred sexual intercourse.

On simple, objective grounds it is impossible to dismiss yoga as just an exercise or to view meditation as only another technique to soothe the troubled soul. In spite of the avowed neutrality ascribed to these disciplines by their practitioners in the New Age Movement, they always emerge with religious overtones. This is especially true when we realize that monism owes its origins to the Hindu religion, and the practices under consideration also have a Hindu background. For those who view these routines from a religious perspective, it is easy to locate religious elements in them. For others who choose to ignore the religious aspects, but still want other benefits from religious rites and ceremonies, these activities may appear nonreligious and merely simple cure-alls for life's disturbing problems.

Hindu religious groups and spiritual leaders rank top on the list that Gordon Melton prepared of those who have identified themselves with the New Age Movement, by way of either publishing related literature or participating in New Age activities.[42] Melton has also listed several Sikh and a few Buddhist-Taoist groups as having New Age affiliation. Groups such as Rajneesh Foundation, Hanuman Foundation, and Vedanta Society would rather not give up their Hindu identity as implied by their names.

Theosophy is another major source from which the proponents of the New Age draw their inspiration. The history of Theosophy began with Madame Helena Blavatsky who travelled the world in search of a certain superior wisdom that governed the universe. As she grew discontented with the church, she broke away from the Judeo-Christian world view and continued her pursuit of truth which to her transcended all religions and traditions. Although the Theosophy Society was founded in 1875 in New York in cooperation with other intellectuals who shared similar dreams, in 1877 Blavatsky and her cohort Henry Olcott moved to Bombay, and in 1882 to Madras in South India. Blavatsky's "hands-on" exposure to Hindu as well as Buddhist ideas from India were then compiled in her famous, sophisticated book, *The Secret Doctrine*.[43]

Blavatsky dedicated her comprehensive two-volume magnum opus to "all true Theosophists in every Country and of every Race, for they called it forth, and for them it was recorded." According to her book, "There is no Religion higher than Truth." Blavatsky herself had been searching for truth, then channeling it for others as a medium. Her search for truth continued perhaps until her death in 1891. The schisms that occurred in the movement since Blavatsky's death, and the splinter groups that emerged thereafter, cause us to wonder if truth, as Blavatsky discovered it, was ever absolute.

Theosophy is an attempt to combine ancient ("secret") wisdom, modern science, certain aspects of Christianity, and Eastern religions. Perhaps inspired by the Darwinian science of the time, Blavatsky rejected the idea of God creating the world.

Nevertheless, God exists, for theosophy is the wisdom *of* God. God is eternal; matter and energy are emanations from him, and all degrees of intelligence are expressions everywhere of his existence. If evolutionary science is true of the physical existence of humans, the soul also goes through another evolutionary process of reincarnation. Both physical science and psychic science offer evidence for a continuity of consciousness which then justifies belief in reincarnation.

For Theosophists death provides awareness of a new and wider realm of existence. Death is consoling and comforting. Death leads into a continued form of existence. When humans die, they enter the astral world where the soul is placed in one of the seven levels tantamount to the degree of karma performed in one's earthly existence. There is no joy and there is no beauty at the lowest level, which is equivalent to hell. Reincarnation enables the soul to work its way through the different levels of the astral plane until its being is perfected. The perfected, moral being will finally enter eternal bliss.

Obviously, Theosophy does not require its followers to give up their own religion. One may remain a Christian, Hindu, or a Buddhist and still be a Theosophist. Humans may savor eternal happiness as they drink from the fountain of that eternal wisdom from which all religions have derived partial truths. Theosophy is an example of how the West turned to the East in search of superior wisdom. The search for wisdom is an acknowledged way to eternal freedom in Hinduism. As Vivekananda said, "Spiritual knowledge is the only thing that can destroy our miseries forever; any other knowledge removes wants only for a time."[44]

We are limited here in going into detail about the many ways in which Hindu ideals and practices have permeated the West, once renowned for its Judeo-Christian heritage and worldview. Christianity, as it enters new cultures and traditions, has been making dramatic changes in its approach to missions, thanks to the good will of Christian thinkers and theologians. On the other hand, Hindu ideals can permeate Western culture and make a significant impact on Western life, without shedding their identity or in any way camouflaging their religious alignments.

We need to note that the Hindu-Christian connection came about mainly as a result of the intellectual exchange that took place between the Hindu elite and Christian theologians. In every instance intellectual encounters between the two faiths occurred through Christian initiative, in the form of dialogues, or in an attempt to "discover" Christ in Hinduism, or even making the claim that Christ is already present in Hinduism. It may be said that, on the spiritual and the intellectual levels, Christian theology often endorsed Hindu ideals, overlooking and ignoring scriptural principles and teachings to the contrary.

Christian theologians have spoken and written extensively about "anonymous Christians." An anonymous Christian is one who in his or her heart believes in Jesus Christ, but who has never come out openly and made a public confession of Christian faith. The disapproving social, political, and religious context in which this person lives, for various practical reasons, makes an open confession impossible. These individuals may not be able to identify with a church, participate in Christian gatherings, or even leave behind any visible symbols of their faith, according to that definition.

That same concept applies to the New Age. Given the scope of Hinduism and given the universal nature of the Hindu paths of knowledge, works, and devotion, the followers of the New Age already may be Hindus, although they would like to remain anonymous.

# 6

# Some Issues in Contemporary Christology

A basic knowledge of the Bible and the direction that Christian theologizing has taken in the last three centuries is essential for analyzing and understanding the New Age and the Hindu connection. In certain theological circles the uniqueness of God's revelation in the person and work of Jesus of Nazareth has been downplayed, and, unfortunately, distorted. Knowing what happened historically in our time to the corpus of Christian doctrine helps us understand to a degree how, over centuries, Hinduism also involved. A major shift occurred in Christian theology as a result of the conscientious effort of some Christian thinkers who, with a view to making the Christian message relevant to the modern era, through their writings projected views that were meant to become "all things to all people."

Recent developments in Christian theology, in the name of objective scholarship, may have hindered rather than helped promote the Christian cause as the contemporary theological enterprise gradually drifted away from the basic biblical perspectives of the Christian religion into modern secularism, religious pluralism, and syncretism. Leaving the historical person and the redeeming work of Jesus Christ as a backdrop, theologians spoke more of the Christ-principle and a kind of Christic consciousness. Into this deep sea of Christological confusion the prophets of the New Age have cast their nets and caught a Christ who satisfies their own whims, a Christ who, like the Buddha, needed his own awakening into Christhood.

Throughout this book the writer does not view Christianity as just another agency of good will for fighting social evil, political oppression, and economic injustice. To be sure, Christianity has always been the first to raise its voice against corruptions and has stood up for the cause of the poor, the oppressed, the widow and the orphan. Nevertheless, the primary mission and purpose of the church of Jesus Christ, even at the end of the 20th century, is to communicate to everyone the free gift of forgiveness and the promise of eternal life.

Our life situation may have changed over the years, and we may be facing a variety of new needs. Yet, since the beginning of the human chronicle the ultimate needs and desires of human beings have remained the same: to run the race here well, and, when the time comes, to depart this world and be where there will be no more tears and no more sorrow. Without pride and without a doubt, Jesus of Nazareth demonstrated to the people of his day that life here is worth living and life hereafter is worth looking forward to for those who put their trust solely in him. Christendom must take pride in presenting to the world the whole Christ, not just the Christ principle. Everyone must rejoice that the entire Christ, and not just the phenomenon of Christ, takes residence in human hearts.

The task of the Christian community is to relate to every generation the mighty acts of God in Jesus Christ. Jesus Christ is the unique means by which God chose to reconcile the entire human race to himself. Through Jesus' sacrificial death on the cross and his resurrection God has granted everyone redemption and life. This is the greatest mystery that the world has ever known. Jesus through his person and work made known to everyone that mystery, and the early church kept spreading that revelation—the only reason for its existence as a separate entity from the rest of the world. A mystery that is known is no longer a mystery. If this is true, why is the mission and message of today's church shrouded in mystery? If the path is known for sure, why deviate from it?

We maintain that an inadequate appreciation of Christ's person and work is at the root of much of today's theological defection in the church. Authentic biblical Christology must occupy the pivotal position in every facet of Christian theology. Christianity hinges on the person and work of Christ. Venturing to downplay the uniqueness of Christ, though done in good faith and sincerity, according to our own way of thinking, results in serious aberrations.

There are perhaps two major misconceptions about Jesus Christ in Christian thought today. One view projects Jesus as the man for others, the eternal God-Man ideal for others to follow, the harbinger of the new humanity, the liberator of the oppressed, and the superstar who holds the victory in every struggle and crisis. The other view is that he is the manifestation of the Christ principle, once revealed in the Jesus of Palestine, then in the Buddha and Krishna. There is no need therefore to witness the Christian Gospel to others, because God has his own mysterious ways of dealing with people everywhere. What caused this major shift in emphasis especially in the modern era?

## Jesus Christ: Man or Myth?

In retrospect, Christians will have to acknowledge that much of the trouble we face today in the Christian church was brewed in our own home. Perhaps there is no other religion in the world that has ever subjected itself to such self-criticism as Christianity. Every change that occurs in the thinking of mankind, any new theological invention, first directs its challenge to Christian faith. That Christianity has outlasted the challenges in the long run is obviously a healthy sign. There always remain good reasons for believing in Jesus Christ in this world of varieties and choices.

# Herman Reimarus

The era of the enlightenment took its toll on Christianity. Hermann Samuel Reimarus (1694–1768), born and raised in Hamburg, Germany, in a family of Lutheran pastors, at a very young age rose to fame as an accomplished philosopher-theologian, and was privileged to serve on the faculty of Wittenberg. Needless to say, Reimarus was heavily influenced by enlightenment thinking in Germany and its attempts to secularize every aspect of human life and thought. As a member of the German intelligentsia, Reimarus was deeply involved in the struggle between faith and reason; and in the end, he simply let his reason take over. Biblical revelation and human reason have nothing in common, nor do they operate on the same premise, Reimarus concluded.[1]

Reimarus maintained that Christianity was based on a fraud propagated by the very disciples of Jesus. He portrayed Jesus as a deist, as one who conformed to the principles of natural religion, with cultic symbols and practices known only to its followers. As a gifted, charismatic teacher, Jesus aroused his followers through his teaching and instruction to improve the nature and morality of human beings. Jesus not only revealed new mysteries, but he "considered the goal of all his work as a teacher to be repentance and the preaching of an upright, active character."[2]

According to Reimarus, Jesus was God's son in the sense in which David, Solomon, and the people of Israel were sons of God. The Jesus of history was a mere man obsessed with the revolutionary drive of the zealots of his time who wanted the Jews to rise in revolt against the existing administration. His hidden agenda was to usher in the messianic era every Jew was awaiting with eager expectation. As part of his strategy, Jesus selected twelve young men, trained them, and sent them out to promote a certain kingdom of heaven. He added further incentive by performing miracles, and his unique preaching in parables.

Reimarus reasoned that Jesus counted on his followers and the entire nation of Israel to proclaim him their king. In fact, Jesus' cousin, John the Baptist, had already announced him as such. This announcement was followed by Jesus' own symbolic entry into Jerusalem early during the week of the great Passover festival. By this impressive performance Jesus anticipated a grand welcome and massive support from the Jewish leadership for his agenda. Unfortunately, the results of this grandiose project were very depressing and disappointing. Jesus' efforts to inaugurate a worldly kingdom ended in tragedy. The catastrophic effects of this aborted mission were echoed at his crucifixion when he cried out in anguish, and against his wish, "My God, my God, why have you forsaken me?" This divulgence "can hardly be otherwise interpreted than that God had not helped him to carry out his intention in attaining his object as he had hoped he would have done."[3]

Because the disciples of Jesus realized that the plot of their master had failed miserably, they made up a story that Jesus rose from the dead on the third day of his death, and then after a while he went up to heaven to be seen in the world no more. Reimarus maintained that the disciples stealthily and quickly got rid of Jesus' body, and, after almost fifty days of silence, began to tell everyone that Jesus would soon return as they had seen him enter the heavens. The disciples could get by with this theory and rally such a large following because the Jews truly believed in the coming of a Messiah. The details of Jesus life and work matched to a great extent the expectations the Jews had of their leader and deliverer. Thus the community of Christians multiplied in membership and influence on the faith and culture of generations to come.

What we see in Reimarus is the frustration of a rationalist who is confronted with the truth-claims of Christian faith. For rationalists who claim to be guided solely by reason, Christianity appears to be a religion made up of people with selfish interests. Since the basic core of the Christian faith, and especially its anchor in the resurrection, fails to match today's norms of reason and science, rationalists allege that its claims are outdated and its veracity subject to scrutiny.

But Reimarus was wrong in assuming that Jesus of Nazareth worked with a political agenda. In fact Jesus did not intend to be a political revolutionary.[4] Like many modernists, Reimarus ignored the biblical context of Jesus' mission, since his sole aim was to rediscover the Jesus of history by means of historical methodology. Thus he thought that the historical Jesus and the Jesus proclaimed by the church were two different, mutually exclusive entities.

## Gotthold Lessing

The world knows Gotthold Ephraim Lessing (1729–1781) more as a critic, poet and dramatist than as a theologian. Lessing himself denied having any expertise in religion or theology.[5] Nevertheless, he fostered the theological insights of Reimarus and popularized them. For generations following, Lessing's writings provided the incentive for other scholars to take a fresh look at the historical origins of the Christian faith.[6]

Lessing saw the Bible as just another piece of literature. In it was information about the early Christian community which acknowledged Jesus as Lord and Savior. Although he doubted the truth of the biblical narratives, Lessing did not think that such doubts should jeopardize faith in Jesus' resurrection. Lessing therefore wanted to begin his work with a free and critical evaluation of the sources for the life of Jesus, namely the four gospels. For him it was a privilege to be in the pursuit of truth rather than claiming to have gained possession of absolute truth. Granting that the absolute is God and with God, Lessing maintained that people must experience an ever-increasing urge for perfection through their own independent search for truth.[7]

Lessing claimed to have discovered, in his own way, the rational content of the Christian religion. He acknowledged that the miracles of the New Testament times may have had a message for the people of the first century. But they were of no particular significance to the people of modern times. Thus, while Reimarus concluded that the life of Jesus was a grand failure, Lessing maintained that the truth claims of the Christian religion, although not verifiable by scientific research, were shaped in and are manifested through history. The distinction that Lessing tried to make between the historical and the religious aspects of the Christian faith prepared the ground for further debate on the historical Jesus and the Christ of faith.

## Karl Martin August Kähler

If Lessing ventured to examine the Christian faith from the point of view of literature, Karl Martin August Kähler (1835–1912) wished to reconsider the person and work of Christ from a philosopher's perspective. Kähler grew up under the heavy influence of the philosophies of Kant, Schelling, and Hegel. Kähler in his research drew a fine line between the Jesus who lived as a historical figure in Israel and the Christ preached by the apostles and the early church. For him the Gospel narratives were detailed stories of Christ's passion with extended introductions.[8]

Thus Kähler saw the need to distinguish the Jesus of history from the Christ of Christian faith. Accordingly, the historical (*historisch*) Jesus, whose earthly life we are able to recount factually and objectively, is not to be mistaken for the historic (*geschichtlich*) Christ of faith, although several points of similarities may still exist between the two.

Kähler feared that ascertaining a purely historical basis for the Christian religion would consign Christianity to historical relativism. According to him, any attempt to reconstruct a biography of Jesus is a lost cause. For purposes of rediscovering the life of Christ there are simply not enough documents we can depend on that can be scrutinized according to the standards of modern historiography.

Unfortunately, the New Testament does not provide adequate biographical information about Jesus. The first three gospels in the New Testament and the gospel of John give us two different perspectives on the life of Christ. The diversity of these available documents hinder, instead of helping increase our knowledge of the historical Jesus. The real Christ, therefore, for Kähler is the Christ who is preached and believed.[9]

Kähler was struggling to discover a correlation between the Jesus of history and the Christ who was preached, a struggle between faith and history. Jesus was determined to influence his disciples and instill in them the idea that he himself was the Christ. The disciples *confessed* this new-found faith which over the years solidified the Christian community as a vital force in society. *"The real Christ,"* Kähler said, *"is the Christ who is preached. . . .* The Christ who is preached is precisely the Christ of faith."[10] Any discussion of Christ must therefore remain purely a confession. The New Testament gospels too were first composed with this idea in mind, because they wanted to project the image of Jesus as a healer and a redeemer. The historical Jesus did not impress Kähler because he maintained that the Christ of faith could not be validated by historical methodology.

# Albert Schweitzer

The Nobel Peace laureate Albert Schweitzer (1876–1965) is well known as a famous French musician, philosopher, physician, and missionary. Schweitzer opened a new chapter in the history of the Christian religion when he revived discussions on the earthly life of Jesus and described his perceptions of the kingdom of God.[11]

Schweitzer devoted his attention in Christian theology to examining the research that had been done until his day on the life of Jesus. Schweitzer was led to believe that such research had been of no avail because it did not in any way help understand Jesus according to the flesh. We must therefore understand Jesus as a "spiritual power in the present" and "be prepared to find that the historical knowledge of the personality and life of Jesus will not be a help, but perhaps even an offense to religion."[12]

History can neither prove nor disprove the truth of the Jesus of Nazareth, thought Schweitzer. All that Jesus Christ is, is essentially a spiritual power in the present, and everyone must claim him and own that power through personal experience. Jesus often spoke of this experience in the sense of being in his kingdom. There was a plot afoot known only to his disciples that Jesus would be the king of this kingdom. This plot, however, ended in failure because Judas divulged it to the Jewish authorities for a bribe. Finally Jesus admitted the charge. Schweitzer suggested that "from start to finish Jesus had been mistaken about himself, about his proclamation, and about the purpose of God—and was great enough to face with unclouded consciousness the realization of his mistake."[13]

Schweitzer developed the idea that Jesus thought of himself as the Son of Man who would on the last days come on the clouds of heaven to establish the kingdom of God on earth. Jesus came anticipating that the people of his day were living in the last hour of the world's history. Furthermore, Jesus thought of himself as being instrumental in bringing about the end of the present order of things, whereby the kingdom of God would be established on earth. But again, Jesus was mistaken.[14]

# Rudolf Bultmann

In explaining the confusion of terms in today's misunderstanding of the person and work of Christ, a name that cannot be ignored is that of the 20th-century New Testament scholar Rudolf Bultmann (1884–1976). Bultmann assumed that a scientific attempt to discover the real Jesus was doomed to failure because he believed that the Bible provided no more than a mythical picture of Jesus. Bultmann showed little interest in the history behind the life of Christ. To him, what mattered most was the significance of the so-called Christ event. In his research Bultmann was using an existentialist approach to delineate the life of Jesus and his message for modern man.

Bultmann viewed myth as "a mode of expression which makes it easy to understand the cultus as an action in which material means are used to convey immaterial power."[15] The New Testament writers made extensive use of the language of myth to convey the meaning of Jesus and his message in existential terms. This was perhaps the best way to communicate the things concerning the spiritual world. Bultmann's thinking, no doubt, was heavily influenced by the existentialist philosophy of his colleague Martin Heidegger.

What we have in the New Testament, according to Bultmann, is a mythologized version of the events that took place in the first century. These documents are of little help for determining the truth of the life and work of Jesus. For modern man to accept this message in its literal sense would require a "sacrifice of his intellect." "It would mean," Bultmann said, "accepting a view of the world in our faith and religion which we should deny in our everyday life."[16] Theology today must therefore engage in the task of demythologizing the message of the Bible, namely, that of stripping the Christian message from its mythological framework.

Bultmann became very skeptical about the biblical portrayal of the historical Jesus. For him the true Christ is the Christ who was and is preached and proclaimed in the church. Nonetheless, at the time of Jesus' earthly ministry, "the proclaimed was at the same time present as the proclaimer."[17] What Jesus proclaimed once must continue to be proclaimed now and hereafter. It is in the proclamation of the Christian message that "salvation-occurrence" continues to take place.

What Bultmann means by salvation-occurrence is the event of the crucifixion of Jesus Christ. People, especially those of our time, are able to appreciate the significance of Jesus' crucifixion only when they listen to what God has to say to them through that event. Furthermore, the crucifixion of Christ (or for that matter, his incarnation or resurrection) is not an event that is limited to the past. It is implanted in each individual as each one is confronted by the preaching of the Gospel, which in turn creates in each one an existential self-awareness.[18]

Thus Bultmann saw the person and work of Jesus Christ only as a sign for future generations. Through Jesus God is extending a call to every human being to make a personal decision. The very embodiment of Christ in the person of Jesus is God's universal summons to decision-making extended to all people. In point of fact, God in Christ is speaking to the inner being of every human being.

In keeping with the above considerations, Bultmann formulated his own version of eschatology, that is, interpreting events of the end time. As expected, even in this aspect of theology, Bultmann reflected his existentialist bent, simultaneously adoring the modern man and revering the present moment. For, "the meaning of history lies always in the present," and "in every moment slumbers the possibility of being the eschatological moment. You must awaken to it."[19] The Jesus of history lived his life with an eschatological awareness, although he could not see the end of the world. We must also live our lives with the same existential awareness, even if we know full well that the world is not coming to its end right now.

## The Significance of Theological Speculation

In summary, several points need to be reviewed here which, we believe, will help identify the historical roots of the New Age interpretation of Christ. At the outset, we need to remember that most people are by nature followers and not leaders, especially in matters of religion. For example, an average Christian may not be aware of, or interested in, the intricacies of the official theology upheld by his or her parent organization. Nor will the person in the pew be equipped to deal with the complexities of theological scholarship. Thus, when new religious ideas surface, especially if they emerge with apparent negative implications for the status quo, they may be able to crush or at least considerably diminish a person's faith in the simple Gospel.

People are prone to pick up quickly the negative aspects of a given religion. Usually such items make headlines in the news media or run as cover stories in news magazines. Rumor flies like wild fire. Much of the growing aversion to religion these days arises not because people have lost their faith in God, but it is the result of "scholarly" interpretations of God and his dealings with people. As great theologians become suspicious and critical of each other, people at the grass roots also begin to grow weary and lose their faith. Good intentions of the scholarly enterprise may not always serve positive purposes for ordinary people.

For purposes of comparison recall Reimarus' interpretation of Christ. First, Reimarus followed a deistic interpretation, a form of natural religion that prospered in Europe in the 17th century. Rejecting the idea of revelation, deists held that God may have created the world, but he then let it run on its own, having nothing to do with it since. If God let the world run on its own, there was no reason to enter it again in the person of Jesus Christ. This led to Reimarus' second conclusion, that Jesus was just a man, a "son of God" like David or Solomon, endowed with great ability. He was a great man, who, as a leader and master, stood a head taller than the rest. Great as he was, his mission ended in failure because he could not rally people after him. Note that the New Age view of Jesus is much like that of Reimarus.

How do Lessing's ideas fit into New Age thinking? As a student of literature he strived to experience the truth of Christ from the gospel narratives. He enjoyed this because it allowed him to transcend historical occurrences and to pursue truth. Lessing's approach matches that of the New

Age because it encourages everyone to embark on an individual search for truth.

The interpretations of Kähler and, following him, Schweitzer and Bultmann, also are matching pieces in the New Age Jesus-jigsaw-puzzle. Kähler made a clear distinction between the Jesus of history and the Christ of faith. Schweitzer's plea to his readers was to find in Jesus the spiritual power for the present. Bultmann maintained that each one of us must live for the present moment, as Jesus did, with a clear conscious self-awareness. What we see here is a ground-breaking theological evolutionary process, which in the end enables modern man to emulate Christ as one among many available principles and models.

## Tillich and the Ground of Being

Paul Tillich (1886–1965), a theologian and philosopher who struggled to mix philosophy with theology, coined the phrase, Christ, the Ground of Being. Tillich was heavily influenced by his teacher Martin Kähler and his colleague, the existentialist philosopher Martin Heidegger. Tillich spoke of his method as correlation, because it involved a skilful blending of reason, dialectic, and paradox to unravel the mysteries of God. According to Tillich, doing theology requires a method of correlating theology and philosophy in order to delineate man's authentic faith relationship with God.[20] He maintained that the theologian must commit himself to relating theology to the concrete situations of modern man.

Tillich described God as the ultimate reality, as "Being Itself," or the "Ground of Being." This Ground of Being was manifested in the person of Jesus Christ.[21] The title "Christ," according to Tillich, is a symbol that represents an aspect of the Christian understanding of divine revelation. The Christian community considers the revelation of God in Christ as unique, normative, and final. However,

Jesus is the Christ for *us* (italics added), namely, those who participate in the historical continuum which determines its meaning. This existential limitation does not qualitatively limit his significance, but leaves open other ways of divine self-manifestations before and after our historical continuum.[22]

Obviously, Tillich deals with the person and work of Christ from a comparative religion point of view. In a similar vein Tillich implies that, just as the Jesus of Nazareth became *Christ* for those who embrace(d) him by faith, other individuals may have become (would be becoming) Christs for other peoples. If Tillich is correct, there is no need to proclaim the Gospel of Jesus Christ to all nations as Jesus himself mandated.

Tillich's theology is a classic model of modern-day universalism. He simply mixes his two favorite disciplines of philosophy and theology and arrives at conclusions that are alien to basic biblical propositions. His view of Christ readily takes on varied shapes, forms, and meanings, adapting the language of contemporary philosophy in order to interpret Christ for modern man. But his conclusions are far removed from the biblical concept of God's unique revelation in Jesus Christ. In this sense Tillich's theology becomes a welcome contribution to the philosophy of the New Age.

Tillich's treatment of the person and work of Christ is not methodologically different from any other part of his system. In fact, he prepares the ground for the above interpretation of Christ on the basis of his own doctrine of the Trinity. Even here Tillich places modern man as his focus:

The questions arising out of man's finitude are answered by the doctrine of God and the symbols used in it. The questions arising out of man's estrangement are answered by the doctrine of Christ and the symbols applied to it. The questions arising out of the ambiguities of life are answered by the doctrine of the Spirit and its symbols.[23]

The above quotation is a sample of what has been popularly known as the "theology from below." It alleges that the people of our day must go through a struggle in order to come to grips with the language of traditional theological discipline. Unfortunately, this theological method lays undue emphasis on *our impressions* of God rather than God's own ways of speaking to, and dealing with us. This method, currently very popular, in effect permits people to create their own God and gives them almost limitless options for interpretation.[24]

Similarly, Tillich offers an existential interpretation of the trinitarian God in humanistic terms. God is obviously the answer to man's every existential question. To those who acknowledge their finitude God represents infinity. To those who suffer from estrangement and alienation Christ epitomizes coherence and harmony. And to those whose lives are in disarray the Spirit offers clarity and focus.

Tillich assumed that the very existence of human beings (on earth) is the sign of their estrangement and alienation from God, the Ground of Being. God is more than essence and existence. Therefore a person who assumes existence is, by definition, estranged from that Ground of Being, from other human beings, and from one's own self.[25] Human beings, once they become aware of this predicament, begin to experience their finitude and are led to despair. Thus in his struggle to reinterpret Christian theology to our age Tillich becomes very skeptical about our existence, as if existence itself is unbecoming of the true self. One wonders if such skepticism does not work its way into the nihilist tendency of repudiating all previously held values and norms.

One wonders also how far Tillich's methodology is removed from the Judeo-Christian appreciation of authentic human existence, and hence more in keeping with the Eastern ideas of maya and monism. For, according to the Bible, man did not experience estrangement when he was first created. Rather, he was happy and content with his environment, surrounded by everything that was pleasing to the eye. To be sure, man was overpowered by his sense of estrangement when he fell from fellowship with his Creator. Thus we wonder if there is not in Tillich's theology a skillful blending of Christianity and Eastern philosophy. Tillich uses a Christian scaffolding to build his theological structure with existential bricks and monistic mortar. As the construction is completed, unfortunately, the scaffolding falls, and the structure retains only its innately monistic disposition.

According to Tillich, Jesus appeared in the world as the New Being. His appearance in this manner was necessitated by man's existential estrangement. The world situation is such that human beings are presently trapped in a hostile environment that is indifferent to our needs and concerns. (Tillich's task of doing theology would have been a lot easier had this estrangement been humbly acknowledged as the result of sin!) In the coming of Christ, the "essential God-manhood," that is, the ideal state of mankind, was disclosed to the world. Doubtless, in Jesus Christ the essential being of man is ideally present. Tillich goes on to say, "There is one man in whom God found his image undistorted, and who stands for all mankind—the one who, for this reason, is called the Son or the Christ." [26]

Tillich finds the term incarnation open to misunderstanding when it is used to depict the event of Christ becoming man. He suspects that there is a certain magical, and therefore superstitious, touch to that expression since other religions make use of the same term to describe different manifestations of the deity. For him the Christian claim that God became man is pure nonsense because

> . . . it is a combination of words which make sense only if it is not meant to mean what the words say. The word "God" points to ultimate reality, and . . . the only thing God cannot do is to cease to be God. But that is just what the assertion "God has become man" means.[27]

Tillich also finds it very difficult to apply the expression "divine nature" meaningfully to the incarnate Christ. In its place he prefers combinations of words such as "eternal

God-man unity" or "eternal God-manhood."[28] While rejecting the idea that the divine and the human natures are united in the person of Jesus Christ, Tillich proposes that "in Jesus as the Christ the eternal unity of God and man has become historical reality."[29] Apparently this is an example of inconsistency in Tillich's Christology. Nevertheless, Tillich feels obliged to resort to this kind of language in the hope of providing a dynamic character to the Christian faith and be more appealing to modern man.

We have noted that in Tillich's reckoning God is the Ultimate, or the Being Itself. In contrast to man who is just a being, God is the ground of everything that has being, and consequently beyond essence and existence. However, Christ, as he was manifested in the person of Jesus of Nazareth is not beyond essence, says Tillich. Evidently Tillich is questioning the divine nature of Jesus although he is the incarnation of Christ.

Not only Tillich, but anyone who wrestles with the Eastern philosophy of God, will encounter difficulty in endorsing without reservation the doctrine of divine incarnation. God always remains the unfathomable mystery in Eastern traditions.

Religions generally require that we humans let God be God. The Judeo-Christian tradition also testifies that no one has ever seen God and yet lived, and he does not live in man-made homes. Even king Solomon, the wisest man who ever lived, wondered if God would really dwell on earth with men (2 Chron. 6:18). The fathers of the Christian faith have repeatedly noted that finite human beings are simply unable to comprehend the infinite Being (God). In fact, God is the True Being, past, present, and future (Ex. 3:14). The mystery of God therefore is the greatest mystery.

However, there is a God in heaven who has revealed himself (Dan. 2:28). The final and the ultimate revelation of him was given once-for-all, and for one and all, in the very person of Jesus of Nazareth (Heb. 1:1–4). Acknowledging Jesus as the revelation of God and the mystery thereof is purely a matter of believing Jesus' own words. To those who have been struggling and wrestling with the God-question, Jesus addressed these comforting words, "Believe me when I say that I am in the Father and the Father is in me." (John 14:11). Once this premise is acknowledged, the incarnation of Jesus Christ will no longer be "nonsense." Moreover, we will be enabled to be conformed to the likeness of Jesus himself (Rom. 8:29). Conformity to the likeness of Jesus is even today the ultimate answer to the perennial question of man's existential self-awareness.

Tillich realized that faith in Jesus as the Christ is fundamental to the Christian religion. Christianity is built on this faith as its foundation. The Christian Church has been kept alive through centuries because it confesses the same faith. Tillich addresses himself to the two aspects of this confession, namely, the *fact* which is called Jesus of Nazareth and the *reception* of that fact by those who receive him as the Christ. In Tillich's words, the receptive side of the Christian faith is as important as its factual side.[30]

Nevertheless, even though Tillich emphasizes the confessional foundation of the person of Christ, he apparently avoids the specific question of the historical person of Christ. For he contends that faith should not be built on something so uncertain that some day historical research might be able to disprove it.[31] Here we cannot but notice how heavily Tillich was influenced by the so-called historical researchers, including his own teacher Martin Kähler.

Thus we must conclude that what Tillich works out in his system is entirely different from the normal systematic appreciation of Christ's person and work. Following his own philosophical guidelines, Tillich finds in Jesus the ideal God-manhood which everyone should seek to follow. Evidently Tillich maintains that it is not the person of Christ but the "Christ principle" that was manifested in the Jesus of Nazareth that brings newness to all creation.

As long as Tillich is able to keep the above observations about Christ as points of reference, he can accept the principles of other faiths as being equal to the truth claims of Christianity. According to him, the rather exclusive nature of modern Christianity is not in tune with its original fabric. He says, "Early Christianity did not consider itself radically exclusive, but as the all-inclusive religion, in the sense of saying, 'All that is true anywhere in the world belongs to us, the Christians.' "[32] Tillich's theology evidently is an exhibit of modern-day universalism. He generously mixes Christian theology with the philosophy of world religions and arrives at conclusions that are alien to simple and basic biblical propositions.

## Chardin and the Cosmic Christ

If Tillich's burden was to make Christology relevant to the modern philosophical mind, Teilhard de Chardin (1881–1955) was struggling to relate Christ to technology and evolutionary science. Teilhard sincerely wished to appeal to the most progressive minds of our scientific era by trying to use the language of science in his writings. A Jesuit priest by calling and a paleontologist and archeologist by profession, Teilhard focused his attention on, and attempted a synthesis of, science and mysticism.

The mixing of the above two categories, science and mysticism, did not really help Teilhard to develop a system of theology. Instead of narrating a specific Christology of his own, Teilhard came up with a "cosmology centered in Christ."[33]

In his writings Teilhard tries hard to establish an underlying unity and coherence for the universe (cosmos) by using certain ideas from the apostles Paul and John in the New Testament. As he argues that all things hold together in Jesus Christ, the "union" of the universe becomes an integral part of Teilhard's thinking. With the premise of the unity of the universe, Teilhard claimed that even "God Himself, in a rigorously real sense, exists only through a process of self-unification."[34]

The unity of the universe was the basic yardstick for Teilhard's theology. He considered Christ to be the unifier of the universe in a very literal sense. Christ is the dynamic center and the cosmic soul of the universe. The *emanations* proceeding from this center penetrate matter itself and keep the creation activity going as a continuous process.[35]

Teilhard's view of Christ is intimately connected with his evolutionary worldview. As a result of the evolutionary process, he anticipated a certain maturity for the entire created order of things. Himself a visionary skilled in both religion and evolutionary science, Teilhard believed that this growth was to take place from within the universe with Christ as its center. In fact, Christ himself puts this whole process into motion, because the universe has a Christic dimension to it. The Christian religion has a very unique role to play in this entire process because, among all the world religions, Christianity alone captures a vision of the future in very clear terms.[36]

In Teilhard's opinion, Christ binds the universe to himself in an intrinsic manner, that is, in a very physical, ontological sense. As the unifier of the universe, Christ is actively involved in the process of its creation as well as consummation. In the language of science, the same Christ is the converging point of all evolution, says Teilhard. Christ is therefore the Omega Point.

Each individual object, presently involved in the process of reaching its full perfection, will finally be united at the Omega Point. Both the universe and the human race are involved in this evolutionary process. The Christ who appeared as the Jesus of Nazareth is the supreme example of perfect humanity. Teilhard understands the same Christ as the converging point of the entire evolutionary process of the universe and humanity. Christ is the final focus of all existence and the catalyst that consummates everything that has assumed existence.[37]

It is this kind of excessive optimism about the future that is the living legacy of Teilhard's mysticism. He was thoroughly convinced that faith will triumph at last over the world. When this takes place, the individual microcosms, through the outpouring of love, will be freed from their respective isolated states and will be converged into Christ, the Omega Point. Each individual should actively cooperate with God in the process of helping the whole universe reach this point of perfection.[38]

Teilhard envisaged two movements running parallel to each other and, at the same time each in its own right, awaiting a dramatic process of transformation. On the one hand, the entire universe is anticipating its own "mystical transfiguration," while on the other, the human race is struggling to converge into its own Omega Point. By definition, mystical transfiguration requires human involvement in the process because, according to Teilhard, "the only subject ultimately capable of mystical transfiguration is the whole group of mankind forming a single body and single soul in charity."[39] Thus humans collectively end up being the savior of both their own race and of the universe.

Teilhard interpreted the Bible to support his assertion that humanity faces the tension between a deep love of God and at the same time a fervent love for the world. The only way to get over this tension is for humans to make a greater commitment for self-development and a willful detachment from the things of this world.[40] To accomplish this Herculean task, Teilhard proposed a "mystique of action," which, when strictly followed, would enable humans to resolve their dilemma of living simultaneously in two different worlds.

Clearly evident in Teilhard's writings is a conscious effort to resolve the dualism between the temporal and the eternal, that is, the things of this world and the things that transcend human comprehension and definition. This scholar of religion and science obviously was capable of recognizing that tension, and, in his own way, suggested a way to defuse that tension. Teilhard recognized that he was dealing with two disciplines that have been at war with each other particularly since the era of the enlightenment.

Teilhard believed that a genuine synthesis of the two disciplines is needed, not a desire to eliminate one or the other. Teilhard believed that such a synthesis would be good for both science and religion. Any course of action to the contrary would be to the detriment of both disciplines. The only way out is for both science and religion to focus on the Omega Point. Christ, the Omega Point, is the animating force behind both religion and science. Teilhard seemed to imply that in this process religion still holds the upper hand when he says, "Neither in its impetus nor its achievements can science go to its limits without becoming tinged with mysticism and charged with faith."[41]

To attain the ambitious goal of the Omega Point, Teilhard suggests what he calls a process of "Christification." That is the means by which each individual at last will be able to become an integral part of Christ's mystical body. That is to say, through this suggested process an incarnation of Christ takes place potentially in each and every human being. The whole human race is involved in the incarnation process as it "makes" and "undergoes" Christ in all things.

Recall that, according to Paul Tillich, the very idea of the incarnation of Christ is nonsense to modern man. To overcome that, Tillich suggested a method of correlation by blending ideas from philosophy and theology. Similarly, to find the relevance of Christ to the modern scientific mind, Teilhard chose the language of mysticism. Unfortunately, Teilhard too was lost in the wilderness of mystical thinking. He surmised that "our salvation is not pursued or achieved except in solidarity with the justification of the whole body of the elect. In a real sense only one man will be saved: Christ."[42] One wonders if both Tillich and Teilhard were not laying the foundation for what might be called a Christian monism (reminiscent of Hinduism).

A thorough criticism of Teilhard's approach to the Christian faith is above and beyond the scope of our present study. The Christian theologian's task should not be esoteric speculation but to apply the biblical truth to specific, real-life situations. Teilhard struggled to relate Jesus Christ to modern man, who is surrounded and overwhelmed by science and technology.

Teilhard spelled out his objective in the following way, "My road ahead seems clearly marked out: it is a matter not of superimposing Christ on the world but of pan-Christianizing the universe."[43] Not surprisingly, Teilhard himself admitted that his ideas about Christ were not necessarily adequate or complete. For him the entire universe was the cosmic body of Christ since it is organically Christic in its constitution. Consequently Teilhard was able to anticipate a certain "super-mankind" to evolve in the future. For Teilhard, the evolution of such a super species of humans is possible through a process of "super-socialization" which in its own right necessitates a "super-personalization." All of this is to be achieved through exercising genuine love, through the most expedient way of "amorization."

Strange, and often confusing, as these propositions of Teilhard appear, he cited biblical support for them.[44] Regarding his assumption that humanity at last will reach a collective maturity, he developed an explanation of things to come at the end of the present epoch. He anticipated this final moment as being a state of heavenly bliss in which all humanity will be able to contemplate God without distraction. In heaven each one of the elect will see God face to face. Such a vision, however, is possible only through "the eyes of Christ" who is "the head and living summary of humanity," Teilhard maintained.

Undergirding the above propositions is, in our view, a deep rooted monistic view of life, and a pantheistic interpretation of the universe. To be sure, Teilhard attempted to give a Christian coloring to largely non-Christian ideas and approaches to life. Perhaps at some risk of caricaturing Teilhard, his views can be summarized as Christian monism. Teilhard's proposals drive his readers to that conclusion as he visualizes the pan-Christianization of the human race and the mystical transfiguration of the universe.

In New Age thinking we also come across the ideas of "Christic consciousness" and a "harmonic convergence." The New Agers also hold to a kind of globalism that presupposes a master plan for building a new world order. Both Tillich and Teilhard reflect these ideas from a Christian point of view.

## The Christ of Hinduism

The Christian religion is no stranger to India. Tradition traces the roots of Indian Christianity to the time of the first apostles of Jesus Christ. The Saint Thomas Christians of the Malabar coast in South India credit the apostle Thomas with having brought them to the Christian faith. Tradition aside, historians have unhesitatingly acknowledged the Christian presence in India at least from the seventh century, and on the basis of objective archaeological data. In the modern era, however, there has been a dramatic increase in the number of Christians in India as a result of the modern missionary movement. Launched when the British ruled India, the modern Christian movement has been misinterpreted by some as the arm of an "oppressor" from the West, forgetting that the Christian religion first took shape and grew on the Asian Continent.

When India became part of the British Empire, Christian missionaries assumed that introducing the people of India to the English method of education would be an effective way of bringing the Gospel of Jesus Christ to them. Although this method did allow many Indians from all walks of life to embrace the new faith, it also gave rise to a significant Hindu revival. Most Indians from an orthodox Hindu background who were exposed to English education saw Hinduism itself as a remarkably advanced stage in human development, not just the vestige of a so-called illiterate paganism. For example, a great thinker like Mahatma Gandhi, the father of Indian independence, could relate Christianity to Hinduism in a way that "begins with a ready acceptance of the God in Christianity, goes on to frank criticism of the extravagances of the Christian claims, and concludes that Hinduism is adequate and satisfactory for the Indian people."[45]

As a consequence of the new Hindu self-awareness, as expressed above in Mahatma Gandhi's words, some Christian leaders began to search for more effective means to relate the Christian Gospel to the adherents of resurgent Hinduism. The result was a summons to Christians to engage in dialogue with people of other faiths.

Dialogue, according to P. D. Devanandan, a pioneer in this approach, is a conversation which is a "frank endeavor to understand, in as far as that is possible, exactly where and how we differ from one another, although we may use the same religious terms such as grace, forgiveness, sin, incarnation and so forth."[46] Genuine dialogue must allow those involved in it to disagree with one another, asserted Devanandan. In recent years, however, this emphasis has changed considerably. As for example, another writer views it, "The purpose of dialogue is a common search for truth. Dialogue [hence] is distinct from proclamation, although it may sometimes give occasion for it."[47] Interestingly enough, most promoters of dialogue understand their task in terms of a common search for truth. According to them dialogue "can lead to the hope that religions will eventually grow together with Christ as their center."[48] Therefore they begin their task with the assumption that there is truth on every side. This is often precarious for Christianity which claims a unique truth revealed in Jesus Christ.

Take the specific example of Raimundo Panikkar, a strong supporter and promoter of inter- as well as intrareligious dialogue. As a student of comparative religion, Panikkar noted that Christians are under obligation to "*somehow* incorporate Hinduism into the universal economy of salvation by God through Christ, of which Christianity is the summit."[49] Panikkar perceived that all non-Christian religions, such as Hinduism, have certain aspects that need to be taken into account as "the footprints of God's redemption."

To be sure, the salvation that God accomplished through his Son Jesus Christ is for all. It is meant for all and has been prepared for all people. Nevertheless, the human predicament is such that, apart from faith in Jesus Christ, humans are unable to measure the magnitude of God's salvific act in Christ. It is in Christ that we hear the word of absolute truth, the Gospel of our salvation. Those who put their trust in Jesus are sealed with the inheritance of eternal life (Eph. 1:13–14).

Panikkar, it may be noted, benefited amply from both the Hindu and Christian world because he was born of a Hindu father and a Spanish Catholic mother. His upbringing in an integrated religious background, along with his scholarly skills, explains his compromising attitude towards other religions. Panikkar encouraged Christians to develop a similar attitude toward other faiths. For him, "the Christian attitude (towards other faiths) is not ultimately one of bringing Christ *in*, but of bringing him forth, of discovering Christ."[50]

According to Panikkar, Christ is already present in Hinduism, though in a cryptic or concealed manner. "Christ is there in Hinduism, but Hinduism is not yet his spouse." Furthermore, Christ still needs to "grow up and be recognized" in Hinduism, and "he still has to be crucified there."[51]

We can't help but notice echoes of both Paul Tillich and Teilhard de Chardin in Panikkar's interpretation of Christ. Tillich did not exclude the possibility that different people could have different Christs. Panikkar also believed that in every religion there is present at its center the same "Christ principle." Perhaps following Teilhard's idea of Christogenesis, Panikkar attempts to bring Christ forth from those religions that are traditionally understood as being non-Christian.

Panikkar deals with the questions relating to the universality of the Christ principle in another volume called *The Trinity and World Religions*.[52] In it he proposes that Christ is a very ambiguous term. Furthermore, the concept of Christ cannot be the exclusive possession of Christians. On the contrary, he is the only link "between the created and the uncreated, the relative and the absolute, the temporal and the eternal, earth and heaven."[53] Obviously, Panikkar did not want to limit Christ to the Jesus of Nazareth. On the other hand, he claimed that "even from right within the Christian faith such an identification has never been asserted."[54] Although at times Panikkar spoke about the universal relevance of the fullness of God's revelation in Jesus Christ, he seemed to be fully convinced that it would be "immoral" to cast doubts on any non-Christian who finds his own faith satisfying apart from faith in Jesus Christ.

Several criticisms of Panikkar's hypotheses should be noted. His daring adventure to "discover" Christ in Hinduism (or any other religion) has no biblical basis. The primary purpose of Christ's (Messiah's) coming into this world was to save sinners (1 Tim. 1:15). The way Christ chose to bring about salvation for all sinners was the way of the cross. True, in the broad and charitable opinion of some Christian students of comparative religion, God's economy of salvation operates in different ways for different people. If, as Devanandan rightly pointed out, different religions attach different meanings to terms such as grace, forgiveness, sin, and incarnation, there can be no unified understanding of Christ and his true significance. In fact, no other religion makes the claim that there is a Messiah who saves people from their sins and their consequences. Panikkar's goal, though sincere, to "bring Christ forth" from Hinduism and "to crucify him there" is wishful thinking and inconsistent with biblical Christianity.

Panikkar's wish cannot be fulfilled because we cannot bring Christ *forth* from a locale where he is not present! The task of the church is indeed to bring Christ *into* the lives of those who do not yet have him. Christ enters a person as Christ's own Word is proclaimed in its truth and received in faith. However, Panikkar believed in what he called the *dekerygmatization* of the Christian faith, perhaps following Rudolf Bultmann's efforts at demythologization.[55]

It is contrary to accepted principles in the study of comparative religions to "incorporate" one religion into another. Incorporation involves assimilation or consolidation of various ideas into a new unified whole, eventually giving way to a new truth not previously disclosed.

Incorporation is the declared purpose of religious dialogue today. We need to remember that most of the pioneers of the dialogue movement are alive today. They will humbly acknowledge that their common search for truth has made its discovery more difficult and even impossible. If truth is one (based on the assumption that dialogue is a common search for truth), truth cannot be relative (what is true to you need not be true to me). If everyone has the truth, why must the search continue?

Panikkar almost repeats Teilhard's error when he proposes that the religions of the world are in an evolutionary process of which Christianity is the summit. As part of this process Panikkar foresaw a need for Christ to be "recognized" and "crucified" in various religions. But the crucifixion and resurrection of Christ is the crux of the Christian faith, and the primary source for information about these events is the Bible. The same source emphasizes that these events will not, and need not, be repeated because they were accomplished once-and-for-all in Jesus Christ of Nazareth.

Panikkar discussed the love of God for all people apart from Jesus Christ and his crucifixion. But true love in the biblical sense is love at God's expense, as Jesus himself says, "Greater love has no one than this, that he lay down his life for his friends." (John 15:13). While it is true that God loves all people regardless of whether or not they love him, people enter into a lasting and trusting relationship with God only through Jesus Christ.

Finally we must note that it is not the term "Christ" that is ambiguous, as Panikkar contends, but it is his own unachievable quest to discover the "Christ-principle" at the center of all religions. Panikkar offers no clear definition of that term, although he considers that it has to do with the "Logos" or the "Lord." Thus ambiguity prevails. Perhaps ambiguity is a sine qua non and inevitable in the study of comparative religion because everyone involved in that endeavor is in search of truth. The New Testament makes the theologian's task much simpler and easier. It states in no uncertain terms that the universal lordship of Christ is not a matter of debate. It is simply a matter of acknowledgment and confession by all people (Phil. 2:10–11). Confession by definition is an expression of faith. Faith, according to the apostle Paul, comes from *hearing* the message, and the message is heard through the word of Christ (Rom. 10:17). Panikkar may have a point in his plea to *dekerygmatize* faith, but faith in the   biblical sense comes from hearing that requires *kerygmatizing* (proclaiming) Jesus Christ as he is revealed in the written Word.

The purpose of this chapter has been to highlight the person and work of Christ from the point of view of a few noted theologians whose views have interesting parallels with Hinduism and the New Age. The above examples show how the view of Christ has kept changing as new ideologies emerged. Some conceived of Jesus as a political messiah, while others denied his historicity. Some considered Christ as a spiritual power present in every existential situation, while others cast serious doubts about his divinity and his resurrection from the dead. Still others considered him as a principle present everywhere in every religion.

Unlike other world religions, the core of the Christian faith rests on the person and work of one person, Jesus Christ. Current trends in much of Christendom today imply that over the years the Christian church has been misleading people all over the world with a message whose full picture was not clear to the church itself. So we ask, What else is new! People will always move on to more religious speculation when they lose their clear biblical moorings. Obviously, this is the reason for the success of the New Age Movement in the West that once sailed the seas to bring Christ to the nations.

# 7

# The Gospel: A Privilege to Proclaim

The New Age in a sense is a new religion. It fills a void, and it fulfills a religious need, ironically of those who aspire to remain religionless. Religion or not, the New Age has already claimed its place in many human hearts where once religion ruled and reigned.

As a religion, the roots of the New Age penetrate deeply into Hinduism. Several significant similarities between the Hindu religion and the New Age have been discussed. Hindu philosophy became familiar to the West chiefly through various encounters between Christianity and Hinduism, launched especially by Christian intellectuals who perceived significant common ground for the two religions. The very movement that once was designed to communicate the Christian Gospel effetively to Hindus later became the channel through which Hindu ideas began to invade the very matrix of the Christian faith.

Responding to the spiritual needs of the New Age with the Christian Gospel, therefore, cannot be altogether different from answering religious challenges posed by the Hindu way of life. Nonetheless, neither of these is an uncomplicated task. Christians have no more powerful and effective tool than the life-giving and transforming Word of God to address these demands. This approach may seem outdated and even out of step with today's ever-improving methods of communication. But the Christian church was called into being and has been nurtured and continues to expand only through the merits of this unusual means. The Word of God has been at work across the lives, languages, cultures, and convictions of various peoples, and so it will be among the New Agers also. The call to heed the Christian Gospel can be even more reassuring for New Agers in the West, especially because for them it is just an invitation to return to their own spiritual roots.

Among the religions of the world, the Christian religion stands out as very unique—one that quickly spreads out and spans the globe by word of mouth. The very makeup of the Christian faith is such that it behooves those who embrace it to share with others what they have been taught and have believed. Salvation by grace through faith in Jesus Christ is still today the core of the Christian Gospel. Communicating that message to others is the primary purpose of the Christian church. There is good news to share, especially with those who have not heard and known about it.

Proclamation of the Gospel is the basic method of Christian propagation as it was first demonstrated, then commissioned to the first believers, by Jesus Christ, the Lord of the church. This continues to be the primary mission of the Christian church even today, after almost 2,000 years of its existence. The urgency of verbalizing the Gospel has not lost its significance in spite of all the changes that may have occurred in the *Sitz im Leben* of human beings.

Preaching and teaching are the two primary, and therefore universally acknowledged, ways of communicating the Gospel to others. These two simple methods are obviously in accordance with the Lord's command, especially as he himself entrusted these privileges to the first disciples and then to the first Christian community. Almost all Christians have continued to uphold these two functions as vital and pivotal in the present order of existence. They have done this either by themselves proclaiming the Gospel to others or delegating that privilege to other trustworthy people. The Christian literature of our time also offers a large supply of the art and science of preaching and teaching the Gospel, to suit the mission of the church to the changing patterns of our society.

Proclamation is basically an act of confession. In the Lutheran tradition, the affirmative theses of the *Formula of Concord* are prefaced by the phrase, "We believe, teach, and confess." Confession proceeds from the human heart, from what has been taught, and believed. The heart of the Christian faith, and therefore of the Christian teaching and confession, is the Gospel. The Gospel is obviously what Jesus first preached and taught and then entrusted to those who followed him also to preach and to teach others. With this idea as backdrop, the Confessions go on to say that

> . . . when the word "Gospel" means the entire doctrine of Christ which he proclaimed personally in his teaching ministry and which his apostles also set forth (examples of this meaning occur in Mark 1:15 and Acts 20:24), then it is correct to say or write that the Gospel is a proclamation both of repentance and of forgiveness of sins.[1]

In the Augsburg Confession, Article V describes the ministry of the church as teaching the Gospel and administering the sacraments.[2] This article follows the great article on justification by grace, for Christ's sake, through faith. As we work our way backwards in the Augsburg Confession (as I have done in the text), we see Jesus Christ who came to the world to save sinners (Article III). Article II describes sin as rebellion against God. And God's existence and his nature are described in the first article. The purpose of these two activities of the church, teaching the Gospel and administering the sacraments, is for people to obtain faith. Faith is the means by which people are justified before God for the sake of Jesus Christ. Christ's involvement in this process is so important that without his life, death, and resurrection there is no forgiveness of sins, and there is no eternal life awaiting anyone. Christ has done for all, and once and for all, what humanity could not attain on its own. Christ took upon himself the punishment for the sin of the whole world to the extent that he was able to free every individual sinner from the wrath of a righteous God.

Christianity presupposes that human beings are sinners. It is sin that stands in the way between God and mankind. Sin is the common human predicament that cuts deeply into every aspect of human existence. The power of sin in human life is such that it causes relationships to break among people themselves, and between God and humanity. Sin is in every individual as an inborn trait that refuses to go away, no matter what treatment the human mind prescribes for it. The powerful grip of sin on human lives has provoked many to deny the fact of sin. Nevertheless, sin continues to be an ever-present reality every human being is destined to deal with, whatever shape or form it may have assumed, or whatever other name it may have been given in various contexts.

Sin presupposes that there is One sinned against. That One is God, according to the Bible. Again, the Lutheran Confessions view sin as the hereditary disease that produces a fundamental aversion to God. It shows itself in the modern tendency to somehow deny God, or to downplay him as just another insignificant entity. The (unredeemed) sinner views God as a certain inconvenience, because he bristles at the very thought of an all-powerful, ever-righteous, and ever-present Being intervening in the daily affairs of the world and interrupting an otherwise presumably smooth-going worldly lifestyle.

Christianity is frequently labeled a religion that besmirches all human beings as sinners. Even many Christians themselves wonder if the idea of sin is not an outdated, and therefore unwarranted, proposition. However, Christianity is not alone in this situation. On a deeper level, all world religions have their own intepretations of sin and propose ways to secure freedom from the power of sin. Even the so-called irreligious people are aware of the stigma of sin, although they would prefer to describe it in nontraditional terms.

To be sure, authentic Christianity understands the problem of sin as a very serious one. It graphically depicts (eternal) death as the inherent consequence of sin. The Christian religion also takes equally seriously the way to freedom from sin, and—this is the most comforting message of the Christian faith—the free offer of the clearance of sin with all its consequences. The religion that claims that "the wages of sin is death" also says that "the gift of God is eternal life through Christ Jesus" (Rom. 3:23). The primary purpose of the incarnation of God in the person of Jesus Christ was to save people from their sin (1 Tim. 1:15).

The Bible presupposes that God exists.[3] God, for the biblical writers, is a given. According to the Bible, the universe is itself proof of God's existence. It is as if a house stands as evidence to the fact that a builder built that edifice. Acknowledging God's existence is a precondition to approaching him in faith. Denial of God and casting doubts on his being and actions therefore are themselves acts of (and the results of) sin. Repudiating God's existence, according to the Scriptures, is a sign of indecent behavior quite unbecoming an intelligent human being. In fact it is the fool who says in his heart, "There is no God." In other words, morally deficient people make up the story of God's non-existence. Such people are corrupt and are unable to do good. They never learn and are unable to understand. These godless oppress the poor and shun the company of the morally and ethically decent and upright.

Nevertheless, it is the more astute and shrewd of this world who are all the more suspicious about the existence of God. God, they surmise, is perhaps a worthwhile proposition for the intellectually immature and the emotionally insecure. Those who have come of age in their mental and emotional make up are not in need of that kind of a support system which projects a father image up in the sky, who, if at all he does exist, is too far removed from, and the least interested in, the daily affairs of mankind, so they maintain. According to them, those who still believe in God are actually making a sacrifice of their intellect (or what is left of it in them).

Debate about God and his dealings with mankind continues. During the Enlightenment, Europe saw little relevance for God and religion. Among the intellectuals of that time, it was no longer trendy to talk about God and religion because these were considered excess baggage. This does not mean that people then by and large hated religion. But, as Rudolf

Otto has pointed out, they "held it in contempt like some-thing for which one no longer had any use. One was cultured and full of ideals; one was aesthetic, and one was moral. But one was no longer religious."[4] This kind of thinking obviously served as the nursery for modern humanism.

Incredibly, in recent years suspicions about God and his interests in the human race were raised more by theologians of the Judeo-Christian tradition than by those of other religious orientation. The two World Wars of the 20th century and particularly the Holocaust during World War II added fuel to the already burning question ignited by the Enlightenment about the existence of God and his relevance for modern man. Undoubtedly, the majority of the victors as well as victims of these appalling battles have been those who were raised in the Judeo-Christian tradition.

In the aftermath of these catastrophic events, and perhaps perplexed by the so-called silence and nonintervention of God in these horrifying world occurrences, a segment of the theological population proposed the idea of the death of God.[5] Before these theologians plunged into the notion of God's death, they should have first asked if, in the course of world history, God was ever *alive* or active in every situation as they expected him to be. Let us take the specific case of the people of Israel, God's own chosen and covenant people. Their destiny as well as their history was shaped more outside their promised (home) land than in it. Their father was a wandering Aramean, and so have they them-selves been as a people. Most of their epoch recounts the story of their lives either as nomads and slaves in foreign lands or as captives under foreign powers in their own homeland. Half a century after the Holocaust, more Jews today live outside of Israel than in it. Many of them have made their home away from home.

Is it not true that we humans invoke the name of God especially when we are in trouble, trouble so deep that we realize that we are deprived of any means other than God to rescue us from that predicament? The seeming irrelevance of God (and religion) today for some people is not that God is becoming more and more an eroding phenomenon (God remains the same, and he does not change like shifting shadows, Heb. 1:12 and James 1:17), but that the human conception of God keeps changing. Human notions about God and human actions in each generation cause the image of God to cloud and to fade. In the present context, much of modern Christian theology is to be blamed for blurring God's image in our society.

According to many modern theologians, God appears to be far removed from the affairs of the people. It is true that the gap between  the people of our time and God is widening more than ever. This situation has emerged not because God is the least interested in the affairs of men, but because we have distanced ourselves from him by exercising our own free will. The human will is so powerful that it even has the ability to silence God. The human ability to silence God cannot be taken as proof of God's inability to do certain things and intervene in human history. Most people today confess that they hear God speaking clearly to them in their moments of silence, when they are away from the clutter and clamor of the environment. Ps. 46:10 also says, "Be still, and know that I am God." God is not dead, though humans have often tried to kill him. God appears to be missing for those who either try to measure him in their own terms, or ignore him when he draws near to them in his own characteristic way.

Neither can the recurrence of massive atrocities and inhuman activites in our world be held against God. God, as we have known him, continues to cause the sun to shine and the rain to fall equally on the righteous and the unrighteous, the godly and the ungodly. If both parties involved in the fight are God's people, on whose side can God be, even when the situation is one like the Holocaust? If Christians themselves fail to care for the poor and if they ignore the cause of the oppressed, those conditions cannot be charged against God.

The cries for freedom *from* religion on the one hand—and the thirst after a religionless Christianity on the other—are the products of a major shift in the theological enterprise today. Much of Christian theology today consciously runs the risk of putting people at its center, thus minimizing the value of a divine-human encounter. For that very reason, theologies of this kind do not endure very long. People-based theologies are vulnerable, as people themselves are vulnerable, and hence they quickly become irrelevant for the very people for whom they are first developed. Some, for example, invoke the name of God, claiming him to be on the side of the poor, the oppressed, and the less fortunate. Such theologizing loses its purpose the moment the oppressed are liberated, and when the poor become wealthy. This has been true of the theology of liberation, of development, and recently in India, of the theology of the poor (Dalit theology).

In the afterglow of the Enlightenment, the German religious thinker Friedrich Schleiermacher (who misunderstood some other essentials of biblical Christianity) rightly called the intellectuals of his day to the greatest need of man, to be in fellowship with God. In his speeches about "religious despisers," he explained that matters of religion are accorded low esteem primarily because people are easily carried away by "false conceptions and devotion to nonessentials." On the contrary, those who seek God stand above those who do not have fellowship with God as the ultimate purpose of life. Schleiermacher saw in the incarnation of God in Christ the uniqueness of the Christian religion. The event of God becoming man makes Christianity the greatest of all religions. To his listeners he said:

> I would, as it were, conduct you to the God that has become flesh; I would show you religion when it has resigned its infinity and appeared, often in sorry form, among men; I would have you discover religion in the religions.[6]

There is no better way for humans to draw near a transcendent God than for God himself to draw near humans through his incarnation. God becoming flesh in Jesus Christ and living among people is the guarantee that, although humans are not God and cannot become God, they can be in fellowship with God while they maintain their own individual identities. Religion in the Christian sense is not an experiment to escape this world of misery and sorrow by contemplating comfort and joy in heaven, but an affirmation that life on earth is worth its struggles and stresses, because it was on earth that God met man in the person of Jesus of Nazareth. In this sense Christianity is a well-rounded religion.

Of course, the event of the incarnation of God in Christ presupposes that God *exists*. The Bible also says that "anyone who comes to [God] must *believe* that [God] exists" (Heb. 11:6). Even in the midst of 20th-century existential self-awareness of humans, scholars have noted reasons to believe that God exists before and outside of our own existence. As one writer put it,

[A] theologian must say not merely "that God is," but also "who God is as such" and what he is in the first instance in himself. Theological statements of this kind . . . should not be immediately mistrusted as metaphysical speculations. . . .Without such "statements" all propositions concerning the relationship of man to God lose their ontological substance.[7]

That God exists before and outside of human beings and the universe is one aspect of the Christian proclamation. The other, and equally important, aspect of Christian preaching is that the same God is not far removed, but is very much interested, and is very much involved, in the lives of people as manifested in his incarnation in Jesus Christ. God is everywhere. He is both transcendent and immanent. He fills heaven and earth. God is near and far away, wrote the prophet Jeremiah (23:23). And in the New Testament we are told that God became man and made his residence among people (John 1:14). His presence on the earth has been so realistic that people were able to hear him, see him, look at him, and even touch him (1 John 1: 1–4). God's presence with people in the person of Jesus Christ is truly ontological. People of every age are privileged to come to an existential awareness of Christ's presence with them as they are confronted by the Word of God and nurtured and nourished by the sacraments. There is no other way to get to know Christ except through the Word.

The rank and file theologians of our day tend to speak disparagingly of those who maintain that the proclamation of the Gospel is still the primary mission of the Christian church. People with that conviction are often caricatured as "Protestantevangelists," implying that such people are not quite capable of handling the weightier matters of the true science of God.

But this criticism ought to be accepted as a compliment. The primary responsibility of the Christian theologian in every age is to proclaim the mighty acts of God. There is nothing mightier or more laudable than Christ's supreme sacrifice on the cross for our salvation. There is no human agency other than the church that has a better grasp of the implications of Christ's death as the ransom for the sin of mankind. It is therefore a privilege for the church to proclaim this news to others. For that very reason Paul, who knew in his heart that he was sent to preach the Gospel (1 Cor. 1:17) "resolved to know nothing . . . except Jesus Christ and him crucified" (1 Cor. 2:2). He was not ashamed of the Gospel because he knew it was "the power of God for the salvation of everyone who believes" (Rom. 1:17). And he would never "boast except in the cross of our Lord Jesus Christ, through which the world had been crucified to [him], and [he] to the world" (Gal. 6:14).

By design, the act of proclamation involves a minimum of two people. There is the one who announces (the news) and the other for whose sake the announcement is made. In this sense proclamation is a relational term. Its purpose is to build relationships. The proclaimers of the Gospel perceive themselves as conveying God's Word of salvation to those who are victims of broken relationships between God and people and among people themselves, caused by sin. This, of course, is one of the most difficult hurdles when confronting the New Age.

New Agers, like the Hindus, do not normally acknowledge the fact of sin the way Christians do. Therefore, for them the coming of a savior figure to redeem the world from sin, and consequently communicating that Gospel to others, may seem irrelevant propositions. However, if we do not want to call it sin, there is nevertheless ever present in this world a powerful phenomenon that causes even well-meaning people to stumble—something that breaks relationships, generates despair, builds walls, and lets everyone down. This failing cripples both the most educated and the unschooled, the pious and the insolent, and the rich and the poor alike. The Christian Gospel offers freely to everyone the ultimate way out of the grip of our unfortunate confinement. To communicate that message is the primary purpose of Christian proclamation.

Proclaiming the Gospel at the end of the 20th century is an awesome responsibility of the church. The world is increasingly shrinking into a so-called global village. Or, is it? Are we not becoming more individualistic and more indifferent to the needs of others? There is perhaps a touch of globalism in today's culture, but certainly not in today's religions. The question is, as people from a variety of cultures and faiths are coming together almost at the speed of light, can the Gospel still claim its relevance in our age of religious pluralism and multiculturalism? Bishop Lesslie Newbigin alerts us to a "triangular pattern of tensions" involved in proclaiming the Gospel in our age.

There is the pull of the traditional culture with its normally powerful religious components; there is the pull of modernization that always means involvement with science, technology, and political ideas that the Enlightenment let loose in the world; and there is the call to faithful discipleship of Jesus Christ.[8]

# The Gospel for the New Age

In confronting the New Age there is a corresponding triangular pattern of tensions. In this case the tension is more acute because the New Age, like the Hindu way of life, is already a composite of popular culture, science, and religion.

M. Scott Peck, in his recent book *Further Along the Road Less Travelled*, characterizes the New Age Movement as a "reaction against the institutional sins of Western civilization."[9] The New Age Movement is prompting a considerable number from the Western upper-middle-class to react against the "sins" of the established systems of modern culture, science, and religion. It is an attack on Western institutionalization. This reactionary process steers them to embrace alternate ways of living—in this case those with an ardent Eastern orientation.

According to Peck, the New Age movement is a reaction against male domination in industry, church, and government. In every walk of life, it promotes the feminist movement in order to curb male supremacy. Followers of the New Age turn away from the Christian church because of the church's "arrogance, narcissism,and blasphemy," which together result in an emptiness of the spirit. Thus searching for true spiritual meaning, and perhaps anticipating authentic spiritual experiences, they turn to Eastern religions and to a miscellany of other ideologies.

The New Age is also an attempt to resist the "sin of science," Peck says. Science touches human lives through modern technology in the form of medicine and other complex methods of modern hospitalization. As alternatives to these methods of caring for the sick, New Agers choose Eastern techniques of holistic medicine, chakras, acupuncture, and other means.

The New Age is also, Peck points out, a reaction against capitalism, imperialism, and the exploitation of people and of the environment. These issues are not limited to one part of the globe. Exploiting the less privileged and the natural resources is an evil that prevails all over the world, even in those communities where Christianity has not entered. These evils have already been operating in nations where Christian missions entered, long before their coming. Even today more people are exploited, enslaved, and dehumanized in other nations than in those that uphold a Judeo-Christian worldview. More acts of charity are performed by Christians all over the world than by any other religion. The question is, How can the church be held responsible for such corruption in the world? And, by holding up such evils as an argument seemingly to justify their falling away from the Christian church, are not the New Agers actually "jumping from the frying pan into the fire"?

To be sure, the church could avoid some criticism if it would be about the business of Gospel witnessing, for which it was first brought into being—a failing for which the church can be held responsible, the sin of not remembering what the true church is all about—more on that later.

But New Agers, in charging that the church backs imperialism, supports capitalism, and ravages the environment, are also making a major and universal mistake by not recognizing that the true treasure of the church is the Gospel of Jesus Christ. The church has always been, among other things, the hospital for sinners, the home of the homeless, and the burden bearer upon which all may cast their loads of anxiety and depression. Unfortunately, the church has never fully lived up to all these expectations in any one given place or time—and that is exactly why the church must always be remembered as a community of both saints and sinners at the same time.

The foundation of the Christian church is Jesus Christ. Jesus had a great appreciation for nature and the environment, as much as any in the New Age. In fact Jesus, like many writers in the Old Testament, exhorted his listeners to learn from nature. He encouraged multitudes of people to fight their worry and anxiety by watching the birds of the air and the lilies of the field (Matt. 6:25–34). Many of Jesus' parables were lessons drawn from nature. But Jesus never attached any divinity to nature. Instead, he wanted people, through their appreciation of the ways of nature, to see the God who made and maintains nature and all that is in it. Jesus also warned his followers that the beauty and glory of nature will fade and go away some day (Matt. 24:35). True, the Jews of old lifted their eyes up to the mountains for help. But they were also wise enough to know that help did not come from the hills, but from God who *made* the hills (Ps.121:1–2). Nature will pass away, but God does not.

Douglas Groothuis describes the New Age as the result of a mutation caused by a "hybrid spirituality," taking "the essence of Eastern religions" (a powerful religious component) and at the same time, retaining "some elements of the Western, Judeo-Christian world view"[10] (the traditional culture of the West). Religion writer and journalist Russell Chandler explains the New Age as "a hybrid mix of spiritual, social, and political forces, [that] encompasses sociology, theology, the physical sciences, medicine, anthropology, history, the human potential movement, sports, and science fiction."[11] As J. Gordon Melton points out, the New Age is "ultimately a vision of a world transformed, a heaven on Earth, a society in which the problems of today are overcome and a new existence emerges"[12] (obviously, the pull of modernization).

Again, Russell Chandler writes, "In many ways, the human mind is the heart of the New Age."[13] The matter of the mind is in itself mind-boggling. It appears that no one has, and has ever had, the mind to understand the mind, because it is, after all, a matter of the mind. While a surgeon may operate on the brain, it takes a psychologist or a psychiatrist to handle the affairs of the mind. Even these may only analyze the workings of the mind and suggest ways to mend its disorders. Ultimately, we are ourselves the custodians of our own mind. The mind wanders. It searches. It never has enough. It knows no limits. And, if Chandler is right, the New Age "bets its money" on the human mind.

In general, Eastern religions deal more with the inner workings of the mind. The mind, itself a mystery, loves mystery. The typical Westerner, who, in the eyes of modern experts, suffers from the left brain syndrome, likes to explore mysteries and analyze them into categories. Or, the Westerner is found good at explaining *away* things, until nothing is hidden, and nothing is left unexplored. And, if there remain unsolved mysteries, they are dismissed as no mystery at all. By contrast, the typical Easterner, who, in the eyes of modern experts, suffers from the right-brain syndrome, prefers to acknowledge mystery, venerate it, and worship it. For the Easterner, it is quite all right to have unsolved mysteries, and unanswered questions in life. This does not mean that Easterners stop exploring mysteries. In fact they do not. They leave the unexplainable mysteries to meditation.[14] They let the mind wander, and thus, as Jacob Needleman said, satisfy the "irrational" need that is in the psyche of everyone.[15]

Christianity is not altogether either an Eastern or a Western religion. Its origins are in the middle (East). If we could stretch the left-brain-right-brain analogy (and if the pun is pardonable), Christianity comes into the middle-brain. There is mystery and transcendence in the Christian religion. There is enough room in Christianity for meditation, for lofty thinking, and even to get lost in the mind of God (Rom. 11:34). But, in an equally convincing manner, the Christian religion speaks the language of ordinary, down to earth, and practical-minded people, especially with its emphasis on God becoming man in the person of Jesus Christ.

The point of God becoming man gives prominence to a "one way traffic" situation. It is as if we need to follow the rules of the road in our spiritual journey. "Flesh and blood cannot inherit the kingdom of God" (1 Cor. 15:50)[6] is one such rule. It does not take a genius to know that in each individual two distinctive and opposite principles are at work. In fact an almost unending battle is going on between them: between good and evil, between the flesh and the spirit. Jesus, in an encounter with a top intellectual of his day

(John 3:1–21), reinforced the same idea. Jesus explained that flesh and spirit do not get along well with each other. There are limitations to the flesh. Earthly, human existence cannot fully comprehend spiritual (transcendental) matters. True, the human mind has a deep desire to know the transcendental and heavenly things. But humans need outside assistance in this regard in order to know the celestial. It takes someone from the transcendental realm to assist us with this information. Jesus also said that no one has ever gone into this realm except the one who descended from there, namely, Jesus himself.

But, the New Age philosophy is highly optimistic that humans, with some serious effort, can enter the transcendental level on their own. To support this position they make the following statement: "Edward was not always king, and Lincoln was not always president, and Jesus was not always Christ. Jesus won his Christship by a strenuous life."[17] But again, this idea is against the rules of spiritual journey. Among the many Edwards who sat on the throne of England, one was defeated in war, another was crowned at age 13, one had a unique sporting style, and yet another abdicated in order to marry. None of them remained kings forever. No one can remain in the office of the president forever, even though he has assumed office "by means of a strenuous life." Jesus, however, claimed that he came from heaven, and, after a strenuous life on earth which culminated in the cross and the subsequent resurrection, he went up to heaven (John 3:13).

Already at age twelve, when according to Jewish law boys were allowed to participate in religious dialogue, Jesus made claims about his divine origin (Luke 2:49). There was talk about Jesus' divine origin already during the early part of his public life (Mark 1:24). In the face of an adamantly strong, conservative community which held that God alone is eternal, Jesus said, "Before Abraham was born, I am" (John 8:58). The great "I am" is the solemn "name by which God wished to be known." Jesus was explaining his eternity and his oneness with God by applying the "I am" in a series of statements.[18]

The "Christship" of Jesus is not something that he claimed on his own, or bragged about. Once when Peter, a disciple of Jesus, declared that Jesus was the Christ, Jesus warned him not to talk about it further (Mark 8:29–30). Jesus did so not because he was not already Christ at that moment, but because among his audience there was the popular notion about Christ (the Messiah) being a political and national hero. Jesus was not intent on "putting the cart before the horse," as it were. He first had to climax his earthly life on the cross in behalf of all, so that through him everyone shall be where he is. He did nothing out of "selfish ambition or vein conceit" (Phil. 2:3). His strenuous work on earth was not something that he practiced with the view to working his way up to Christship, or better, Christhood. Jesus' divinity and his Christhood are not ranks which he strived to attain. Rather, by becoming man he was humbling himself for the sake of all who would put their trust in him and *confess him* as Christ and Lord (Phil. 2:1–11).

*The Aquarian Gospel* puts these words in Jesus' mouth, "What I have done all men can do, and what I am, all men shall be."[19] This too is against the rules of the spiritual journey. Human beings do have the desire to be like God. This is actually the first recorded temptation of man. The life of Jesus in the true Gospels is to be trusted more than the Aquarian Gospel which originated with someone in our generation, two thousand years removed from the time of Jesus. The gospels show that Christ did much more than any human being can do and has ever done. History tells of no one else who did—or came anywhere near to doing—what Jesus did. The desire and the claim to be able *to do every-thing* is just a reflection of the human desire to be God.The true spiritual attitude in this case ought to be, "I can do everything *through [Christ ]* who gives me strength" (Phil. 4:13), because Jesus himself said, "Apart from me you can do nothing" (John 15:5) and *"I will do* whatever you ask in my name" (John 14:13).

Jesus did not say (as the Aquarian Gospel claims) "*What* I am, all men shall be," but he only said, "You may also be *where I am* (John 14:3). Jesus said that he was the way *to* God and that through him people are drawn to God, into his presence. The spiritual principle does not allow created objects to become God. God, however, became man within the created order so that through him humans may be brought to where God is, where humans cannot enter on their own. This is a rather difficult principle to abide by for those who maintain that the human mind is capable of everything.

All through time human beings have been fighting this difficulty. Christians are aware of this human predicament as much as anyone else. In order to emerge victorious out of this situation the New Testament calls for nothing short of a *renewing of the mind* or a spiritual transformation (Rom. 12:2). Spiritual transformation is a metamorphosis of the mind—of the "heart" (the mindset) and the will—which, in the language of faith, is also known as repentance. Repentance must continue as an ongoing process, because the human mind is always subject to change (for better or for worse). The Bible maintains that God, through His Spirit, assists humans in effecting this transformation individually in each person. It is comforting to know that this help is available from God, because God alone has an unchanging mind as his prerogative.

Repentance calls for a life for the better, not for the worse. This better life is initiated, offered, and prospered by the Spirit of God. The Spirit leads people to the true knowledge of God and continues to keep them in that knowledge. Unsolved mysteries are unveiled by the Spirit of God. Knowledge that ignores the mystery of Christ's crucifixion and resurrection—and its relevance for all—is weak and, unassisted by the Spirit of God, will remain incomplete. The knowledge that has been revealed in Jesus, the wisdom of God, is already much more than humans can understand (John 16:12).

Repentance offers a new life in the Spirit. Those who live in the Spirit also have their minds set on what the Spirit desires. They are controlled by the Spirit, because they have the Spirit of Christ living in them (Rom. 8:1–17). The Spirit of Christ is not "Christ-consciousness" or "Christic consciousness." Rather, it is the privilege of being directed, controlled and led by God each moment of our lives. It is a matter of our relationship with God, where God remains God and we remain ourselves. In this relationship we can do what God wants us to do, not as slaves, but as free people. As Paul wrote, "Where the Spirit of God is, there is freedom" (2 Cor. 3:17); and "since we live by the Spirit, let us keep in step with the Spirit" (Gal. 5:25).

Freedom in the Spirit and, consequently, walking in the same Spirit are the privileges of a Christian. These experiences transcend culture. A person is not required to break away from his or her culture in order to enjoy these privileges. For the greatest mystery of all is the revelation of God in Christ who takes residence in every individual who acknowledges him as Savior and Lord. Those who enter into this kind of relationship with God make their presence known in the world as the church, symbolizing their unity in this faith. For there is "one Lord . . . one God and Father of all, who is over all and through all and in all" (Eph. 4:5–6).

# The Kingdom of God

The prophets of the New Age, unlike the faithful followers of the Hindu way of life, anticipate the ushering in of a new era of peace and harmony on earth. Accordingly, they are engrossed in the veneration and preservation of Mother Earth, a universal brotherhood, a harmony and convergence of universal peace and justice, and, ultimately, the monistic fusion of all into one.

New Agers are not pioneers in this kind of thing. All of the above, except perhaps the idea of monism, are part of the package of all major world-affirming philosophies of modern times. Throughout history, splinter groups have broken away from the world's major religions, proposing an identical, affirmative-action plan—if for no other purpose, to cherish the dream of making the world a better place to live. On the part of Christians, some modern interpretations of the idea of the kingdom of God also have contributed amply to this new enthusiasm.

In recent years, there has been a dramatic shift in the focus of Christianity. Christians of the 19th century demonstrated a great and unusual zeal for evangelizing the whole world with the Gospel. However, many Christian thinkers in the post-World War II era have been speaking about merging the Christian faith with the cultural, social, and political aspects of contemporary human life. While Christians of yesteryears trumpeted the free gift of forgiveness to all and the salvation of the souls through faith in Jesus Christ, modern Christians consider as their *primary* mission standing up (and fighting) for a more just society and for a more fully "human" life for all on this earth. The Christian focus has shifted from the *other* world to the present one. Theology today has left the impression that Christianity is just another agency of good will ready to fight against social and political injustice.

There is hardly a human concern today to which modern Christians have not spoken—whether of a social, political, economic, or ecological dimension—often with the primary purpose of trying to *identify* the Christian faith with the practical situations and the needs of people. In an effort to see the work of God in the events of world history, many Christians look at Christianity as a world movement that operates outside and without the framework of religion. Because much energy is expended for such purposes, they also seem to preempt the primary mission of Christians, which is proclaiming to others the good news of salvation in Jesus Christ. Thus Christians are facing a potential challenge to be *of* the world, instead of being *in* the world (but not of it), as mandated by Jesus himself (John 17:15–18).

We should note that Christians have always stood up for the cause of the poor, the widow, and the orphan. Even today, the majority of the membership of worldwide Christendom is comprised of the economically poor and the socially lower sections of the human race. Christians have always been behind the social, and cultural revolutions in the world. These are healthy reflections of responsible Christian citizenship. However, there is no guarantee that the church's endorsement of the struggle against exploitation and injustice will somehow help build a more just and fully "human" society. God's saving act in Christ does not entail the promise that the present world will be transformed into an arena of eternal peace and justice. Instead, it does promise a perfect life in God's kingdom forever, the foretaste of which can be experienced in the present world, and it offers the power to cope with the problems of the world, come what may.

Many well meaning Christians are optimistic about the coming into being of a harmonious, just, and peaceful society on earth truly reflecting the ideals of the kingdom of God. They are also enthusiastic about the endless possibilities for human beings to change the world, if only they put their mind to it. However, such thinking tends to neglect the fact that our resources to build a better world and better society are limited because of our rebellion against God. Sin has brought such a curse upon us that we fall short of the skills to tame the world for our purposes. Unfortunately, sin has shaped our destiny to be "restless wanderer[s]" on this earth (Gen. 4:12). The earth is not in a friendly relationship with humans no matter where we are. This situation is more than we can handle on our own, in spite of all the positive attitudes we might be able to project.

Because of man's sin all of creation must face God's judgment. The cosmic scope of man's sin continues to persist. The enduring nature of sin in the world and among people shows that the religious thrust of the saving act of God in Christ must take precedence over its other aspects. Because of sin, the world as we have known it is bound to disappear. The growth of the kingdom of God will culminate in the judgment of the present order of things and not in its improvement. The kingdom of God operates on the belief that "Christ died for all in order that all men may die to themselves to live in him in the light of the new covenant that he has made with them in his death and resurrection."[20]

Discussions about the kingdom of God have occupied a central place in modern Christian theology.[21] The topic runs through the length and breadth of the Bible. It was also the central theme of the life and teaching of Jesus on earth. In fact Jesus' speeches were designed to alert people to realize how difficult it is to enter this kingdom (Matt. 5:20; 7:21). By using parables to speak about the kingdom, Jesus added a certain zest to its mysterious or secret nature. He used object lessons from nature and drew examples from human experience to explain the nature and scope of the kingdom of God.

An important purpose of Jesus' miracles was to demonstrate to his listeners that the kingdom of God had come upon them. The miracles of Jesus are called the signs of God's coming kingdom.While speaking about and performing the signs of the kingdom, Jesus also taught his disciples to pray for the coming of the kingdom. Following the model of the disciples, Christians continue to pray for its coming when they pray the Lord's Prayer. The above implies that human beings by themselves are unable to bring about God's kingdom. They can neither hasten nor delay the coming of the kingdom of God. The kingdom is God's and so is its execution.

If that is the case, what is the meaning of *the kingdom of God*? Modern scholarship has attempted to answer that question in a variety of ways. Students of the Bible, such as Adolf Harnack, maintained that the kingdom of God is a kind of inward power that lays hold of the individual soul by coming into it. He did not see a difference between God and his kingdom when he said God's kingdom is "God himself in power."[22] Harnack obviously viewed the kingdom idea as a purely spiritual principle.

Others like Albert Schweitzer have maintained that the kingdom of God is an altogether future and supernatural event that will be ushered in at the end of world history.[23] According to Schweitzer, Jesus knew full well that he himself was the Messiah who would usher in the kingdom of God at a later date. But he kept this fact secret from his first disciples and his first listeners. Jesus was preparing a people for this purpose, and he expected that the final hour of the world would come in his lifetime, when the mystery of the kingdom would also be revealed to all.

Another student of the New Testament, C. H. Dodd, proposed that the kingdom of God has come in the person of Jesus Christ.[24] Dodd saw a true paradox in the whole discussion on the kingdom of God. This is the paradox of Jesus (the king of the kingdom) going through the terrible experience of his own suffering and death (on the cross) so that through that unique event his kingdom may finally set in. The true mystery or the secret of God's kingdom therefore is the mystery of the cross of Jesus Christ. The culmination of that kingdom is a matter of actual human experience with Jesus. Those who reject Jesus also reject his kingdom which is ultimately God's kingdom.

Recently, a more secular interpretation has been given to the concept of the kingdom of God. It holds that the purpose of Jesus was to teach an ideal pattern for human society. Jesus attacked the rich and the wealthy of his day especially as they exploited the poor and took away their freedom. The proponents of this view base it on their interpretation of the New Testament. According to this view, the kingdom of God is a classless society, a new social order that will eventually transcend all apparent inequalities and bring about an even distribution of wealth and well-being to all. All people must work hard to achieve that goal for which a master plan was outlined in the teaching and ministry of Jesus.

The kingdom of God presupposes the obvious idea that *God* is the king of this kingdom. The kingdom of God is where God is. The benefits of the kingdom are available to all and must be enjoyed by all who are with God. If God is eternal and everlasting, his kingdom also must be eternal and everlasting. If God is not the God of the dead but of the living (Matt. 22:32), his kingdom also is not the kingdom of the dead but of the living.

In his trials before the Roman governor Pontius Pilate, Jesus was charged with claiming to be the king (of a kingdom). Pilate, with his limited knowledge of the Jewish religion, cross-examined Jesus to see if in fact Jesus was the king of the Jews (John 18:33–37). Jesus countered with a more personal question, "Is that your own idea . . . or did others talk to you about me?" Pilate's response to that was another query and a blunt announcement, "Am I a Jew? . . . It was your people and your chief priests who handed you over to me." Jesus cleared the air with this emphatic statement, "My kingdom is not of this world . . . . my kingdom is from another place." It is true that Jesus is *the* king and his kingdom is *the* eternal kingdom. But God does not bring about his kingdom either by might or by power but by his Spirit.

The kingdom of God is evidence of God's kingship and his kingly rule, brought about by the Holy Spirit. It refers to God's rule of grace.[25] God's grace, then, is the first characteristic of the kingdom of God. Grace means that human beings can contribute absolutely nothing to the coming of God's kingdom. Mankind can neither hasten its coming nor prevent it from coming.

Second, the kingdom of God means that God in his mercy chose to forgive peoples' sins because of the sacrifical death of his Son Jesus Christ on the cross. God's kingdom is made accessible through the cross of Jesus Christ. God redeemed the Old Testament people of Israel from the land of slavery, and in his infinite mercy made them a people to live in his presence. Similarly, God, in Christ's work of redemption, has created a community of believers who are called to live in his presence through Immanuel (God with us, Christ).

And third, the kingdom of God is the "kingdom of priests," built on the principle of a covenant relationship with God. It is a community set apart to do God's will in a life of service to God and fellow human beings. As priests, the citizens of this kingdom reflect the kind of holiness that is accorded them by divine favor. As offerings, they dedicate their lives to God and represent God before others in all their actions involving their body, mind, and soul. God's kingdom is where faith in God becomes active in love.

The apostle Paul's understanding of the kingdom of God is worth noting here. Paul explained both sides of the spectrum as to who will and who will not enter the kingdom of God. For example, he wrote that "the kingdom of God is *not* a matter of eating and drinking, but of righteousness, peace and joy in the Holy Spirit" (Rom. 14:17). Paul was reminding his readers that there are deeper and greater needs than what are often understood as the basic needs of life. A fulfilled life does not depend on, and cannot be measured by, the quality of food we eat and our wardrobe. Rather, lasting peace and abiding joy are experienced by those who are made righteous and who lead a morally pure and ethically wholesome life.

Paul further explained that the kingdom of God is *not* a matter of talk, but of power (1 Cor. 4:20). Life in God's kingdom involves a life of dedication, powerfully demonstrating the fruits of the Spirit as Paul describes them elsewhere.[26] Christian believers can claim this power because through baptism the Spirit of God has taken residence in them. The church, the community of believers, in spite of all its failures and weaknesses, has been entrusted with the awesome responsibility of combating the forces of evil in the world. This has often been called the warfare of faith. The God-given weapons of this warfare are only those of prayer and the sword of the Spirit—the Word of God.

Paul wrote to the Christians at Colossae that the kingdom of God is truly the kingdom of Christ, God's Son. This kingdom is in sharp contrast to the kingdoms of the present world where the powers of darkness and of evil prevail. Again, God's kingdom is one in which satanic forces cannot prevail. Christians, under the lordship of Christ, are no longer caught in the clenching grip of these forces because under the cross of Christ they enjoy the life of forgiveness and freedom.

God's rule is also at work outside his kingdom of grace. This divine activity is often described as pertaining to his kingdom of power. Here is where the secular governments and other authorities fit into God's plan. Those who hold such offices are also serving God's purposes for mankind under divine providence, whether they know it or not. All authorities are ultimately responsible to God since God exercises His power over them too. The kingdom of power is in fact the continuation of the divine order of creation. As such it is established for the conduct of an orderly life in the present world. Accordingly, God may use (and he continues to use) nonbelievers also as his servants to execute his rule of power. It is our Christian duty to submit to administrators because God has placed them as authorities over nations and kingdoms (Rom. 13: 4–5). The kingdom of grace, on the other hand, operates on God's work of redemption, and only believers enter it.

## The Community of Believers

The New Age is the age of discovering the self. The desire to find a person's true self, and its alleged ultimate oneness with the divine, presupposes naturally a sense of lostness in the present existence. Accordingly, in both the Hindu way of life and the New Age philosophy, independent existence of individuals is just a phenomenon that needs to be beset by (a series of) incarnations. This is not at all a contradiction to those who embrace such worldviews, because monistic philosophy undermines any authentic existence beyond and outside of the Eternal One.

As a spiritual principle, this idea may be appealing to many, especially with its notion of every person being a potential god and ultimately One (God). But an irony is hidden in this fantasy, because it works as a double-edged sword. We exist (temporarily) on earth as humans with our needs, wants, desires, and emotions. But when we depart this world we shall lose ourself (or find the true self). If oneness with the ultimate is the ultimate goal, it damages the idea of the individual self and grants little meaning to its present existence. Persons and names carry no specific message (contrary to the Christian belief that our names are written in heaven). Individuals together with everything that surrounds them, are reduced to abstracts and become relativistic. There are no real persons, and there are no relationships. There is no communication. All is silence.

Christianity, on the other hand, is a religion of relationships. Its basis is a personal relationship of the individual with God through Jesus Christ. In the broader context, the same relationship spreads to others also, especially to those who believe in Jesus as their Lord and Savior. For that very reason the Christian faith is able to transcend races and cultures, and it continues to grow even in those cultures that have little love for the West.

The cross is the universally acknowledged and the most familiar symbol of the Christian faith. While some Christians worry that the sign of the cross is widely misused in the world of fashion and business, recent efforts in the United States to remove this symbol from public places proves that the primary message conveyed through the cross is still the message of Christ. This is appropriately so. Christ's willing submission to the cross and his subsequent resurrection from the dead marked the beginning of a new life for all, in fact a new creation. The idea of the new creation is anchored in the cross of Christ. It was on the cross that the great mystery of God's eternal plan of salvation was finally and fully revealed.

The New Testament speaks of the Christian life as a new beginning, the result of a new creation.[27] In that context the apostle Paul, following his own Jewish tradition, calls Jesus Christ the second Adam. Jesus is the new Adam who calls the new creation into existence. In Jesus Christ a new genesis has already begun. Through him all the wounds and the divisions caused by human sin are healed.

The idea of Jesus as the second Adam goes back to the Old Testament and to the Jewish tradition. Judaism maintained that Adam was a kingly figure. However, he was stripped of that splendid existence when he sinned. Jesus Christ in his incarnation demonstrated to the world the kind of man God wanted Adam to be. Christ did all that Adam failed to do. Christ through his death brought life where once Adam through his sin brought death. Christ revealed the true image of God which Adam failed to keep because of his sin. The curse that Adam's sin brought upon mankind and the whole creation has now been removed because of the willing and innocent death of the new Adam. The church is the community of believers that live in and benefit from the blessings of the new creation.

Church in the Christian sense has a very unique meaning. Unfortunately, the business and yellow pages of the telephone directory use *church* as a generic term for a place of worship. And so they use *church* as an umbrella term for listing the places of worship of Christians (of all denominations), Hindus, Jews, Muslims, Sikhs, and so on. *Church* in its original sense had two basic meanings. One is the local congregation of Christian believers who gather around the Word and sacraments. And the other is the church universal, consisting of all believers in Christ from all over the world. In the language of the Bible, the church is the body of Christ, which continues to grow, be nourished and sustained by the Lord Jesus Christ.

The Christian church, while it may try to justify becoming involved in every human and humanitarian endeavor as its calling in the world, still has a primary mission to perform what no other human agency can do. This is simply the proclamation of the Gospel of Jesus Christ. The church of today is undoubtedly the product of that same proclamation in times past. The Christian community has taken root, grown, and survived in those cultures where the word of God was preached and was demonstrated in actions of love, peace, and forgiveness. There was a time when multitudes of people joined the church because it was fulfilling their basic physical needs. History even called them "rice Christians"or "milk powder Christians." Such Christians also left the church when the supply of rice and milk powder ceased. More people are drawn to the church of Jesus Christ when they are confronted by the Word of God and nourished by the sacraments than by any other means.

The true Christian community is the *fellowship* of believers in Christ. In fact, Christians are part of the prototype of the fellowship all believers in Christ will enjoy in God's everlasting kingdom. Christian fellowship therefore runs contrary to the New Age attempts to inject in humans a conscious awareness that they are part of a cosmic whole, whose destiny is to merge with and finally become one with the eternally One. It is perhaps better for Christians today to identify themselves more as the fellowship of believers than a community. The apostle John wrote that the purpose of proclamation is to draw people to Christian fellowship (1 John 1:3). Christian fellowship involves the believer's spiritual solidarity with Christ and with other fellow believers. It is a bond of inner communion that people are able to experience with God and with other people. Each individual has direct access to this experience without the assistance of intermediaries because Christ himself reaches out and offers his nearness directly to all.

When Christians today stress social and political activity as the church's primary responsibility, for the most part, they are heavily influenced by and maintain a strong affinity to Marxist ideology. We need to remember that Karl Marx viewed all religious movements as being of no avail for finding solutions to human misery and sorrow. Yet, ironically, Marxism itself owes its revolutionary ideas to the book of the Acts of the Apostles. In fact, Friedrich Engels, a collaborator of Marx, found all the ingredients of the socialist movement in the life of the early Christian community. He was convinced that Christianity was the best form in which to establish socialism because he saw in the history of Christianity several notable points similar to the modern working class movement. Engels concluded that both

Christianity and socialism were originally a movement of the oppressed people, that both preached a forthcoming salvation from bondage and misery, that both are persecuted, discriminated, and despised, and that both forge victoriously, vigorously, and irresistibly ahead.[28]

What Marx and Engels (and because of them other revolutionary movements of similar orientation) fail to acknowledge is the activity of the Holy Spirit in the life of the Christian church. Most Christians of the early centuries were from the socially and economically poor and even oppressed classes of society. Nevertheless, they emerged victorious against all odds, and they turned the world upside down, not by their skills to organize themselves against the forces of oppression, but by the Holy Spirit's power working in them. As the Spirit worked through them, they boldly and fearlessly proclaimed the good news of salvation for everyone. Thus for example Peter, a fisherman from Galilee, became so bold as to speak to Cornelius, a Roman military commander, about the free gift of forgiveness through Christ (Acts 10). As long as they acted according to the dictates of the Spirit they succeeded (Acts 2:42–47), and all those who tried to test the Spirit of the Lord met with serious consequences (Acts 5:1–10).

The true Christian community, like the kingdom of God, is where the grace of God is in operation. Grace is God's undeserved favor that extends to all mankind through Jesus Christ, God's Son. Christians do notice a difference between God's grace and his goodness in the material world. Proof of God's goodness is seen in the created order of things. The various ways in which the physical and material needs of humanity are satisfied can be considered evidence of God's goodness. A great family, a well-balanced diet, friendly neighbors, good government, and universal peace and justice are part of the goodness of God. On the other hand, God's grace is a purely spiritual matter. It operates on the principle of God's forgiving love. There is no explanation for the way in which God extends his *grace* to humanity. Grace is God's prerogative. God sets the rules for its operation.

Grace in this sense is not available to anyone apart from Jesus Christ.

The community of believers therefore is privileged to proclaim God's grace revealed, enacted, and offered through Jesus Christ. This is a privilege that Jesus Christ entrusted to his first followers. This was the primary purpose for the first believers to gather as a community, a church. Proclamation of God's grace in Jesus Christ has been at the center of all apostolic preaching. So that this grace might reach the hearts of Jews and Gentiles alike for their salvation, the apostle Paul was willing to become all things to all people (1 Cor. 9:19–23).

What the church confesses is primarily the message of eternal salvation. Confession is closer to the New Testament way of describing the *mission* of the Christian Church, for the words *mission* and *missionary* are not in the Bible. In their place Holy Scripture speaks of proclaiming and bearing witness to the good news. The strength of the Christian church lies in its bold confession of the mighty acts of God in Christ. The church, like any other human agency of good will in the world, is never without its struggles against inequalities and injustices. While the Christian community itself suffers from such weaknesses, there is no practical reason to hope for the emergence of a worldwide community of equality, peace and harmony.

The church exists as a corporate entity in the world for the specific purpose of confessing the faith and serving humanity. This is how the church demonstrates to the world by word and by deed that the kingdom of God has drawn near. The dawning of the kingdom does not mark the beginning of a social upheaval, but of a different kind of revolution, of repentance and faith. In faith turning first to the Lord of the church and of the universe—and then with the vision of the Lord to neighbors and their needs—is the only way to restore the broken relationships between God and fellow human beings. This is the way to let the world know that the kingdom of God is within us and among us.

True spiritual fellowship and lasting relationships in communities, therefore, are the tangible marks of Christianity. These two fundamental virtues add meaning and credibility to our independence as individuals and interdependence as communities. Independence is a prized possession every human being wants to cherish forever, if possible, even in eternity. Independence obviously fosters self-confidence and self-reliance. New Age thinking, however, runs contrary to this model, claiming individuality for the present existence, but willing to let go of that privilege in the next.

## Christ Is All and in All

Christianity is a religion of paradoxes. To many, it involves apparent inconsistencies and contradictions. It expresses spiritual things—about God, spirit, sin, death, faith, heaven—things that make sense only if they are understood in a metaphysical way. For some, Christianity is a lot of preaching, a lot of talk. For others, Christianity is not spiritual enough to be a religion. This is true especially of many Easterners (and those suffering from the right-brain disposition) who think that Christians are, for the most part, libertinists, this worldly, beer drinkers, and meat eaters.

Christianity is a religion of those who are at the same time sinners and saints. Christians live *in* this world, but do not become *of* the world. It is not the Christian design to live a life of resignation from the world in order to become more religious and more spiritual. Nor is it the Christian ideal to indulge in the affairs of the world with the view that a moment of lost pleasure is a moment lost forever. Authentic Christianity takes away the *fear* of being *religious* by letting the spirit take control of matter lest matter control spirit.

The universal lordship of Christ is part and parcel of the Christian religion. Perhaps the oldest and the most original Christian confession, "Jesus Christ is lord," pretty well sums up this fact. Christ's lordship entails his absolute authority and dominion over all things. In Jesus Christ, human beings are to see the divine intention for them as it has been ever since God created the first man. Christ is everywhere, but everything is not Christ (a point to remember against Christian monism). Everything is *under* him and controlled by him.

In the New Testament, Jesus Christ is described as "the image of the invisible God, the firstborn over all creation" (Col. 1:15). That is, Christ is the perfect revelation and true reflection of his prototype, God. Jesus is also the perfect reflection of how God first created man, in his own image (Gen. 1:27). However, man, since he first sinned, has been unable to face God, nor has he been able to exercise authority and dominion over himself and the rest of the universe as Christ continues to do. Sin caused man to walk away from God's presence, though God has still been reaching out to man in spite of man's sin (Gen 3: 8–19). Christ, being without sin, continues to be what man, because of sin, continues to fail to be. Christ alone continues to reflect and illuminate God's true essence and existence.

Jesus Christ is the firstborn over all creation. In the Old Testament, the idea of the firstborn is that of a privileged person who enjoys that status purely on account of his birth. The firstborn son was the legal heir of the father's wealth and possessions (Gen. 25:29–34; 2 Chron. 21:3), and for that very reason took precedence over others in the family. Christ reigns supreme. And he is the only custodian of all the divine rights.

The concept of the firstborn reflects the origin of Jesus and his unique status. God the Father has entrusted Jesus Christ with the responsibility for exercising authority over the entire creation. As God's firstborn, Christ is not part of the created universe (an argument against monism and eclecticism), and he is different from all that has been created. Everything was "created *by* him and *for* him" (Col. 1:16). The universe and Christ exist in a relationship, not in a state of fusion or union, as, for example, Teilhard de Chardin envisioned. Doubtless, Teilhard's writings on the cosmic

Christ have had a strong influence on New Age thinking. Many Hindus also find his interpretation of Christ interesting and acceptable to them. Christ , however, is the *head* of the cosmos, and all things are held together in him. Christ sustains everything that has been created.

The coherence of all things must be seen as something that takes place *in* Christ. This is important to note because not only is the universe created in Christ and for Christ, but its whole existence depends on him. The unity of the cosmos is something that is knit together (quilted together) in Christ (with Christ at its center) in such a way that the identity of each component part is retained as an individual unit. In the setting of the human race, this unity is to be seen as fellowship with one another, generated, nourished, and consummated by God's Spirit.

Generally speaking, the superstructure reflects the quality of the foundation of a building. Accordingly, when an edifice appears in bad shape or leaning, serious questions are asked about the status of its foundation. At least two major distortions are visible in the edifice of "religion," specifically in modern interpretations of Christ and his work of redemption. One is the recurring temptation to *discover* a certain Christ-principle in all religions in the name of God's universal economy of salvation. The other is a growing consensus within theological circles to interpret wrongly the meaning of salvation. Both trends are the consequence of an inadequate appreciation of the uniqueness of the incarnation of Christ in Jesus of Nazareth.

Examples of attempts to discover the Christ-principle in other religions have been discussed. Among the educated, and among those who have access to modern methods of communication, it is next to impossible to visualize individuals who have not heard the name of Jesus Christ. They have heard him, and they continue to hear about him, through literature, art, radio, television, and through well-meaning Christian involvement in social and political activities. All such exposures may lead a person to what we would call the natural knowledge of Jesus Christ.

That kind of knowledge about Jesus is really not different from the natural knowledge of God. Such information might, in some instances, cause a person to believe that Jesus Christ is God. However, knowledge serves its true purpose only when it makes a person "wise for salvation through faith in Christ Jesus" (2 Tim. 3:15). Faith, as Paul reminds us, "comes from hearing the message, and the message is heard through the word of Christ" (Rom. 10:17). The tendency to find the Christ in all religions is advanced largely by those who are in some way engaged in the study of comparative religion. They also operate on the notion that religions are attempts on man's part to search for absolutes. Accordingly, they propound the idea that potentially all religions lead ultimately to the same God. Thus, they accuse traditional Christianity of being particularistic and exclusivistic by pointing out that salvation is found in Jesus Christ alone.

The last point above is precisely what both Hinduism and the New Age movement have to criticize about Christianity. The Christian religion is acceptable to most people until the uniqueness of Jesus Christ as the savior of the world is brought into the picture. And, if this point is either ignored or watered down, Christians perhaps have no other distinctive message to share with others in our open world. The Christian proclamation may cause people to stumble. But it remains the only message that enables everyone to draw water from the wells of salvation (Is. 12:3).

The greatest confusion among students of comparative religion (which, we surmise, is at the root of the New Age) has been about where (and how) to draw the line between God's revelation and his act of salvation. Clearly reflecting this dilemma, Paul Tillich said that "the question of salvation can be asked only if salvation is already at work, no matter how fragmentarily."[29] Elsewhere Tillich wrote,

Man is given a revelation, a particular kind of experience which always implies saving powers. One never can separate revelation from salvation. There are revealing and saving powers in all religions. God has not left himself unwitnessed.[30]

There is only one reason for such failure to distinguish the divine facts of creation from salvation. Human nature does not want to acknowledge the need of a savior. As long as this attitude prevails, it is also impossible to humbly acknowledge the New Testament witness of Jesus Christ. The apostolic witness of Jesus Christ speaks emphatically to Christ's involvement equally in creation and salvation. Salvation in the Christian perspective is a special revelation with a universal application. That is why Jesus himself commissioned the church to proclaim the Gospel to all nations. The Gospel is the power of God to everyone who believes (Rom. 1:16).

Those who hesitate to separate God's acts of creation and salvation do so because they maintain that salvation is coextensive with the events of world history. This idea assumes that salvation for the whole world is being revealed progressively and that humans cooperate with God for its fulfillment. This view is current especially among those Christian humanists who refuse to acknowledge that salvation is entirely an act of divine grace.

God's message to the people of the world is Christ. Christians are blessed with the privilege of proclaiming to the world "Christ and him crucified" until all people everywhere acknowledge him as Lord and Savior. Life situations keep changing. What we need most is the repeated assurance that God is in control of the whole universe and that he has already worked out his plan of salvation for all in his Son Jesus Christ.

# Notes

## Introduction

1. Roland E. Miller, "A Lutheran College Approach to the Study and Teaching of Religion," *Currents in Theology and Mission,* XIX:1, February 1992, 35.

### Chapter 1: Theories of Religion (pp. 17–36)

1. Emile Durkheim, *The Elementary Forms of Religious Life, The Classic Sociological Study of Primitive Religion.* Translated from French by Joseph Ward Swain (New York: Collier Books, 1961), 478.

2. E. E. Evans-Pritchard, *Theories of Primitive Religion* (London: Oxford University Press, 1965), 100.

3. "Hinduism Gains a Foothold in America," *Christianity Today* February 8, 1993, 50.

4. The Brahmo Samaj is the end product of a Spiritual Association first established in 1815 by a great Hindu religious reformer Ram Mohan Roy. In response to the Christian Missionary Movement that sent deep roots into Indian soil, Ram Mohan Roy defended the religion of India by subjecting to Hindu scrutiny the Christian doctrines of the Trinity and the atonement.

    The person who provided the Arya Samaj with definitive leadership was Sri. Ramakrishna (1836–1886). It was understood that, as a result of practicing the Hindu way of devotion, Ramakrishna attained perfection which in turn enabled him to experience union with Christ. After that this great thinker proposed that all religions are equal. Swami Vivekananda emerged as Ramakrishna's faithful disciple and worthy successor, and in 1897 founded the Ramakrishna Mission.

5. Vivekananda's address in this assembly hinged on the theme that India had prepared the ground plan for the coexistence of all world religions. According to Vivekananda, all religions are manifestations of the one supreme religion, that is, of Hindu non-dualism (*Advaita Vedanta*).

6. In this regard, a landmark event that attracted world attention was the demolition of the mosque in Ayodhya by militant Hindus and its rippling effect on the entire nation. The ill-fated Hindu-Muslim antagonism surfaced worldwide, though short lived, in neighboring Pakistan and in such faraway lands as England.

7. Durkheim, 466.

8. Garadus van der Leeuw, *Religion in Essence and Manifestation* (New York: Harper & Row, 1963), vol. 2, 679.

9. Secular humanism is widely understood to be a religion, based on a 1961 United States Supreme Court ruling, *Torcaso v. Watkins*, 367 U.S. 4951 (1961). For a review of the decision and subsequent discussion in religion circles see David McKenzie, "The Supreme Court, Fundamentalist Logic, and the Term *Religion*," *Journal of Church and State*, 33:4 (1991), 731–46.

10. This definition is from the Dictionary's 1990 edition. According to *The Oxford English Dictionary* (1989), modern scholars see the force of our word in the Latin *religare*, inasmuch as it means *to bind*, and hence the view that religion is essentially something that binds people together.

11. W. Richard Comstock, "Toward Open Definitions of Religion," *Journal of the American Academy of Religion*, LII/3 (September 1986), 499.

12. For a discussion of how ancient societies understood power, see especially the first two chapters in G. van der Leeuw. The author says that the idea of *power* often forms the basis of religion and "the Power in the Universe was almost invariably an impersonal Power," 27.

13. Don Reisman (Senior Editor), *Religions of the World*, Third Edition (New York: St. Martin's Press, 1993), 115.

14. The people of Israel understood God's nearness to them in several different ways. During their journey from the land of slavery to the promised land, God manifested his presence with them in pillars of cloud and fire. The ark of the covenant, the temple, and the synagogue symbolized for them God's presence at various times.

15. Rudolf Otto, *The Idea of the Holy, An Inquiry into the Nonrational Factor in the Idea of the Divine and its Relation to the Rational,* trans. by John W. Harvey (London: Oxford University Press, 1952).

16. See *Religions of the World*, 4.

17. David Mckenzie, 735.

18. Mckenzie, 738.

19. For an updated edition of his work see William James (1842–1910), *The Varieties of Religious Experience* (Cambridge: Harvard University Press, 1985).

20. Sigmund Freud, *The Future of an Illusion* trans. by W. D. Robson-Scott, revised and newly edited by James Strachey, Revised Anchor Books Edition (New York: Doubleday & Company, 1964).

21. Carl Gustav Jung, *Psychology and Religion* (New Haven: Yale University Press, 1938), 4.

22. We must note that neither Freud and Jung nor Marx were professionals in the study of religion. Karl Marx, a political scientist, spoke very little on religion in proportion to his other writings. His criticism of religion, however, has had such a powerful influence on people that for a long while it served as a platform for most critics of god and religion.

23. Karl Marx and Friedrich Engels, *On Religion* (New York: Schocken Books, 1964) 42.

24. *On Religion*, 41.

25. Jacob Needleman, *The New Religions* (New York: Crossroad, 1987), especially 1–22.

26. Needleman, 7.

27. Frederick Engels, *Ludwig Feuerbach and the Outcome of Classical German Philosophy*, Marxist Library, Works of Marxism-Leninism, XV (New York: International Publishers, 1984), 44.

28. Emile Durkheim, 466. For Durkheim, society is the basis for all religions, and therefore, for all other human endeavors. And he concludes, "Religious forces are therefore human forces, moral forces."

29. *Christianity Today*, February 8, 1993, 49.

30. Stewart Sutherland, Leslie Houlden, Peter Clark & Friedhelm Hardy, eds., *The World's Religions* (Boston: G. K. Hall & Co, 1988), 7.

31. Eugene A. Nida, *Religion Across Cultures, A Study in the Communication of the Christian Faith* (Pasadena: William Carey Library, 1968), 44.

32. Quoted in *Eerdmans' Handbook to The World's Religions* (Grand Rapids: William B. Eerdmans Publishing Company, 1982), 248, 246.

33. Robert S. Ellwood, *Many Peoples, Many Faiths: An Introduction to the Religious Life of Humankind*, Fourth edition (New Jersey: Prentice-Hall, 1992), 129.

34. *Eerdman's Handbook to the World's Religions*, 185.

35. So we have gods of wisdom, good fortune, and beauty; gods of fire, war, and sacrifice. Rama, Krishna, and Buddha, and Matsya (The Fish), Kurma (The Tortoise), and Varaha (The Boar), all came into this world to accomplish a specific purpose.

36. Is. 65:1, quoted in Rom. 10:20.

37. Col. 1:26, 27.

*Chapter 2: The Religion of the New Age* (pp. 37–61)

1. For an appraisal of the modern theory of deconstruction see Gene Edward Veith, Jr., *Modern Fascism: Liquidating the Judeo-Christian Worldview* (St. Louis: Concordia Publishing House, 1993), 135–144.

2. Rom. 2:14, 15a.

3. For example see Douglas Groothuis, *Unmasking the New Age* (Downers Grove, IL: InterVarsity Press, 1986); and Douglas Groothuis, *Confronting the New Age* (Downers Grove, IL: InterVarsity press, 1988). For a comprehensive description of New Age thinking including the events in history that led to its emergence see J. Gordon Melton, Jerome Clark and Aidan A. Kelly, *New Age Almanac* (New York: Visible Ink Press, 1991), including an extensive bibliography. Cf. also Walter Martin, *The New Age Cult* (Minneapolis, MN: Bethany House Publishers, 1989); and Elliot Miller, *A Crash Course on the New Age Movement: Describing and Evaluating a Growing Social Force* (Grand Rapids, MI: Baker Book House), including a bibliography by categories.

4. See the far-reaching effect of the first-century Rabbi Gamaliel's comment in Acts 5:33–39.

5. Janet and Stewart Farrar, *A Witches Bible Compleat* (New York: Magickal Childe Publishing, Inc., Fourth printing, 1991).

6. Anna Riva, *Powers of the Psalms: Occult books—Curio—Supplies* (Los Angeles: International Imports, 1992 reprint).

7. *Unmasking the New Age*, 131.

8. Joan Borysenko, *Guilt is the Teacher, Love is the Lesson* (New York, NY: Warner Books, 1990), 119.

9. See for example Psalms 8 and 121.

10. Jean K. Foster, *New Earth New Truth, A God-Mind Plan for Saving Planet and Man* (Kansas City: Uni*Sun, 1989). *The Trilogy of Truth* was published also by Uni*Sun: *The God-Mind Connection* (1987), *The Truth that Goes Unclaimed* (1987), and *Eternal Gold* (1988).

11. *New Earth New Truth*, 188.

12. Ibid., 46.

13. Ibid.

14. For further discussion of this topic see chapter 7 below.

15. Matthew Fox. *The Coming of the Cosmic Christ* (San Francisco: HarperColins, 1988.

16. *The Cosmic Christ*, 235.

17. Gloria D. Karpinski, *Where Two Worlds Touch* (New York: Ballantine Books), 59.

18. Ibid., 59.

19. Paul discusses this point in great detail in Ephesians 2. He begins that chapter, "You were dead in your transgressions and sins, in which you used to live when you followed the ways of this world .... but because of his great love for us, God who is rich in mercy made us alive with Christ even when we were dead in transgressions." This contrast is seen all through the Pauline corpus.

20. See Rev. 3:20. In Col. 1:27 Paul writes that Christ lives in the hearts of those who believe in him. See also Rom. 8:10. Furthermore, the New Testament refers to the fact that a believer lives *in* Christ (see, for example, 2 Cor. 5:17 and John 15:5).

21. *The Coming of the Cosmic Christ*, 209.

22. Borysenko, *Guilt Is the Teacher*, 153–57.

23. See also Acts 17:30; Rom. 2:12–16; Col. 1:15–20; 1 Tim. 1:15; and Titus 3:7, 8.

24. Matthew Fox, *Original Blessing: A Primer in Creation Spirituality* (Santa Fe, NM: Bear and Co., 1983), 33, quoted in Borysenko, 154.

25. Compare the verses of Psalms 19 and 8.

26. See John 9:4; Rom. 1:21; 1 Cor. 7:29, and 1 John 2:9–11.

27. The concepts reviewed here are selected from those in the glossary in *New Earth New Truth*, 185–192.

28. *Eerdmans' Handbook to the World's Religions* (Grand Rapids, MI: William B. Eerdmans Publishing Company, 1982), 236.

29. For a discussion of these issues see chapters 5 and 6 below.

30. *Brahman* is neuter and *Brahma* is masculine. The Upanishads, which are the philosophical discussions on the Vedic teachings, make use of the masculine and the neuter in a progressive manner. Interpreting the ultimate in gender terms (Brahma) limits the scope of reality. Once it is understood as neuter (Brahman), there are no limitations to it. For an understanding of the Upanishadic teaching see *The Thirteen Principal Upanishads*, tr. by R. E. Hume (London: Oxford University Press, 1934), and S. Radhakrishnan, *The Philosophy of the Upanishads* (London: George Allen & Unwin, 1924).

31. Chandogya Upanishad 6.12, 247.

32. David S. Noss and John B. Noss, *Man's Religions*, (New York: Macmillan, 1984), 88.

33. The 13th-century Hindu philosopher Madhava taught *dvaita* (dualism) as opposed to Sankara's monism. Madhava distinguished between the Supreme Soul and the individual soul. He also talked about heaven and hell, the destiny for the soul for the hereafter. According to Madhava, salvation came through the wind-god (Vayu). Scholars see a possible Christian and Islamic connection with this kind of thinking because at this time these faiths were not foreign to India. For example, see Noss and Noss, 193.

34. *Eerdmans' Handbook to the World's Religions*, 175.

35. Hinduism suggests three ways of salvation from this situation that we will discuss briefly in the next chapter.

36. David Christie-Murray, *Reincarnation: Ancient Beliefs and Modern Evidence* (Dorset: Prism Press, 1988), 259. For a Christian appraisal of the reincarnation concept see Mark C. Albrecht, *Reincarnation: A Christian Critique of a New Age Doctrine* (Downers Grove, IL: InterVarsity Press, 1982).

37. Noss and Noss, 90.

38. Noss and Noss, 90. The authors quote *Chandogya Upanishad* 5.10.7 in support of the position that "those who are of pleasant conduct here—the prospect is, indeed, that they will enter a pleasant womb, either the womb of a Brahmin, or the womb of a Kshatriya, or the womb of a Vaisya. But those who are of stinking conduct here—the prospect is, indeed, that they will enter either the womb of a dog, or the womb of a swine, or the womb of an outcast."

39. Norvin Hein in *Religions of the World*, 107.

40. For example see Elliot Miller, *A Crash Course on the New Age Movement*, 17–18.

41. Mercea Eliade, *Yoga: Immortality and Freedom*. Translated from the French by Willard R. Trask, Bollingen Series LVI. (Princeton University Press, 1969), 12.

42. Mircea Eliade, 12.

43. *Eerdmans' Handbook to the World's Religions*, 62.

44. This quotation from Helen Keller is printed for the month of August in the 1993 Calendar published by Half Price Books Record Magazines Inc., 1992.

45. *Sacred Books of the East*, Vol.XXV, *The Laws of Manu*. Translated by G. Buhler (Oxford: Clarendon Press, 1886), 484, 496–98; XX.9, 54–67. Quoted in Noss and Noss, 90.

46. Rom. 7:7–25.

47. Compare Ezek. 18:2. "The fathers eat sour grapes, and the children's teeth are set on edge," and Jer. 31:30, ". . . whoever eats sour grapes—his own teeth will be set on edge." While the New Age appears to teach the former, Christians boldly acknowledge the latter and find its remedy in the Savior.

*Chapter 3: Hindu Openness—A Fascination for the West* (pp. 62–86)

1. S. Radhakrishnan, *The Hindu View of Life* (New York: The Macmillan Company, 1924), 17.

2. S. Radhakrishnan, 11. See also Kshiti Mohan Sen, *Hinduism: The World's Oldest Faith* (Baltimore: Penguin Books, 1961), 14.

3. S. Radhakrishnan, 13.

4. K. M. Sen, 14.

5. K. M. Sen, 21.

6. Diana L. Eck, Darsan: *Seeing the Divine Image in India*. Second Revised and Enlarged Edition (Chambersburg, PA: Anima Books, 1985), 27.

7. S. Radhakrishnan, 34.

8. Gover, *The Folk Songs of Southern India* (1871), 165, quoted in S. Radhakrishnan, 35.

9. David R. Kinsley, *Hinduism: A Cultural Perspective*. Second Edition (New Jersey: Prentice Hall, 1992), 10.

10. Raymond Hammer, "The Eternal Teaching: Hinduism," in *Eerdmans' Handbook to the World's Religions*, R. Pierce Beaver et al. Consulting Editors (Grand Rapids MI: Wm. B. Eerdmans Publishing Company, 1982), 189.

11. For the Hindu idea of a personal God and the personal nature of God see below. In Philosophical Hinduism the understanding of God as person is considered rather immature and at a lower level of reasoning.

12. Klaus K. Klostermaier, *A Survey of Hinduism* (Albany: State University of New York Press, 1989), 71.

13. *Mandukya Upanishad*, quoted in Klaus K. Klostermaier, 71.

14. Mircea Eliade, *Yoga: Immortality and Freedom*. Tr. from the French by Willard R. Trask. Bollingen Series LVI. Second Edition (New Jersey: Princeton University Press, 1969), 5.

15. Mircea Eliade, 3.

16. Mircea Eliade, 361.

17. I Cor 8: 1–3. Compare Prov. 3:5 Trust in the Lord with all your heart and lean not on your own understanding.

18. Troy Wilson Organ, *Hinduism: Its Historical Development.* Barron's Compact Studies of World Religions (New York: Barron's Educational Series, Inc. 1974), 57.

19. For further explanation of these and similar illustrations see David S. Noss and John B. Noss, *Man's Religions.* 7th Edition (New York: Macmillan Publishing Company, 1984), 184. See also the ninth edition of this work under the new title, *A History of the World's Religions* (New York: Macmillan College Publishing Company, 1994), 84-160.

20. What follows is a summary of Klaus K. Klostermaier, 189-191.

21. Klaus K. Klostermaier, 190.

22. For a reconstruction of these principles see Eliot Deutsch, *Advaita Vedanta: A Philosophical Reconstruction* (Honolulu: East-West Center Press, 1969), 103-10.

23. Norvin Hein, "Classical Hinduism: The Way of Knowledge," in *Religions of the World.* Third Edition. Robert K. C. Forman, General Editor (New York: St. Martin's Press, 1993), 119.

24. Compare the apostle Paul's statement in I Cor. 13:12: "Now I know in part, then I shall know fully, even as I am fully known."

25. According to the Code of Manu compiled sometime from 200 B. C. and on, Brahman created four classes of people, namely, Brahmins, Kshatriyas, Vaishyas, and Shudras. Of these, the first three are the "twice-born" who have a greater chance of attaining nirvana. Accordingly it also appears that, of the three, the Brahmins have the best chance as the Brahman created them especially for teaching, studying and officiating at sacrifices. Nevertheless, we must note that unlike in the old era, scriptures and knowledge are open today for all people regardless of caste. This kind of openness will easily attract New Age thinking to the Hindu way of knowledge because, after all, knowledge is the way to become one with the cosmic soul.

26. K. M. Sen, 25.

27. Klaus K. Klostermaier, 149.

28. Troy Wilson Organ, 27. Professor Organ quotes *Brihad-Aranyaka Upanishad,* 4.4.22 and 4.4.6.

29. Klaus K. Klostermaier, 149.

30. Denise Lardner Carmody and John Carmody, *The Story of World Religions* (Mountainview, CA: Mayfield Publishing Company, 1988), 291-93.

31. Leonard J. Ballas, *World Religions: A Story Approach* (Mystic, CT: Twenty-Third Publications, 1991), 167.

32. Leonard J. Ballas, 167.

33. The Hare Krishna Movement surfaced in the United States in the 1970s with its attractive dancing and chanting of the Krishna Mantra: Hare Krishna, Hare Krishna, Krishna Krishna, Hare Hare. Hare Rama, Hare Rama, Rama Rama, Hare Hare. The movement was founded in India by Sri. Chaitanya (ca. 1486-1533) and shaped into a modern enterprise in the late 1960s by A. C. Bhaktivedananda Swami Prabhupada (1896-1977).

34. J. Gordon Melton, *Encyclopedic Handbook of Cults in America* (New York & London: Garland Publishing Inc., 1986), 161.

35. Sri. R. G. Bhandarkar, *Vaishnavism, Saivism and Minor Religious Systems* (Varanasi, India: Indological Book House, 1965), 46. Bhandarkar quotes from a Jain work called *Dharmapariksha Amitagati.*

36. Robert S. Ellwood, *Many Peoples, Many Faiths*, Fourth Edition, (New Jersey: Prentice Hall, 1992), 88, 89

37. David R. Kinsley, 2,3.

38. John B. Noss and David S. Noss, 208.

39. Klaus K. Klostermaier, 183.

40. Klaus K. Klostermaier, 181.

41. Klaus K. Klostermaier, 182.

42. John B. Noss and David S. Noss, 207.

43. Mohandas Gandhi, *Young India*, 1919-1922 (New York: Huebsch, 1923), 804, quoted in John B. Noss and David S. Noss, 208.

44. *Atharva Veda* 10.8.44. Edgerton Translation. Quoted in Troy Wilson Organ, 87.

45. V. S. Agrawala, "Mother earth," in *Nehru Abhinandan Grandh,* Nehru Abhinandan Grandh Committee, 1949), 490ff. Quoted in Klaus K. Klostermaier, 276.

46. Klaus K. Klostermaier, 276. See also the various references he cites in this connection.

47. Devi is the feminine of the masculine *Deva*, which means god.

48. Quoted in Klaus K. Klostermaier, 261, from *Sri Aurobindo on the Mother*, 447.

49. Klaus K. Klostermaier, 261.

50. Klaus K. Klostermaier, 261. Klostermaier quotes *Devimahatmya I*, 75ff. directly from *Markandeya Purana*, 81.

51. Klaus K. Klostermaier, 414.

*Chapter 4: Philosophical Hinduism and Its Resurgence* (pp. 87–119)

1. Lewis M. Hope, *Religions of the World*, Third Edition. (New York: Macmillan, 1983), 168.

2. Wulf Metz, "The Enlightened One: Buddhism" *Eerdmans Handbook to the World's Religions* (Grand Rapids: William B. Eerdmans Publishing Company, 1982), 232.

3. Lewis M. Hope, 213.

4. Chakravarti Rajagopalachari, *Hinduism: Doctrine and Way of Life*, Bhavan's Book University, (Bombay: Bharatiya Vidya Bhavan, 1970), 18.

5. See for example Anand K. Coomaraswamy, *Hinduism and Buddhism* (New York: Philosophical Library, n. d.), 3–9.

6. Quoted in Troy Wilson Organ, *Hinduism: Its Historical Development*. Barron's Compact Studies of World Religions (New York: Barron's Educational Series, Inc., 1974), 243.

7. Troy Wilson Organ, 245.

8. Swami Nikhilananda, *Hinduism: Its meaning for the Liberation of the Spirit*. World Perspectives, Vol. 17 (New York: Harper & Brothers Publishers, 1958), 89.

9. Troy Wilson Organ, 252.

10. C. Rajagopalachari, *Hinduism: Doctrine and Way of Life* (Bombay: Bharatiya Vidya Bhavan, 1970) 83.

11. C. Rajagopalachari, 79.

12. C. Rajagopalachari, 79–80.

13. Troy Wilson Organ, 118–19.

14. Sarvepalli Radhakrishnan, Kalki (London: Kegan Paul, 1929), 58, quoted in Stanley J. Samartha, *Introduction to Radhakrishnan: The Man and His Thought* (New York: Association Press, 1964), 72.

15. Maitri Upanishad, quoted in John B. Noss and David S. Noss, *Man's Religions*, 7th edition. (New York: Macmillan Publishing Company, 1984), 87.

16. Taittiriya Upanishad 2. 6, quoted in Troy Wilson Organ, 264.

17. Troy Wilson Organ, 265.

18. C. Rajagopalachari, 66.

19. Robert Ernest Hume, *The Thirteen Principal Upanishads* (London: Oxford University Press, 1954) 2, quoted in Troy Wilson Organ, 103.

20. Troy Wilson Organ, 102–05. Organ supports his position with references from the Vedas and the Upanishads.

21. Troy Wilson Organ, 103.

22. Noss and Noss, 192.

23. Troy Wilson Organ, 106.

24. C. Rajagopalachari, 69.

25. Muslim rulers from Turkey and Afghanistan made inroads into India through present-day Pakistan, which was part of India until 1947. Early Muslim conquests were focused mainly on the wealth in kind of the Hindu temples, and the Punjab, the bread basket of India. For an appraisal of such events see Romila Thapar, *A History of India*, vol.1 (New York: Penguin Books, [1965], 1985), and Percival Spear, *A History of India*, vol. 2 (New York: Penguin Books, [1965], 1985).

26. Physical contact between high caste Hindus and the outcastes was considered taboo in traditional Hinduism. High caste Hindus limited their public appearances to a minimum for fear that they would come in physical contact with the outcasts, the untouchables such as the farmers, hunters, potters, scavengers and so on. When contacts did occur, though by accident, the high

caste person went through ceremonial cleansing before reentering the house.

27. M. M. Thomas, *The Acknowledged Christ of the Indian Renaissance*, Indian theological Library No. 4, (Madras: Christian Literature Society, [1970] 1976, 1.

28. Noss and Noss, 211.

29. M. M. Thomas, 3. Thomas gives a complete list of major sources available on Raja Rammohan Roy, his teachings and writings.

30. Tantrism stands for sex acts performed as a religious ritual. Tantric activities are associated with the interaction between Shiva and his cohorts, manifestations of his female counterpart Shakti. Viewed in this way, ideal sexual union transcends the mere physical act between male and female and takes on spiritual proportions. Tantric practices of the New Age Movement have their religious base in Hinduism.

31. For an appraisal of Ramakrishna's teachings see *The Gospel of Ramakrishna*, New York: Vedanta Society, 1907.

32. Noss and Noss, 213.

33. *Cultural Heritage of India* (Belur Math, Calcutta), II, 494, quoted in Robin H. S. Boyd, *An Introduction to Indian Christian Theology*. Indian Theological Library. (Delhi: ISPCK [1969] 1975), 59.

34. Quoted in Troy Wilson Organ, 355.

35. For example see Raymond Hammer, "Men and Movements," in *Eerdmans' Handbook on World Religions*, 177.

36. *The Complete works of the Swami Vivekananda*, 5th ed. (Almora, 1931), vol.I, xiii, quoted in M. M. Thomas, 124.

37. M. M. Thomas, 124–28.

38. M. M. Thomas, 195. Gandhiji expands these concepts in his famous autobiography, *My Experiments with Truth* (London, 1945).

39. M. M. Thomas, 197.

40. *Young India*, 4 November 1926. Quoted in M. M. Thomas 198. Gandhiji edited the weekly news paper *Young India* from 1919 to 1931.

41. M. M. Thomas, 199. Thomas quotes from C. F. Andrews, *Mahatma Gandhi's Ideas* (London, 1929).

42. M. K. Gandhi, *The Message of Jesus Christ* (Bombay: Christian Missions, Ahmedabad, 1940). Quoted in M. M. Thomas, 200–01.

43. M. K. Gandhi, *The Message of Jesus Christ*, 35.

44. M. K. Gandhi, *The Message of Jesus Christ*, 21.

45. M. K. Gandhi, *The Message of Jesus Christ*, 6f.

46. R. C. Zaehner, *Hinduism* (London: Oxford University Press, 1962), 224.

47. See for example Stanley J. Samartha, *Introduction to Radhakrishnan: The Man and His Thought*, New York: Association Press, 1964.

48. Sarvepally Radhakrishnan, *Eastern Religions and Western Thought* (London: Oxford University Press, 1939), 75.

49. Radhakrishnan draws support for his argument from the writings of St. Augustine, from John Bunyan's *The Pilgrim's Progress*, and from various Church Fathers. He quotes extensively from the New Testament, the sayings of Jesus and the writings of the apostles. For example, Jesus said, "Remain in me and I will remain in you" (John 15:4). Obviously, Radhakrishnan, following his advaitic instinct, fails to see the difference between mystical union and Christian fellowship.

50. *Mysticism and Ethics in Hindu Thought*, 69.

51. Sarvepalli Radhakrishnan, *An Idealist View of Life*, Herbert Lectures for 1929, Third Impression (London: Allen & Unwin, Ltd., and New York: The Macmillan Company, 1947), 279.

52. Stanley J. Samartha, 24–37.

*Chapter 5: The Hindu-Christian Connection* (pp. 120–149)

1. Modern missionary movements brought into India representative missionaries from the world's major Christian denominations. Indian Christians, however, had long felt the need to unite themselves on the basis of the common faith they share in Jesus Christ, transcending denominational barriers. This was important especially because Christianity had to shed the impression of being an imported religion, and Indian Christians

are a religious minority, consisting mainly of people from the lower castes. The first of such attempts was made already in 1908, between the Congregationalists and the Presbyterians of south India, resulting in the formation of the South India United Church. Later in 1925 the Wesleyan Methodists joined this group after negotiations. After almost a generation of deliberations, the Church of South India came into being. In a similar manner the Church of North India was formed in 1970, comprising various denominations in the north.

2. The State of Kerala in the south was the first to elect the communist party to power in 1957. In fact this was the first time in world history that communism gained power to rule a state through the democratic process. Later, West Bengal and Tripura, two other states in the northeastern section of the Indian republic followed. Interestingly enough, all these states are strongly influenced by the Christian religion. Beginning with the tradition of St. Thomas Christians, almost a third of Kerala's population is Christian. Bengal was the mission field of William Carey, one of the greatest missionaries of modern times. In Calcutta, West Bengal, Serampore University is the one autonomous Christian university that awards degrees in Christian theology. Both Christianity and Marxism seem to appeal to minds with similar dispositions.

3. For a detailed account of the history of Jesuit Missions in India see C. B. Firth, *An Introduction to Indian Church History*, Indian Theological Library, revised edition (Madras: The Christian Literature Society, 1976 [1961]), 109–29.

4. It may be noted that Gandhiji turned away from Christianity because he could not appreciate the way in which Christians failed to practice their faith. According to him, Christians, for the most part, lived for pleasure in terms of eating meat, drinking and reveling, with little concern for upholding moral principles, while they were overtly conscious of a gracious God. He also believed the Christian lifestyle (which he believed was Western) was not becoming a true follower of Jesus Christ. It was also true that during Gandhiji's time many Christians in India were also adopting a Western lifestyle. By contrast, almost 300 years ago, de Nobili proposed that the Gospel be applied to Indian cultural situations.

5. For example, Raymond G. Panikkar, *The Trinity and World Religions* (Madras: The Christian Literature Society, 1970). For an appraisal of these attempts by great Indian Christian thinkers see also R. H. S. Boyd, *Khristadvaita: A Theology for India* (Madras: The Christian Literature Society, 1977).

6. S. Radhakrishnan, *The Hindu View of Life* (New York: The Macmillan Company, second printing 1968), 82.

7. Robin H. S. Boyd, *An Introduction to Indian Christian Theology* jointly published by the Indian Society for the Promotion of Christian Knowledge, Delhi and Indian Theological Library Trivandrum, India 1969. This work, one of its kind, is the source material for understanding the development of Christian theology in India in the context of the modern Christian missionary movement. Boyd himself, raised in India as son of a Christian missionary, and later missionary and professor of theology, vividly presents several cases of theological thinking, heavily accenting their Indianness.

8. For example, C. B. Firth narrates the story of the first Protestant mission, noting that the Protestant Churches of Europe did not entertain the vision of preaching the Gospel to other nations until King Frederick IV of Denmark, himself a Lutheran, made a giant move. The king, having been unable to find suitable men from his country for the task at hand, through his court chaplain, found Bartholomew Ziegenbalg and Henry Pluetschau from Germany. In 1706, although they boarded the ship to India with the kings's blessings, they were most unwelcome creatures to the ship's commandant Hassius. Firth writes, "It was three days before they could get a boat to take them ashore from the ship, and when at last they did get to land and presented themselves at the entrance to the fort with their papers addressed to the Danish commandant, these were taken from them and they were kept waiting there from ten o'clock in the morning until four in the afternoon. Then the commandant, J. C. Hassius, appeared with some members of the council and the two Danish chaplains of the place, to ask them their business. Receiving a grudging permission to enter, they followed the official party to the marketplace, only to be left there standing in the street." C. B. Firth, *An Introduction to Indian Church History*, Indian Theological Library, Revised edition, [1961] 1976, 131f.

9. H. A. Krishna Pillai (1827–1900) was a well-known Tamil Christian poet who wrote the Christian epic *Rakshanya Yatrikam* (literally Salvation Journey) and *Rakshanya Manoharam* (The Splendor of Salvation). Krishna Pillai was born a non-Brahmin high caste Hindu, and embraced the Christian faith while he was serving on the faculty of the CMS College in Tirunelveli, South India. For other great contributions of this poet and others like him see R. H. S. Boyd, *Indian Christian Theology*, 110 ff.

10. P. G. Kuruvila, *Bharatiya Christava Darsanangal* (Tiruvalla: The Christian Literature Society, 1986) 9–27.

11. Kaj Baago, *Pioneers of Indigenous Christianity*, (Bangalore: The Christian Institute for the Study of Religion and Society 1960), 6.

12. A landmark event in this connection for Indian Christianity was the missionary conference held in Thambaram, Madras, India, in 1938. In that meeting of the minds, Hendrik Kraemer presented an essay on "the Christian Message in a Non-Christian World" in which he claimed that the Christian message must be interpreted in non-Christian terms in order to effectively communicate Christianity to non-Christians. Kraemer advised that theologians must incorporate into Christianity factors from African and Asian religions without jeopardizing the Christian revelation. He went on to say that Western Christianity itself evolved in its present form as the Christian faith entered Western culture long ago.

13. R. H. S. Boyd, *Indian Christian Theology*, 92.

14. R. H. S. Boyd, *Indian Christian Theology*, 93.

15. F. Heiler, *The Gospel of Sundar Singh* (1927) quoted in R. H. S. Boyd, *Indian Christian Theology*, 93f.

16. *Indian Christian Theology*, 95. Boyd quotes from Heiler.

17. B. H. Streeter and A. J. Appasamy, *The Sadhu* (1921), 132, quoted in *Indian Christian Theology*, 97.

18. These and other examples of Sundar Singh's parabolic preaching style are described in R. H. S. Boyd, *Indian Christian Theology*, 101ff.

19. Quoted in R. H. S. Boyd, *Indian Christian Theology*, 100.

20. R. H. S. Boyd, *Indian Christian Theology*, 103, quoted from Heiler, 166.

21. In fact, Sundar Singh said that "Christianity is the fulfillment of Hinduism. Hinduism has been digging channels. Christ is the water to flow through these channels." What we see here is the spiritual struggle typical of those who became Christians for the first time from an orthodox non-Christian religious background. People can be "religious" and still be looking for ways to fill the spiritual void in their lives. As they begin to taste the fullness of life in Christ, they  also experience the fact that their spiritual search has now been completed. Sundar Singh's views should not be mistaken for the popular notion that all religions, including Christianity are in a process of development which will ultimately lead to one world religion as, for example, proposed by William Hocking in his *The Coming World*

*Civilization.* Many leading theologians in India, including Christian missionaries, have viewed Christianity as the fulfillment of other world religions. In the Indian context they see Christ as the fulfillment of Hinduism. For example, see J. N. Farquhar, *The Crown of Hinduism*, Oxford, 1913.

22. For an appraisal of Appasamy's theology see Boyd, *Indian Christian Theology*, 118–143. Boyd includes an extensive bibliography on Appasamy.

23. Quoted in, *Indian Christian Theology*, 123.

24. For selected examples of Christian devotional writings in this category see R. H. S. Boyd, *Indian Christian Theology*, 112–18. What follows is a summary of such illustrations.

25. Boyd, 115.

26. Boyd, 118.

27. The reference is to *Taittiriya Upanishad* 2.6.2. Appasamy's position on this item is explained in his famous book, *Christianity and Bhakti Marga* (1928), quoted in Boyd.

28. *Christianity and Bhakti Marga*, 43, quoted in Boyd, 125.

29. A. J. Appasamy, *What is Moksha?* (1939), 174, quoted in Boyd, 125.

30. A classic example in this connection is Stanley J. Samartha, long time professor of theology in various theological colleges in India and for ten years director of the Program on Dialogue with People of Living Faiths and Ideologies of the World Council of Churches. He writes extensively on this topic and is currently on the advisory council of the Christian Institute for the Study of Religion and Society, and is visiting professor at United Theological College, Bangalore.

31. P. G. Kuruvila, *Bharata Christava Darshanangal*, 186–88.

32. M. M. Thomas, *The Acknowledged Christ of the Indian Renaissance*, 251.

33. In addition to *The Acknowledged Christ of the Indian Renaissance*, Dr. M. M. Thomas has written extensively on related topics in the form of books and in various publications. Among them are *Secular Ideologies of India and the Secular Meaning of Christ* (Bangalore: CISRS/CLS, 1978); *The Christian Response to the Asian Revolution* (London: SCM, 1969); and *Salvation and Humanization* (Bangalore: CISRS, 1971).

34. Boyd, 262.

35. C. S. Lewis, *Mere Christianity* (New York; Macmillan Publishing Company, 1952), 41.

36. According to Vivian Worthington, a former Secretary General of the British Wheel of Yoga, who spent over 40 years researching and lecturing on the subject, three of which were in India itself. See his *A History of Yoga* (London: Arkana, 1989).

37. Vivian Worthingtion, 1.

38. Mircea Eliade, *Yoga: Immortality and Freedom.* Tr. from the French by Willard R. Trask. Bollingen Series LVI (New Jersey: Princeton University Press, 1990), 294.

39. Eliade, 145f.  Eliade quotes from  Sacred Books of the East, XCVII, 11–14, tr. Julius Jolly, *The Institutes of Vishnu*, 285–90.

40. His Holiness Maharishi Mahesh Yogi, *Science of Being and Art of Living* (Washington DC: Age of Enlightenment Publications, 1968).

41. See Josh McDowell and Don Stewart, *Handbook of Today's Religions* (San Bernardino, California: Here's Life Publishers, Inc., 1991), pp.80–85.  In 1982, The United States Supreme Court has ruled Transcendental Meditation to be a religion.  Yoga in its pure form is not just an exercise, but a religious rite because it still invokes the names of different gods in the Hindu religion even when it is practiced in the USA.  In contrast to what Christian missionaries did to the Christianity in India with a view to indigenizing it to the Indian context, Yoga techniques do not let go of their Hindu identity.  Unlike tennis, or jogging, Yoga in its pure form is more than just an exercise.

42. J. Gordon Melton, *Encyclopedic Handbook of Cults in America* (New York & London: Garland Publishing Inc, 1986), 120.

43. Helena Petrova Blavatsky, *The Secret Doctrine: The Synthesis of Science, Religion, and Philosophy* (New York & Madras: The Theosophical Publishing Company, 1888).

44. Swami Vivekananda, *Karma Yoga and Bhakti Yoga* (New York: Ramakrishna-Vivekananda Center, 1982), 32.

*Chapter 6: Some Issues in Contemporary Theology* (pp. 150–178)

1. Several volumes are available in English that supply detailed biographical information on Reimarus and his major writings. See for example Ralph S. Fraser, trans. *Reimarus: Fragments*, ed. by Charles H. Talbert, Lives of Jesus Series (Philadelphia: Fortress Press, 1970); and H. S. Reimarus, *The Goal of Jesus and His Disciples*, introduction and tr. by George Wesley Buchanan (Leiden: E. J. Brill, 1970).

2. H. S. Reimarus, "Concerning the Intention of Jesus and His Teaching" in *Reimarus: Fragments*, 72.

3. *Reimarus: Fragments*, 150.

4. See chapter 7 for an appraisal of the Kingdom of God as Jesus taught it.

5. For a biography of Lessing, see H. B. Garland, *Lessing: The Founder of Modern German Literature* (London: Macmillan & Co., 1962).

6. See for example Henry E. Allison, *Lessing and the Enlightenment* (Ann Arbor: University of Michigan Press, 1966), 83, 96.

7. Henry Chadwick, *Lessing's Theological Writings: Selections in Translation* (Stanford: Stanford University press, 1956), 42–44.

8. Martin Kähler, *The So-Called Historical Jesus and the Historic, Biblical Christ*, trans. by Carl E. Braaten (Philadelphia: Fortress Press, 1964).

9. Kähler, 52.

10. Kähler, 66.

11. Schweitzer's landmark book is his *Von Reimarus zu Wrede: Eine Geschichte der Leben-Jesu-Forschung*, which appeared in English as *The Quest of the Historical Jesus: A Critical Study of its Progress from Reimarus to Wrede*, trans. by W. Montgomery (New York: Macmillan Publishing Co., 1975). For a discussion on the kingdom of God see chapter 7.

12. Albert Schweitzer, 400–401.

13. Stephen Neil, *The Interpretation of the New Testament 1861–1961* (London: Oxford University Press, 1964), 198.

14. Schweitzer, 337.

15. Rudolf Bultmann, "New Testament and Mythology" in *Kerygma and Myth*, ed. by H. W. Bartsch (New York: Harper & Row, 1961), 10, n. 2.

16. Rudolf Bultmann, 4.

17. Rudolf Bultmann, *Theology of the New Testament*. 2 vols., trans. by K. Grobel (New York: Charles Scribners, 12951), 1:33.

18. Bultmann, *Theology of the New Testament*, 303.

19. Rudolf Bultmann, *History and Eschatology: The Presence of Eternity* (New York: Harper & Row, 1957), 155.

20. Paul Tillich, *Systematic Theology*, 3 vols. (Chicago: University of Chicago Press, 1957), 2: 91.

21. Tillich, *Systematic Theology*, 3: 285.

22. Tillich, *Systematic Theology*, 2: 101.

23. Tillich, *Systematic Theology*, 3: 286.

24. For example see below our discussion on some of M. M. Thomas' and Raimundo Panikkar's propositions.

25. Tillich, *Systematic Theology*, 2: 44–45.

26. Paul Tillich, *The Eternal Now* (New York: Scribners', 1963), 76.

27. Tillich, *Systematic Theology*, 2: 94.

28. Tillich, *Systematic Theology*, 2: 148.

29. Tillich, *Systematic Theology*, 2: 148.

30. Tillich, *Systematic Theology*, 2: 99.

31. Tillich, *Systematic Theology*, 113–14.

32. Paul Tillich, *Christianity and the Encounter of World Religions* (New York & London: Columbia University Press, 1963), 35.

33. Numerous studies on Teilhard's theology are available. See for example Robert Hale, *Christ and the Universe: Teilhard de Chardin and the Cosmos* (Chicago: Franciscan Herald Press, 1972); George A. Maloney, *The Cosmic Christ from Paul to Teilhard* (New York: Sheed and Ward, 1968); Eulalis R. Bultazar, *Teilhard and the Supernatural* (Baltimore-Doublin: Helicon, 1966).

34. Quoted in Robert Hale, 71.

35. Pierre Teilhard de Chardin, *The Divine Milieu: An Essay on the Interior of Life* (New York: Harper, & Row, 1960), 25–30.

36. Pierre Teilhard De Chardin, *The Phenomenon of Man* (New York: Harper & Row, 1959), 269-99.

37. Pierre Teilhard de Chardin, *The Phenomenon of Man*, 294.

38. Pierre Teilhard de Chardin, *Divine Milieu*, 121–22.

39. Pierre Teilhard de Chardin, *Divine Milieu*, 126.

40. Pierre Teilhard de Chardin, *Divine Milieu*, 21.

41. Pierre Teilhard de Chardin, *The Phenomenon of Man*, 284.

42. Quoted in Eulalis R. Bulldozer, 124.

43. Quoted in Robert Halle, 77.

44. For example see 1 Cor. 15:28: "God shall be all in all"; Col. 2:19, "He it is who fills all"; other texts are Col. 1: 16, 17; 3:11; and Eph. 4:9. For an interpretation of all these and similar concepts see Teilhard de Chardin, *Science and Christ*, trans. by Rene Hague (New York & Evanston: Harper & Row, 1965).

45. Paul D. Devanandan, *Preparation for Dialogue* (Bangalore: The Christian Institute for the Study of Religion and Society, 1964), 96.

46. P. D. Devanandan, 141.

47. Marcus Braybrooke, *The Undiscovered Christ* (Madras: CISRS-CLS, 1973), 30.

48. Marcus Braybrooke, 30.

49. Raymond Panikkar, *The Unknown Christ of Hinduism* (London: Darton, Longman & Todd, 1964), 34.

50. Panikkar, 48.

51. Panikkar, 17.

52. Raymond Panikkar, *The Trinity and World Religions* (Madras: CISRS-CLS, 1970).

53. *The Trinity and World Religions*, 52.

54. *The Trinity and World Religions*, p. 52.

55. Rudolf Bultmann argued for a demythologization of the Christian faith because he believed that modern man is unable to accept the claims of the New Testament on its own terms. Bultmann believed that Jesus had a message to proclaim to his hearers, but those who heard him first (the early church) began to proclaim him. Thus in Bultmann's own words, "The proclaimer became the proclaimed." According to Panikkar, "The real Christ is not the kerygma of the Lord, but the Lord himself. The naked Christ also means the dekerygmatized Christ." See Raimundo Panikkar, *The Intrareligious Dialogue* (New York, N. Y./Ramsey, N. J.: Paulist Press, 1978), 57.

56. Leslie Newbegin, *A Faith For This One World?* (London: SPCK,1961), 65.

57. Stanley J. Samartha, *The Hindu Response to the Unbound Christ*, Inter-religious Dialogue Series (Madras: CISRS-CLS, 1974), No. 6, 7.

*Chapter 7: The Gospel: A Privilege to Proclaim* (pp. 179–214)

1. *The Book of Concord, The Confessions of the Evangelical Lutheran Church*, tr. and ed. by Theodore G. Tappert (Philadelphia: Fortress Press, 1959), 478.

2. Article V of the Augsburg Confession describes the ministry of the church, which is teaching the Gospel and administering the sacraments. This article follows the great article on justification by faith, for Christ's sake. As we work our way backwards (as I have done in the text), we see Jesus Christ who came to the world to save sinners in Article III. Article II describes sin as rebellion against God. And God's existence and His nature are described in the first article.

3. For example, the Bible begins with the statement, "In the beginning God created the heavens and the earth." The entire Bible is a record of God's actions. The Wisdom Literature especially calls the reader's attention to the wonder of God's handiwork on earth as well as in the sky. In the text I have used references particularly from Psalm 14 and the Book of Hebrews.

4. Rudolf Otto, "Introduction to Friedrich Schleiermacher," *On Religion: Speeches to Its Cultured Despisers*. Tr. by John Oman (New York: Harper & Row, 1958), ix.

5. See Thomas J. J. Altizer, ed., *Toward a New Christianity: Readings in the Death of God Theology* (New York: Harcourt, Brace & World, Inc., 1967).

6. Friedrich Schleiermacher, *On Religion*, 211.

7. Heinz Zahrnt, *The Question of God: Protestant Theology in the 20th Century*, tr. from the German by R. A. Wilson (New York: Harcourt Brace Jovanovich, Inc, 1966), 279. In this book Zahrnt evaluates and criticizes various modern viewpoints on the existence of God that emerged in the context of existentialist philosophy, and the subsequent death of god theology. Zahrnt's quotations are from Helmut Gollwitzer, *Die Existenz Gottes im Bekenntnis des Glaubens*, (Munich, 1963).

8. Lesslie Newbigin, Preface to *Toward the 21st Century in Christian Mission*, ed. by James M. Phillips and Robert T. Coote (Grand Rapids, MI: William B. Eerdmans Publishing Company, 1993), 5.

9. M. Scott Peck, *Further Along the Road Less Travelled: The Unending Journey Toward Spiritual Growth* (New York: Simon & Schuster, 1993), 196.

10. Douglas R. Groothuis, *Unmasking the New Age* (Downers Grove, IL: InterVarsity Press, 1986), 131.

11. Russell Chandler, *Understanding the New Age* (Grand Rapids MI: Zondervan Publishing House 1993), 17.

12. J. Gordon Melton, *Encyclopedic Handbook of Cults in America* (New York and London: Garland Publishing, 1986), 113.

13. Chandler, *Understanding the New Age*, 31.

14. In some traditional societies where the gurus impart special knowledge to their disciples, certain gurus used to retain selected principles or techniques (for example, in martial arts) solely to themselves. They would not teach these techniques even to their most favorite disciples. It was supposed to be the privilege of the gurus to have in their possession some kind of secret wisdom. These would be shared with selected ones at the end of the guru's life. But again, there was a very good possibility that these were never shared at all with the next generation, and no one could benefit from it after the guru.

15. Jacob Needleman, *The New Religions* (New York: Crossroad, 1987).

16. For the meaning of the Kingdom of God, see below.

17. Walter Martin, Ph. D. *The New Age Cult* (Minneapolis, MN: Bethany House Publishers, 1989), 29, quoted from Levi, *The Aquarian Gospel*, 13–14.

18. In the Gospel of John we read a series of the "I Am" statements from Jesus: "I am the living water," "I am the bread of life," "I am the light of the world," "I am the door," "I am the gate," "I am the good shepherd," "I am the resurrection and the life." Also to the woman from Samaria (whom Jesus confronted with her sins), who was from among those who were expecting the coming of the Messiah (the Christ), Jesus said, "I am (the Christ)" John 4:26.

19. Quoted in Martin, *The New Age Cult*, 28.

20. Stephen Neill, *Salvation Tomorrow: The Originality of Jesus Christ and the World's Religions* (Nashville, TN: Abingdon Press, 1976), 59.

21. For an appraisal of the kingdom of God, the reader is referred to two monographs that appeared very timely when they were first published. They came out in a context in which the church was seriously rethinking its mission to the modern world. Cf. John Bright, *The Kingdom of God: The Biblical Concept and its Meaning for the Church* (New York: Abingdon-Cokesbury Press, 1958); and Norman Perrin, *The Kingdom of God in the Teaching of Jesus* (London: SCM Press, 1963).

22. Adolf Harnack, *What is Christianity?* English trans. by T. B. Saunders (Harper & Row, 1957).

23. Albert Schweitzer, *The Kingdom of God and Primitive Christianity*, trans. by L. A. Garrard (New York: Seabury Press, 1968).

24. C. H. Dodd, *The Parables of the Kingdom*. Revised Edition. (New York: Charles Scribner's Sons, 1961).

25. What follows is a summary of the items discussed in Martin H. Scharlemann, *Proclaiming the Parables* (St. Louis: Concordia Publishing House, 1963), 34–36.

26. In his letter to the Christians in Galatia, Paul lists love, joy, peace, patience, kindness, goodness, faithfulness, gentleness, and self control as the fruit of the Spirit (Gal. 5:16–26). Paul also explains how these are constantly at odds with what he calls the desires of the sinful nature. In 1 Cor. 15:15, following the great description of the resurrection of the body, Paul unequivocally states that flesh and blood cannot inherit the kingdom of God, nor can the perishable inherit the imperishable.

27. For example 2 Cor. 5:17. This reference must be compared to other passages such as Rom. 5:12; 6:11; 13:14; Gal. 3:27; Col. 2: 11–15; Eph. 2:15; and others. The context of the verse from 2 Corinthians clearly explains that the new creation is the result of Christ's death on the cross, and the ministry of the church is to proclaim that unique message to others.

28. Friedrich Engels, "On the History of Early Christianity," in *Marx and Engels on Religion* (Moscow: Foreign Language Publishing House, 1957), 313–43.

29. Paul Tillich, *Systematic Theology*, 3 vols. (Chicago: University of Chicago Press, 1957), 2:80.

30. Paul Tillich, *The Future of Religions* (New York: Harper & Row, 1966), 81.

......................................................................

A. R. Victor Raj was born in 1948 of Christian parents in Trivandrum, Kerala, South India. He graduated from Gurukul Lutheran Theological College and Research Institute in Madras and received the Bachelor of Divinity degree from the Senate of Serampore College, Calcutta, West Bengal. He also holds the Master of Sacred Theology (1976) and the Doctor of Theology (1981)from Concordia Seminary, St. Louis.

He served the India Evangelical Lutheran Church (IELC) in an urban parish in Cochin and parishes in Trivandrum, as Director of Youth Ministry, as Director of Renewal of the IELC, and as President of Concordia Seminary, Nagercoil. Since 1990 he has been professor and chairman of the Division of Theology, Concordia University Wisconsin.

Dr. Raj and his wife, Anie, live in Cedarburg, Wisconsin, and have three sons.

......................................................................